The United States and China

The United States in the World:
Foreign Perspectives
Akira Iriye, Series Editor

Already published:

The United States and Britain
H. G. Nicholas

**France and the United States:
From the Beginnings to the Present**
Jean-Baptiste Duroselle
Translated by *Derek Coltman*

Russia and the United States
Nikolai V. Sivachev and *Nikolai N. Yakovlev*
Translated by *Olga Adler Titelbaum*

The United States and Mexico
Josefina Zoraida Vazquez and *Lorenzo Meyer*

Arnold Xiangze Jiang

The United States and China

94-58

The University of Chicago Press
Chicago and London

The University of Chicago Press, Chicago 60637
The University of Chicago Press, Ltd., London

97 96 95 94 93 92 91 90 89 88   5 4 3 2 1

Library of Congress Cataloging-in-Publication Data

Chiang, Hsiang-tse.
    The United States and China.

    (The United States in the world, foreign perspectives)
    Bibliography: p.
    Includes index.
    1. United States—Foreign relations—China.   2. China—
Foreign relations—United States.   I. Title.   II. Series.
E183.8.C5C4355   1988   327.73051   87-30059
ISBN 0-226-39947-8

ARNOLD XIANGZE JIANG is professor of
history at Zhongshan University in
Guangdong.

To Dr. and Mrs. F. David Roberts

Contents

Series Editor's Foreword

This book is a volume in the series entitled The United States and the World: Foreign Perspectives. As the series title indicates, it aims at examining American relations with other countries from a perspective that lies outside the United States. International relations obviously involve more than one government and one people, and yet American foreign affairs have tended to be treated as functions of purely domestic politics, opinions, and interests. Such a uninational outlook is not adequate for understanding the complex forces that have shaped the mutual interactions between Americans and other peoples. Today, more than ever before, it is imperative to recognize the elementary fact that other countries' traditions, aspirations, and interests have played an equally important role in determining where the United States stands in the world. As with individuals, a country's destiny is in part shaped by the way other countries perceive it and react to it. And a good way to learn how foreigners view and deal with the United States is to turn to a non-American scholar of distinction for a discussion of his country's relations with America.

Professor Arnold Jiang, who teaches history at Zhongshan (Sun Yat-sen) University in Guangdong (Canton), is uniquely qualified to offer such a perspective. He is a preeminent historian in contemporary China, but he also holds a doctorate from the University of Washington and knows the United States quite well. He has spent many years studying the history of U.S.-Chinese relations. When I approached him several years ago with the idea of contributing a volume to the series, he was eager to do so, knowing fully well that there were certain risks involved in writing such a book in English. He has since visited the United States on two separate occasions to do research and begin work on the book. He has examined American sources, both primary and secondary, in addition to Chinese ones, but he has presented his own views of past trends and episodes in the fascinating, often tortuous, story of U.S.-Chinese relations. These views are his own, and should not be taken as representing "the party line." Occasionally the two may coincide, but some of his interpretations would provoke controversy in the People's Republic. American readers, for their part, may take strong exception to his presentation of certain events. But this is as it should be. Here one finds a record of a courageous contemporary historian who has defied odds in completing a work that is dedicated to promoting better understanding between the two peoples.

In bringing this project to fruition, I am grateful to a number of assistants (Anthony Cheung, Marnie Veghte, Barbara Welke) who helped edit the manuscript, and especially to Professor David Roberts, a close friend of the author, for contributing an insightful introduction.

AKIRA IRIYE

Introduction

David Roberts

Jiang Xiangze brings together in this work his skills as a historian and his Chinese perspective to present a Chinese interpretation of the history of the U.S.-Chinese relations. Jiang was born in 1916 in the Guizhou Province of South China. After attending the University of Nanjing in Chengdu, he earned a Ph.D. from the University of Washington in the United States in 1951. Jiang's dissertation, *The Nien Rebellion,* was published by the University of Washington Press in 1954. Since completing his doctorate, he has taught at Zhongshan University in Guangzhou.

Drawing on primary and secondary Chinese and U.S. sources, Jiang here presents the history of U.S.-Chinese relations from approximately 1783 through U.S. recognition of the Peoples' Republic of China in 1978. His work offers the student, teacher, and policy-maker critical insight into the Chinese interpretation of events, which have often been viewed only from an American perspective. Although the reader may not agree with Jiang's view of many events, an awareness of the differing interpretations that two peoples draw from a set of shared events is crucial for understanding the relationship between those nations. Moreover, viewing events from a different perspective should provide the reader an opportunity for reevaluation of accepted interpretations.

In Jiang's chronological approach, three themes emerge to characterize U.S. relations with China. The first and most central is that, between the two aims that defined U.S. policy toward China—a generous friendship and an aggressive self-interest—the latter dominated. Thus, Jiang describes the Sino-American relationship as a history of "United States aggression and Chinese resistance." Beginning with the 1844 "Treaty of Peace, Amity & Commerce" (Treaty of Wangxia), he sees the United States as playing a major role in a "long, humiliating process, the reduction of China to a semicolonial country." John Hay's Open Door Policy, first articulated in 1899, did not stem the tide of Western aggression in China. Rather than condemning spheres of influence, Jiang argues, the Open Door Policy was a tool to enhance America's economic dominance and "open up the way for an American hegemony in the Far East."

The process Jiang sees as characterizing the U.S.-Chinese relationship from its beginning continued into the twentieth century. Thus, he interprets the 1922 Washington Conference as a continuation of America's pursuit of aggressive self-interest in Asia and argues that when "America's dream of hegemony in China came true" in the 1946 Treaty of Friendship, the United States, in an aggressive policy of "military encirclement, political isolation, and economic blockade," sought to prevent Mao Zedong from destroying that dream.

The second main theme emerging from Jiang's interpretation of the U.S.-Chinese relationship is that the United States was a consistent supporter of corrupt, unpopular, and repressive regimes in China. Jiang points to U.S. assistance of the Qings in strangling the Taiping insurrection; the dispatch of forces to quell the popular Boxer Rebellion; the U.S. role in undermining the revolution led by Sun Yat-sen; and the financial and military support given to Chiang Kai-shek's corrupt government in an attempt to suppress the Chinese Communist Party. In his description and analysis of the reactionary and corrupt regimes that the United States supported, Jiang brings to bear both a Chinese perspective and the informed view of a scholar of Chinese history.

The third main theme developed by Jiang is that the United States, in pursuing its twofold policy of friendship and self-interest, often became involved in contradictions and unrealities. As Jiang makes clear, the Open Door Policy itself rested on an inconsistency and an illusion: it proclaimed both "respect for the sovereignty . . . and territorial integrity of China" and the protection "of all rights guaranteed to friendly powers by treaty and international law." "The two points," Jiang emphasizes, "were self-contradictory." Moreover, the U.S. guarantee of China's integrity yielded to Japan's aggressive designs on China as highlighted in the Root-Takahira and Lansing-Ishii agreements. As Jiang interprets events, the United States lacked the will as well as the power to stop Russian and Japanese encroachments on China's integrity.

Jiang also stresses the contradictions and unreality of U.S. support for Chiang Kai-shek in the 1940s and the use of Taiwan in the 1950s to undermine the People's Republic of China. Although, as Jiang carefully documents, the United States was aware of both the corruption in Chiang's regime and his policy of preserving his forces to fight a civil war against the Chinese Communist forces after the end of the Pacific War rather than fighting against the Japanese, it continued to provide him with arms and financial support. Moreover, American fear of Communism and the conviction that Communism was a "passing phase" meant that U.S. support of Chiang's regime continued even after he had escaped to Taiwan. "Americans," writes Jiang, "did not know or want to know of the strength, maturity, tenacity, and popularity of the Chinese Communists, nor that they were completely independent of the Soviet Union."

Jiang's work deserves careful reading, discussion, and thought. Whether the reader agrees with Jiang's interpretations or not, this book should both broaden and deepen most readers' understanding of a historic relationship that is also of great importance for the future.

1

From "Peace and Amity" to "Cooperation"

Before the birth of the United States of America, its merchants hoped to break the monopoly of the British East India Company and do business directly with China. Immediately after the Peace of Paris of 1783 between America and Britain, merchants in Boston and other major ports prepared to develop the China trade. Since 1784, when the first American ship, the *Empress of China,* reached Guangzhou (Canton), American trade had rapidly gained ground, leaping in the early nineteenth century to a position second only to Britain. In spite of the rigid restrictions which the Chinese government set up for governing foreign trade, the American merchants were content with the trading system and had no serious complaints. Through such an intercourse, Americans acquired Chinese products prized in the United States and Europe—silk, nankeen cotton cloth, porcelain, and above all, tea. For its part, China usually enjoyed a favorable balance of trade. During this first phase, the commercial relations between the two countries were equal and mutually beneficial. Nevertheless, certain developments after the turn of the century doomed this mutual relationship to a short life.

In the seventeenth and eighteenth centuries, when Western Europe became ever more capitalistic, China under the reign of the Qing (Manchu) Dynasty remained a feudal society in which the landlord class possessed most of the arable land and exploited the peasant masses. The close integration of small-scale farming with domestic handicraft constituted a self-sufficient economy. It was a society in rapid decline, one beset in the nineteenth century by crises of ever greater intensity. Across all China, peasant uprisings broke out, one after another. Depravity, corruption, and ineptitude paralyzed the bureaucratic ruling machine.

As China's ruling class decayed, in Great Britain, thanks to the Industrial Revolution, the ruling class grew wealthier, more powerful, and more capitalistic. British merchants sought vigorously to expand their trade and influence in China. The Chinese government, however, not only refused to relax its restrictions on foreign trade, but it also imposed a ban on opium trade and confiscated the opium which British merchants smuggled into Guangzhou. To end these restrictions and to win commercial privileges, the British government launched a war against China in 1840. By 1842 Britain had brought the decadent Qing government to submission.

Since Britain did not dare openly to use an immoral trade in opium as a pretext for war, it complained that the Chinese government subjected British traders in China to many kinds of "unequal treatment." That the Qing government imposed restrictions on foreign trade is true;[1] but also true is the fact that all countries have the right to regulate foreign trade through their own ports. Furthermore, many of the Qing government's regulations involved considerations of self-defense. During the sixteenth and seventeenth centuries, European merchants prowled the coastal areas of Guangdong and Fujian provinces engaging in piratical activities. The government could not but adopt defensive measures. An American historian admits that

the early intercourse in its own ports with these nationalities [i.e., the Portuguese, Dutch, Spanish] and the English, so marked by violence and bloodshed, led the Chinese authorities to stringent measures in the seventeenth century, which resulted in the closing of all ports except that of Canton, and even at that port foreign intercourse was conducted under very onerous conditions.[2]

No system of international law justified Britain's resorting to war because of China's trade system. It was a war of aggression.

Most American merchants were exultant at the results of this unjust war, for they too wished to "open up" China. In the early part of the nineteenth century, changes had also taken place in the American-Chinese trade. In pursuit of exorbitant profits, American merchants had smuggled opium into China since 1804, in which pursuit they were soon second only to the British. Although they continued to export sea otter skins, sandalwood, and other exotic natural products to China, after 1826 these items gradually gave way to manufactured goods—products of America's expanding capitalist economy. This tendency made selling to China more important than buying from it. From then on, American government officials and merchants envisioned an unlimited market in China for American economic expansion.

In 1839, before the Sino-British War, American merchants had requested their government to send warships and diplomats to China to extract commercial privileges. The United States, however, did not yet have the ability to dispatch expeditionary forces to remote countries. Nor was this step necessary. The British not only would do the job, but they would also share the war booty with other nations. When negotiating the peace treaty at Nanjing in 1842, the British envoy, Henry Pottinger, told his Chinese counterparts that if various countries won China's consent to trade at the treaty ports,[3] Britain would not stop them in order to seek exclusive gains.[4]

The American government was aware of Britain's attitude. Edward Everett, American minister to England, who supplied his government with all the news he could collect, reported that whatever advantage accrued to England as a result of the Treaty of Nanjing would be shared with the other powers.[5] The American government responded to the merchants' request for warships and diplomats by sending to China a squadron under Lawrence Kearny. In October 1842, more than a month after the signing of the treaty between Britain and China, Kearny sent a letter to Qi Gong, governor-general of Guangdong and Guangxi, demanding that American citizens "be placed upon the same footing as the merchants of the nation most favored."[6]

The Chinese government, in the face of this demand, could not delay making a policy to cope with nations other than Britain. The Qing court instructed the imperial commissioner Yilibu to reject Kearny's demand, but Yilibu dissented, arguing that

prohibition would give rise to complications and perversely cause the various countries to complain on account of England. Furthermore, it is feared that if England joins them and all alike come to trade, it will also be hard for us to prevent them and, perversely, the kindness would derive from the [English] barbarian leaders. Then the various countries would be well disposed toward England and resentful to China.[7]

Qiying, governor-general of Jiangsu, Jiangxi, and Anhui, held a view identical to that of Yilibu, and advocated "treating all with equal kindness." "If the United States and other countries are determined to trade in Fukien, Chekiang, and Kiangsu, it would seem that we could allow them likewise to draw up regulations and allow them to go where they will."[8] The Qing court, unable to extricate itself from the mire, accepted the two officials' suggestions. Yilibu died before he could meet with Kearny, who went back to the United States without knowing Yilibu's opinion. But Kearny's demand for unilateral most-favored-nation treatment and Qiying's policy of "treating all with equal kindness" had already predestined that China would become a common colony of several powers.

Before Kearny came home, the American government had decided to send to China a formal diplomatic mission to demand "equal footing," which would be consolidated by a treaty. Caleb Cushing, a strong friend of the merchants engaged in the China trade, was appointed commissioner. Secretary of State Daniel Webster gave him an instruction, which reads in part:

A leading object of the mission in which you are now to be engaged is, to secure the entry of American ships and cargoes into these ports on terms as favorable as those which are enjoyed by English merchants. . . . Your constant aim must be to produce a full conviction in the minds of the Government and the people, that your mission is entirely pacific; that you come with no purpose of hostility or annoyance; that you are a messenger of peace, sent from the greatest Power in America to the greatest Empire in Asia to offer respect and good will, and to establish the means of friendly intercourse. . . . It is hoped and trusted that you will succeed in making a treaty such as has been concluded between England and China."[9]

This instruction was the first declaration of America's policy toward China. Although it definitely prescribed that the supreme task of the mission was to secure all the privileges wrung from China by British gunboats, it still repeatedly stressed the necessity of maintaining peace and amity toward China. For the next century this two-pronged strategy was to characterize America's China policy.

Before Cushing arrived at Macao on February 24, 1844, Qiying had made it clear to all foreign merchants that they enjoyed "the imperial favor" and were authorized to proceed to the various ports and engage in trade on an equal basis.[10] There thus should have been no difficulty for Cushing to perform his task. But he wanted more. His real wish was to outstrip rather than just equal the British. According to his instruction, besides negotiating a treaty, he should proceed to Beijing to deliver a letter from the President of the United States to the Chinese Emperor, "if practicable"; if not, he might "consider the propriety of sending it to him."[11] It is obvious that this added request was only secondary and conditional. But Cushing, in order to exact further concessions, made this request a leading object and used it to intimidate the Chinese authorities who dreaded the fact of foreigners coming to the capital. Cushing, in a communication of April 16 to Cheng Yucai, acting governor-general of Guangdong and Guangxi, said that he intended to leave immediately for Beijing, and added that Western states would consider the refusal to receive the embassies of friendly states as a "just cause of war," and that perhaps "it would be necessary for my government, in the first instance, to subject the people of China to all the calamities of war."[12] Then, on learning that Qiying had been appointed imperial commissioner and was coming to Guangzhou to meet him, Cushing revealed his real intention. In a dispatch to Secretary of State Abel Upshur, he wrote:

So far as regards to objects of adjusting in a proper manner the commercial relations of the United States and China, nothing could be more advantageous than to negotiate with Tsiyeng at Canton, instead of running the risk of compromising this great object by having it mixed up at Tien Tsin, or elsewhere at the north, with questions of reception at Court.[13]

Nevertheless, though he finally negotiated with Qiying at Wangxia (a village near Macao), he still insisted on going to Beijing and continued to talk menacingly of this "momentous subject—perhaps involving the question of peace or war between the two countries."[14]

On April 9, a week before Cushing exerted pressure on Cheng Yucai, the Qing court had already delegated power to Qiying to negotiate a treaty with the American envoy. But Cushing's threats, though coming after this delegation, were not superfluous; because of them, Qiying indicated an unusual readiness to make concessions, particularly if the American envoy gave up his projected journey north. When Cushing did announce his abandonment of the project, one which he had never intended to carry out, he then won, on July 3, 1844, the imperial commissioner's signature to the Treaty of Wangxia.

While actual force was needed to win the Treaty of Nanjing, a mere threat of such won the Treaty of Wangxia. Besides gaining all privileges stipulated in the former, the Treaty of Wangxia imposed on China more concrete and harsher obligations in regard to extraterritoriality, fixed tariff duties, and unilateral most-favored-nation treatment. According to the treaty, China did not even have the right to interfere with disputes in China between citizens of the United

States and the subjects of other nations. While the Treaty of Nanjing only stipulated that a fair and regular tariff "shall be publicly notified and promulgated for general information," the Treaty of Wangxia provided that if the Chinese government desired to modify the tariff, such modifications should be made "only in consultation with" American officials.[15] It also provided for additional privileges, such as the revision of the treaty after twelve years and permission for American warships to enter China's ports. It was "greatly superior to the English agreement," wrote the historian Tyler Dennett, "so superior that it became immediately the model for the French treaty negotiated a few weeks later."[16]

This so-called "model treaty," together with other unequal treaties concluded in these years, marked the beginning of a long and humiliating process, the reduction of China to a semicolonial country dominated, with the cooperation of the Qing regime, by foreign powers. This development involved the Chinese people in a twofold struggle: one against the imperialism of the foreign powers, the other against feudalism.

Two days after the signing of the Treaty of Wangxia, Cushing complacently wrote:

I recognize the debt of gratitude which the United States and all other nations owe to England, for what she has accomplished in China. From all this much benefit has accrued to the United States.

But, in return, the treaty of Wang Hiya, in the new provisions it makes, confers a great benefit on the commerce of the British empire; for the supplementary English treaty stipulates that any new privileges conceded by Chinese to other nations shall be enjoyed also by England, and there is a similar provision in the treaty of Wang Hiya; and thus, whatever progress either government makes in opening this vast empire to the influence of foreign commerce, is for the common good of each other and of all Christendom.[17]

Cushing candidly confessed that the United States, like Great Britain, not only wanted the right to trade, but also wanted special privileges—and quite extraordinary privileges at that, privileges that meant, in fact, subjection to Western imperialism. No wonder that the canny among the Chinese realized that the United States and Britain were birds of a feather, and no wonder that the U.S. would become one of the chief targets of the Chinese people's struggle against imperialism. From 1844 on, United States aggression and Chinese resistance defined the Sino-American relationship.

Yet there was a difference in form between America and the other imperialist powers. The American warships which accompanied the diplomats had not, after all, fired a shot, nor was the Treaty of Wangxia a settlement whose purpose was to terminate a war. It was officially called the "Treaty of Peace, Amity, and Commerce." Such flaunting of peace and amity was to play a unique role in subsequent events.

The signing of the treaties did not mean that the aggressors were completely satisfied with the privileges they had exacted from China. The area legally opened to foreign trade was, for example, limited to only five treaty ports, all situated on the southeast coast. The Chinese government still excluded all foreigners from the north coast and from the vast interior, and refused to permit foreign diplomatic personnel to reside in Beijing, considering that a concession on this question would be tantamount to a declaration to the Chinese people that the all-powerful Qing throne had bowed to the foreigners. When signing the treaties, the foreign powers left this question pending for the time being. Gradually, however, they came to the conclusion that in order to both deal effectively with and extend their influence over China, they must secure the right for their envoys to reside in Beijing.

Like the other treaty powers, America yearned for rapid expansion along China's north coast and penetration into the interior. After concluding the Treaty of Wangxia, American trade with China started to boom: from 1845 to 1860 total volume increased from $9.5 million to $22.5 million.[18] The prospect that China would offer an unlimited market became much brighter. After the United States' westward expansion reached the Pacific coast of their own continent, the Americans even became confident that they were destined to dominate the trade of East Asia. But there still remained crucial restrictions preventing trade with the whole of China. To end those restrictions, the Americans found in the Treaty of Wangxia a convenient handle. The last clause of that treaty said:

inasmuch as the circumstances of the several ports of China open to foreign commerce are different, experience may show that inconsiderable modifications are requisite in those ports which relate to commerce and navigation: in which case, the two governments will, at the expiration of twelve years from the date of the said convention, treat amicably concerning the same by the means of suitable persons appointed to conduct such negotiation.[19]

The Americans thought they could draw on this provision to demand the revision of the treaty and the opening up of the whole of China. Even an old-type mandarin like Yiliang, governor-general of Jiangsu, Jiangxi, and Anhui, could point out that this provision "implied nothing more than certain adjustments at the five ports necessitated by changed circumstances, certainly not major changes."[20] The American minister, William Reed, a lawyer, also admitted that the invoking of this provision was "the weak point of our case."[21] Unequal treaties, however cautiously spelled out, could still, in the hands of the powerful, be forged into ever more binding fetters. For aggressive diplomats, even a weak point could be used to serve their purpose. By invoking the most-favored-nation clause, Britain and France claimed that they also had the right to make major changes in their treaties. So, in the early 1850s, the three powers banded together and demanded a treaty revision.

At the very time of these demands, a violent storm burst out over China. The Taiping Insurrection of 1850/51–1864 was an explosion of peasant anger, a deep and intense anger. In less than three years it enveloped six provinces, and in March 1853 the Taiping Heavenly Kingdom established its capital at Nanjing. China was divided into two states.

Though the diplomats and governments of the three powers were now unanimous that the moment was propitious for a treaty revision, they still, for the time being, preferred to watch and wait, and to plan those measures that would best extend their treaty rights.

In May 1853, the American commissioner, Humphrey Marshall, suggested to his government a two-China policy which would recognize "the new government at Nanking de facto and the old one at Peking de jure." He said that the purpose of his policy was "to seize advantage for my country," and to find out which one of the two governments would grant more privileges.[22] Later he recommended that the United States should support the Qing government on condition that it make concessions.

The American government did not immediately adopt Marshall's proposal. It instructed his successor, Robert McLane, to negotiate a new treaty with the Qing government, but it also allowed him, if the Qings refused his demands, to deal with the Taipings. In May 1854, McLane made a trip to Nanjing and Wuhu in search of firsthand information. After the tour, he became convinced that the success of the Taipings would in no way benefit the foreign powers. In his report to Secretary of State William Marcy, he said:

[The Taipings] are composed almost exclusively of the ignorant
unenlightened population of the interior . . . whose origin was a
band of robbers in the interior, . . . unworthy of respect of the civi-
lized world, and perhaps incapable of consolidating civil government beyond the walls of the cities captured and pillaged by
a multitude excited to the highest pitch of resentment against
all who possess property or betray a partiality for the Imperial
authorities.[23]

Obviously, McLane was on the side of those who possessed property,
and considered the toiling masses represented by the Taipings as his
real enemy in China. It is thus not surprising that he believed that
the Taiping government would not fulfill the present treaty obligations or make the same concessions as granted by the Qing government.[24] So he decided to negotiate with the Qing authorities, though
not without trying to intimidate them by threatening negotiations
with the Taipings.

Unable to get satisfaction from local governors, McLane and the
British minister, John Bowring, sailed north and reached Dagu, at
the mouth of the Beihe River, on October 16, 1854, where they
called for direct negotiations with the central government. Emperor
Xianfeng dispatched a lesser official, Conglun, to deal with the foreigners. They presented Conglun with their demands for the free
navigation of the Changjiang (Yangtze) River, the right to trade and
reside in any part of China, the right to fish in the Chinese coastal
waters, payment of custom duties in gold, and permission for foreign
diplomats to reside in Beijing. Then they combined inducements
with threats:

Here are the ministers of two of the greatest of . . . nations, who
would approach the emperor with friendly disposition and rejoice to
see his throne upheld and peace and order restored throughout his
realm. But if his Majesty rejects them under such circumstances,
they may go to the rebels themselves.[25]

These inducements and threats, however, produced little result.

After the outbreak of the Taiping revolution, the Qing government
had decided that, come what may, it would never compromise with
the "insurgents" but would instead fight to the bitter end. It was thus
a foregone conclusion that the government would go to any length to
appease the aggressive demands of the foreigners, an appeasement
that would give the Qings the freedom to wage an all-out struggle

against the Taipings. But, at the same time, the government feared that the foreigners would ultimately aid the "rebels," because of a number of foreign missionaries and merchants who, in the first years of the Taiping revolution, had sympathized with the Taipings in the hope that this new political force, which professed Christianity, would open China up to them. The Qings thus became uncertain whether concessions could really win the foreigners over. In August 1854, Jierhanga, governor of Jiangsu, requested the Emperor to commission "a minister of long experience and great distinction to come and conclude suitable regulations" with McLane.[26] In an edict, the Emperor refused the request, reprimanded Jierhanga, and ordered that armed forces should closely guard the ports on the lower reaches of the Changjiang River to prevent foreign warships from forcing their way up the river and making "illicit alliances with rebels."[27] This edict reveals that the Qing court still suspected that the foreign powers might cooperate with the Taipings. It thus hesitated, during the Dagu negotiations, to grant all the demands raised by the two envoys, though it was ready to make partial and minor concessions. Because of these hesitations, the 1854 negotiations for treaty revision came to nothing, and the two envoys returned empty-handed to Shanghai.

As the envoys told Conglun, their departure did not mean that the powers would abandon the Qing regime for the "rebels." On the contrary, following McLane's mission the American government had decided to have nothing to do with the Taipings. So had the British. McLane's claim that the Taipings were ignorant, unworthy robbers by origin, and incapable of government reflects an attitude toward China's revolutionaries defined by both a white man's sense of supremacy and a capitalist's high regard for property. Only the Qing regime could safeguard and extend their treaty rights. In October 1855, Secretary of State Marcy told the newly appointed commissioner, Peter Parker, that he was to "consider the Emperor as the Sovereign of China. To him and his Government alone can we look for the faithful execution of the treaty now existing between the United States and China."[28] The foreign powers would uphold the Emperor's throne and help him to restore "peace and order," but not now. First they needed to teach him a lesson in servility.

Britain and France were ready to resort to force. In late 1856, after the end of the Crimean War, these two European powers, using minor incidents as pretext, unleashed another war against China and in December 1857 occupied Guangzhou. The United States, beset by the slavery issue and other international problems, decided to take no part in the war, but its diplomatic representative was instructed to "unite with them in their efforts for a revision of the existing treaties."[29] In his instruction to William Reed, the first minister accredited to China, Secretary of State Lewis Cass said that President Buchanan recognized the goals which Britain and France sought as just and expedient, and that "so far as you can do so by peaceful cooperation, he expects that you will aid in their accomplishment."[30] In February 1858, Reed sent a letter to the Qing government, defending the allies' military action and offering "to interpose his mediation to avert the miseries which war inflicts even when mercifully conducted."[31] America was no longer satisfied to follow behind the British gunboats and collect their dividends. Its diplomats now wanted to help the allies accomplish their common objectives by playing the part of "mediator."

Russia also interfered in the affair. In 1857 it sent an envoy to Hong Kong to consult with the British, French, and American ministers on how to bring pressure on China. In his letter of February 1858 Reed had told the Qing government that America and Russia "have always been, and are yet the friends of China."[32] When the Anglo-French fleets sailed northward, all four envoys—of both the enemies and the so-called "friends"—accompanied the invading forces.

In April they arrived at Dagu. Shocked by this turn of events, Emperor Xianfeng directed the governor-general of Zhili, Tan Ting-xiang, to proceed to Tianjin to supervise the negotiations. Now America's strategy of peace and amity demonstrated its efficacy. The Emperor specially enjoined Tan that "as the American chief never helped the evildoers, he can be received affably" and should be distinguished from the British and French.[33] When Tan arrived at Dagu on April 28, 1858, the American and Russian ministers expressed their willingness to meet with him for peaceful negotiations, disregarding the allied ministers' refusal to do so. Encouraged by American friendliness, Tan begged Reed to act as mediator, and went to great lengths to satisfy Reed's demands in the hope that his mediation would help China. But Tan's hopes were in vain. He had to confess, in his own blunt words, that "England and France openly show malice; America and Russia secretly foster crime. While their strength and weakness vary, they are all in one category in their insatiable greed."[34] Tan came to the conclusion that "their manifold schemes combine plots against us."[35]

Begging for mediation had only laid bare the Qing government's weakness and fed the arrogance of the British. On May 20, the allied warships bombarded the Dagu forts, destroyed them, and forced their way to Tianjin with little resistance. The American and Russian envoys followed the invading forces. The Emperor quickly sent two imperial commissioners, Guiliang and Huashana, to negotiate with the four envoys. In spite of Tan's disillusionment, the Qing court still hoped that if the commissioner would "reason with them [i.e., the American diplomats] they [might] be able to induce England and France to conclude the affair."[36] The next day, in the first interview with Reed, Guiliang found that the Americans "utilized the English barbarians to frighten us. . . . The items they proposed were many more than those presented to T'an T'ing-hsiang and it is impossible to think of having them intercede for us with England and France . . . the Russian and American barbarians merely want to get the fishermen's [i.e., the third party's] profit."[37] Yet Guiliang continued to implore Reed to mediate, even inserting in the new American treaty a clause which provided for American good offices in times of trouble. He did not hesitate to pay a high price for this mediation, accepting almost all of America's demands. But despite these efforts, the British remained fierce and arrogant. Like Tan, Guiliang could only bewail the fact that the Americans and Russians "are actually in the same category as the English and French."[38]

Tan and Guiliang were bound to be disappointed. America's policy was precisely what Guiliang said it was, an attempt to "get the fishermen's profit." From the outset Secretary of State Cass had stated the American case very clearly in his instruction to Reed:

During the hostilities which now exist in China, we may be able to avail ourselves of this fortunate position, not only for the benefit of our countrymen who reside there, or who have extensive interests there of a commercial character, but in order to facilitate also the general objects sought to be accomplished by a revision of the existing treaties.[39]

Given America's candid desire to revise the treaty to its own benefit, the question arises as to why the Chinese officials persisted in seeking mediation. The root cause of this unusual course lay in that, in this second war, the Qing government preferred to compromise with the foreign aggressors so that it could use all its resources in the war against the Taipings. Since real resistance was out of the question, the most it could hope for was that mediation would lessen the

foreigners' demands. Even though they learned that American prom-
ises were made of straw, they preferred to clutch at them rather than
strike out on a new path. Both enemies and mediators could thus
exploit the Qings' weakness and gain all that they desired. In June of
1858, each power obtained a new treaty, which increased and extended the many privileges China had, from 1842 to 1844, granted
to the foreigners.

A year later, in June of 1859, the British, French, and American
ministers again came to Dagu and expressed their desire to proceed
to Beijing to effect an exchange of the ratifications of the treaties of
Tianjin. The Chinese agreed, but only if the emissaries came over a
prescribed land route. The British and French refused and ordered
their fleets to bombard the Dagu forts. The Chinese garrison could
not but return the fire. The Anglo-French forces suffered heavy casualties, retreated, and prepared to take revenge in a larger military
effort. Yet the battle of Dagu did not mean that the Qing government's policy had changed; the allied defeat was as much a surprise to
the Qing court as to the British and French. The Emperor was still
bent on reconciliation with the foreign powers.

Unlike the British and French envoys, the American commissioner,
John Ward, traveled to Beijing by the land route prescribed by the
Chinese government. During the Dagu skirmish, American sailors,
with Ward's approval, had come to the rescue of the British and had
joined the British in loading the guns. Though the Emperor knew of
this, he still ordered Hengfu, the new governor-general of Zhili, to
give Ward the most friendly of treatments so that Ward would persuade the British and French ministers to come to Beijing for the
exchange of the ratifications. Ward completed the procedure of the
exchange in a peaceful manner. The British and French, however,
chose a different course. In 1860 they sent a larger expeditionary force
to Beijing, burned the Summer Palace, and, in October, forced the
Qing government to sign the conventions of Beijing, which confirmed the provisions of the treaties of Tianjin and imposed further
obligations on China.

China now sank deeper into the quagmire of semicolonialism. A
new relationship grew up between the foreign powers and the Qing
government, as the foreigners found it necessary and possible to
support the Qing regime and turn it into an instrument to serve
them. To enjoy without any molestation the privileges which the new
treaties granted in all parts of China, the powers had to bolster up the
Qing regime rather than see it crumble. At the same time, after they

had brought the Qings to their knees, they found that the latter were now "disposed to maintain order and our treaty rights."[40]

Anson Burlingame, the first American minister to reside in Beijing in conformity with the provisions of the Treaty of Tianjin, thus made every effort to uphold the Qing government. He held the opinion that

the Imperial Government should be treated not only as the de jure power in the land, but sustained for the sake of humanity in its desperate struggle with anarchy by whatever moral support was allowable in a diplomatic agent.[41]

For Burlingame "anarchy" was synonymous with "Taiping," and he urged the foreign powers to give all the aid they could to the Qing government in its effort to wipe out that insurrection. This proposal fitted well with the desire of Prince Gong, the Emperor's brother, who, after signing the conventions of Beijing, took charge of foreign affairs. He had suggested in a memorial of May 1861 that "if we unite with them [i.e., the foreign powers] to suppress the rebels, it will not be difficult gradually to wipe out the latter."[42] At this time, though, the United States was involved in its own civil war. The other powers were also unwilling to become bogged down in a long struggle against the Taipings. Burlingame thus proposed that the Qing government should "organize its own defense taking only foreigners for instructing in the arts of peace and war."[43]

In 1860, some Chinese officials and merchants in Shanghai had already hired Frederick Ward, an American mercenary, and asked him to enlist foreign soldiers for the war against the Taipings. In 1861 they changed the scheme and asked Ward to enlist Chinese recruits and have them trained in the use of modern weapons by American and British instructors. After the conclusion of the conventions of Beijing, with the official blessing of the Qings and the open support of American and British diplomats, Ward's army took an active part in fighting the Taipings. It was an army that conformed in every respect to Burlingame's idea. In September 1862, Ward died from a battle wound. Burlingame, in a special report to the State Department, expressed his deep sorrow over Ward's demise. "Indeed, he taught the Chinese their strength," wrote Burlingame, "and laid the foundations of the only force with which their government can hope to defeat the rebellion."[44] Burlingame recommended another American, Henry Burgevine, to succeed Ward. But Burgevine failed and was dismissed and replaced by the British officer Charles Gordon.

Subsequently, Gordon's army played an important role in the strangling of the Taiping revolution. America's financing and equipping of the Nationalist troops from 1945 to 1949 in order to suppress the Chinese revolution was thus no innovation: eighty-five years before, Ward and Burlingame had set the precedent.

Burlingame's second measure for the maintenance of the Qings required that the treaty powers cooperate in a unified plan of joint support. He laid great stress on such cooperation because it would also preserve the balance of power among the foreign nations in China. Before Burlingame, two other American commissioners to China, Alexander Everett and Humphrey Marshall, had feared that Britain would disrupt and dominate the Chinese Empire. Both therefore advocated, as did Burlingame, a policy of preserving the balance of power in China that would allow each foreign state to exert an equal influence and to enjoy equal opportunities. The outlook of all the commissioners reflected America's traditional policy toward China, one that had held sway since the Opium War. The achievement of equal opportunity for all required both the continued cooperation of the foreign powers and the preservation and use of the Qing regime as a common instrument of the powers.

These were the two conditions that Burlingame strove most energetically to create. In 1863, a year after his arrival in China, he wrote Secretary of State William Seward that Britain's control of the Chinese customs administration and of the affairs at the treaty ports had aroused the suspicion and rivalry of the treaty powers. To counter this tendency, he proposed a policy of cooperation. Since the interests of the treaty powers in China were identical, he argued, they should forget their rivalries, present a united front to the Chinese government, and defend their treaty rights against all who might violate them. At the same time, the powers should give their joint moral support to the Qing government and should in no way interfere with its jurisdiction over its own people, nor even menace the territorial integrity of the Chinese Empire.[45] The Qing government, for its part, must faithfully "cooperate" with its masters.

The Qing government was only too willing to undertake this obligation. Before Burlingame's arrival, Prince Gong had written, in a memorial of January 1861, that since the foreigners "are not going to make any claim either on our territory or on our people, they can yet be won over with good faith and tamed."[46] Since the foreign powers still had a use for the Qing government and were not inclined to supersede it, Prince Gong concluded that it was a paying proposition to make friends with them. But others wondered if any ill effect would arise from a policy of collaboration with foreign powers. Before coming to a definite conclusion, the central government instructed its provincial governors to give their opinions. Zeng Guofan, governor-general of Jiangsu, Jiangxi, and Anhui, and an influential figure of that time, considered the United States the ideal country to cooperate with, because "the Americans are of pure-minded and honest disposition and long recognized as respectful and compliant towards China."[47]

Burlingame, aware upon arriving in Beijing of this favorable disposition, immediately got on best terms with Prince Gong, Wenxiang (a member of the Grand Secretariat), and other high-ranking officials who favored the policy of collaboration. Under their direction, the newly established Board of Foreign Affairs set as its guideline in dealing with foreign powers "better accommodation than rupture."[48] The gratitude and confidence shown to Burlingame by the Qing official circle became fawning and so ludicrous that, when in November 1867 Burlingame was due to leave his post, the Board of Foreign Affairs made him their "Minister for the Management of Chinese Diplomatic Relations with the Powers" and placed him at the head of a mission to visit various foreign countries. The aims of the mission were to state China's difficulties and to inform the treaty powers of the sincere desire of the Chinese to be friendly and progressive.[49] But none of the treaty powers made allowances for China's difficulties. Except for the conclusion of a treaty with the United States that actually legalized the traffic in coolies, the mission made no noticeable dent in the policy of the powers. When the mission arrived in Russia, Burlingame fell ill and died, and the farce came to an end. So too did the "policy of cooperation."

"Peace and amity" thus developed into "cooperation," but a cooperation that contained at least two irresolvable contradictions. First, though under certain circumstances and at certain periods the aggressors could cooperate with one another regarding their common interests, the cooperation would break down when the underlying rivalries and suspicions became too intense. At such moments their unity would collapse and the balance would be upset. Even Secretary of State Seward, who approved Burlingame's policy, warned him that his proposed plan of cooperation would be precarious.[50] The greed of aggressors was insatiable, and most of the concessions of the compliant Qing government only whetted their appetite, making them unable to rest content with extorting economic privileges but rather inspiring them to encroach still further upon China's territory.

Second, for the Qing government, the rulers of a semicolonial country, cooperation with the treaty powers meant serving them, by maintaining order and upholding their treaty rights. But in the long run, these two functions were incompatible. While the foreign powers hoped to use the Qing officials to curb the people, and the imperial court to curb both the officials and the people,[51] at the same time, they wished to keep the Qings corrupt and impotent, and thus subservient and amenable to concession. As a result, the Qings were discredited and weakened. The more servile they became, the less capable they were of curbing the people.

2

The last three decades of the nineteenth century saw the rapid development of industry in various countries of Western Europe and in the United States. In these decades, as monopoly capitalism grew powerful, so did the appetite of these countries for colonies. They partitioned Africa, consolidated holdings in Southeast Asia, seized islands in the Pacific and Caribbean, moved into the Near East, and expanded their economic penetration into South America. Technologically superior, unrivaled in wealth and power, restless and intense rivals of one another, they sought to extend their influence throughout the globe, including China.

In the five years following the 1894–1895 Sino-Japanese War, the imperialist powers scrambled to acquire leased territories in China, to establish spheres of influence, and to increase their investments. By 1899, Germany had grabbed Jiaozhou Bay and taken control of Shandong Province; Russia had occupied Dalian (Dairen) and Lüshun (Port Arthur) and regarded Northeast China (Manchuria) and Mongolia as its sphere of influence; France had compelled the Chinese government to agree to its special privileges in Yunnan and Guangxi provinces and had also leased Guangzhou Bay; Great Britain had seized the port of Weihaiwei and made the Changjiang (Yangtze) Valley its own sphere; Japan had further compelled the Chinese government to declare that it would never cede Fujian Province to any other country.

The United States had not participated in cutting up China: it sought to realize its ambitions through other means. In the 1890s it was no less eager than the European powers for overseas expansion, and, under the guise of rescuing colonies from Spanish misrule, it did not hesitate to wage war against Spain, from which it gained Guam and the Philippines in the Pacific. Throughout that decade America's interest in China grew ever greater. Though trade with China was relatively small, only 2 percent of America's total foreign trade, it was expanding and showed promise. In the fervor for expansion, businessmen and politicians regarded China as a new frontier, one which would keep American commerce competitive with Europe and would relieve America's industrial glut by absorbing its surplus goods. Interest in China constituted one of the reasons for America to retain the Philippines; and the retention of those islands in turn heightened enthusiasm for expansion in China. The Philippines would furnish a political and military base for the ultimate domination of the "new frontier."

But, unlike the Philippines, China was not a colony of a declining Western power, but a field of competition among several major powers. When the powers divided China into spheres, America was at first occupied with the Spanish war and then, later, with the insurrection of the Philippine people. When it did shift its attention to China, it found that its existing interests were in danger. The spheres of influence, especially those controlled by Russia and Germany in north China, threatened to deny American capital opportunities for profitable investment and potent channels of trade and political influence. American business interests and diplomatic representatives thus urged their government to take a strong hand in Chinese affairs.

But America was not strong enough to oust the powers from their respective spheres. It considered some plans to obtain a leasehold, but did not earnestly carry them out. Disdaining to take a mere fragment of the Chinese melon, it sought instead to use its formidable economic power throughout the whole of the China market. In the 1890s America's industrial production had already surpassed that of Germany and Britain and assumed the leading position. In 1899 manufactured products began to account for more than 90 percent of American exports to China. The absolute volume of manufactured exports also experienced a sharp rise, multiplying four times between 1895 and 1899, from $3.2 million to $13.1 million.[1] In the expansionist psychology of the 1890s, these statistics bolstered the widespread expectation that, given an open door to China's market, the United States could become economically dominant. Even the cautious John Hay, secretary of state from 1898 to 1905, claimed in a public letter that "in the field of trade and commerce we shall be the keen competitors of the richest and greatest powers, and they need no warning to be assured that in that struggle, we shall bring the sweat to their brows."[2] The best alternative to leasehold and spheres of influence, therefore, and the most promising for America's expansion, was for all the powers to open their spheres to the trade of every other nation.

On September 6, 1899, Hay dispatched instructions to the American ambassadors in London, Berlin, and St. Petersburg informing them that the United States desired that England, Germany, and Russia pledge their support of an open door policy in those Chinese territories in which they were dominant. A few days later he circulated the same note to Japan, Italy, and France. The note requested that every power claiming a sphere of influence in China make a formal declaration that they (1) would in no way interfere with any treaty port or any vested interest, (2) would maintain an equitable administration of the Chinese customs tariff, and (3) would levy no discriminatory railway rates or harbor dues on merchandise or vessels belonging to other nations.[3]

The open door policy, as reflected in these requests, did not mean that the United States was opposed to aggression in China. In 1895, at the end of the Sino-Japanese War, American businessmen and diplomats were as delighted with the Treaty of Shimonoseki between China and Japan as they had been, fifty-three years earlier, with the Treaty of Nanjing. This newest of the unequal treaties opened seven new Chinese ports and three new rivers, abolished some internal taxes, and, above all, granted foreigners the right to create within China their own industrial enterprises. By the unilateral most-favored-nation clause, these provisions would widen the market not only for merchandise but also for investment. An American consul-general in Shanghai thought that the missiles of war had made "a decided opening . . . in the opposing wall of Chinese conservatism, and that a widening market may be expected for Western production."[4]

Even before the end of the war, American capitalists swarmed over China, preparing to invest in railroads, banking, and mining. Reporting to the State Department on these enterprises, the American minister, Charles Denby, expressed optimism about their future prospects:

As some indication of the work done here it may be stated that first at this moment the accomplishment of great plans, by which railroad building and mining and other matters connected therewith will, it is hoped, be carried on by Americans, is on the eve of becoming assured. . . . I am satisfied that if the plans now awaiting the decision of the American negotiators are consummated this almost limitless field of financial and industrial operations will be occupied, dominated, and controlled by Americans.[5]

A year later, the tone of Denby's reports had changed. A general partitioning would, he said in a more pessimistic vein, make "prohibitive duties" a certainty and "would tend to destroy our market."[6] If the powers exercised greater and greater control in their spheres, the Chinese market, widened by the Treaty of Shimonoseki, would soon be either narrowed or closed to American businessmen. Hay's note of September 6, 1899, was an attempt to counter this tendency, not to counter aggression. On the contrary, it was an effort to preserve the fruits of aggression.

The open door policy was not a challenge to the existence of spheres of influence. In fact, it recognized and accepted such spheres—areas where the controlling power would have commercial privileges, superior investment rights, and a concomitant political influence. Though the policy sought to preserve equal opportunities for trade within the spheres, it did not mention equal opportunities for investment. Hay's objective in 1899 was of a limited nature. He wanted only guarantees for a trader's equality.

The "open door" did not imply a policy opposed to that of the other powers. Britain had all along assumed the most influential position in China. What it feared was not free competition but restrictions which might result from definite spheres of influence. As early as January 1896, it had consulted and won France over to an agreement that both countries should have equal rights to all concessions secured in Yunnan and Sichuan provinces. During 1898, Britain had repeatedly asked the United States to cooperate in opposing all tendencies that would restrict freedom of commerce in China, whether it be by imposing preferential conditions or by obtaining the cession of coastal territory. But the United States preferred independent action to any alliance with a European power.

The open door policy itself was drafted on the basis of a memorandum presented by the Englishman Alfred Hippisley, a longtime official in the Chinese customs. Both the United States and Britain saw Russia as the chief enemy of the open door policy; Hay's note, in fact, was directed primarily against that nation. But even the Russian government had, in August 1899, issued a ukase which announced that no restriction would be imposed on foreign commerce in the Russian sphere. (Indeed, Hippisley confessed that it was after reading the Russian ukase that he drew up his memorandum.)[7] Earlier, Germany too had published a white paper, declaring the port of Jiaozhou a free one. After receiving Hay's note, every power agreed to an equality of trade and navigation in their spheres, though not without reservation. Britain added the remark that America's proposal "was in substantial conformity with the policy and spirit" of the British government.[8] Indeed, the open door policy was not opposite to, but in conformity with, the more or less common stand then taken by the powers.

The basic reason why they supported such a policy was that no one of the imperialist powers was strong enough to swallow all of China. As for partitioning China into colonies, there was much talk of it, but the powers' conflict of interests in China was very complicated, far more so than in Africa. Moreover, for centuries China had been a powerful and unified country; outright partition would have aroused the fiercest opposition from the people. Each of the powers thus reasoned that it would be most advantageous to maintain the principle "Let's all share in equal opportunities" in order that one power would not be crowded out by the others. And as for further expansion, all would await the future, and all would wait in concert.

Equality of opportunity and influence—such was the gist of the open door policy. President McKinley himself had defined the policy as meaning "no advantages in the Orient which are not common to all."[9] An appeal to the controlling powers to open up their spheres to all, the policy was not an appeal to China, whose doors the foreigners had already thrown open after the Opium War. "Equal treatment to all" was now the business of the foreign powers. Neither the United States nor the other powers deemed it necessary to sound out the attitude of the Chinese government, even though the matter directly concerned that country. China had become a passive object. In fact, the United States even neglected to inform China of its actions until international rumors provoked the Chinese to make an official inquiry. In answering the inquiry, the American minister told the Zongli Yamen (Board of Foreign Affairs) that the open door policy had insured China's "integrity," and therefore, to reap this bounty, China should faithfully discharge its treaty obligations.[10] China's business was only discharging obligations; every nation but China had an opportunity.

It is ironical that the Qing government accepted the open door as a bounty. Since the Opium War, the Qing officials in charge of foreign affairs had, time after time, resorted to the ancient tactic of "playing the barbarians off against one another."[11] Their recourse to American mediation in the 1850s, however fruitless, was still an attempt to use the Americans to counter the British. To outmaneuver one's enemies by exploiting the contradictions among them is an astute idea, but it can succeed only if one stands on one's own feet and takes the initiative. After China had slipped into the mire of semicolonialism and after the Qing regime had become the vassal of imperialist powers, "playing off the barbarians" meant basing China's survival on the unpredictable contradictions among the great powers.

The Qing officials, especially Li Hongzhang, practiced precisely these tactics. Li had built himself up in the government by taking a major part in the suppression of the Taiping revolution. For thirty years after 1870 he had, as governor-general of Zhili and a minister of the Board of Foreign Affairs, directed China's foreign policy. He had also done much to modernize China's national defense. He bought machinery abroad to set up factories, arsenals, and shipyards, and foreign warships and arms to build up China's naval and land forces. But all these undertakings were based on a rotten autocracy and bureaucracy—they were modern in name but not in reality. Li himself was well aware of his own weakness. Afraid of committing his army and navy during the war crisis of 1894 between China and Japan, he resorted to the old tactic of wooing the major powers, imploring them, one by one, to mediate the crisis. But in vain: the Japanese attacked, and Li's "modern" navy and army disintegrated.

After the conclusion of the Treaty of Shimonoseki, however, which ceded the Liaodong Peninsula to Japan, Russia, France, and Germany did intervene, forcing Japan to return the peninsula to China. Thus for Li Hongzhang and his colleagues, the old tactic still paid off. They regarded the three powers as "saviors." Li even concluded a secret alliance with Russia in 1896, with a view to using Russia to check Japan. But soon Germany, Russia, and France—the three "saviors"—extorted their own rewards, in terms of generous leaseholds and spheres of influence. The other powers followed suit and demanded, on the grounds of equality of concessions and a balance of influence, their own leaseholds and spheres. The situation had reversed itself; now, instead of China exploiting the contradictions among the powers in order to save its territory, the powers exploited China's weakness and used its territories to adjust their contradictions. The imperialists' scramble for spheres revealed the bankruptcy of the strategy of "playing off the barbarians."

It was at this juncture, and to the surprise of the Qing officials, that the United States urged the policy of an open door. If China had become the colony of a single, powerful, ruling state, the Qing regime would have ceased to exist. But in a China "open to all," even the Qings could remain the rulers of an "integrated" country. They realized that if they accepted the common control of the powers, they could also enjoy their joint protection. So the Qings prized the open door policy highly and even attempted, as the next chapter will show, to pursue an open door policy of their own.

In the northern provinces, the intensification of aggression turned the Chinese people's indignation into a peasant movement known as the Boxer Uprising, with militant slogans directed against the foreigners and their religion. The Qing rulers, who had cringed before the foreign powers and believed that no external crisis would arise, suddenly found themselves, in 1899 and 1900, confronted with crisis at the heart of their realm. At first the movement terrified them. Later, as they found it impossible to check the movement's spread, they adopted a policy of deceit to turn it to their own interest. This impelled them to stiffen their attitude toward the foreign powers, though only as a gesture. In June 1900, when the Boxers had extended their activities to the vicinity of Beijing, the imperial edicts still called them "mobs" or "bandits" and declared that they should be suppressed.[12] But all efforts either to exterminate or to pacify the Boxers failed. On June 21, the Qing court, in an imperial rescript, declared war on the foreign powers and drove the Boxers to attack the foreign legations. But four days later, in reply to memorials from the governors-general of the southern provinces, new imperial rescripts explained that the earlier rescripts had been issued against the rulers' will, issued only because the Boxers had "turned up even in the neighborhood of the imperial palace." They then added that since an extermination campaign might have led to unexpected consequences, it seemed "more advisable to make use of [the rebels] so as to avert a crisis."[13] At the same time, they instructed their envoys abroad to tell the respective governments that "China, even unaware of its own limitations, would not go to the extent of opening hostilities with all the powers simultaneously and would not depend on the rebel mobs to fight the powers."[14]

The Boxer Uprising also took the foreign powers by surprise. In June, when the Boxers entered Beijing and became the virtual rulers of the capital, the powers realized the seriousness of the situation. On June 17, 1900, a combined naval squadron of the powers took Dagu and laid siege to Tianjin. They then had to fight the hardest battle they had so far experienced in their aggressive wars in China, because the mounting anti-imperialist sentiments had stirred the people to heroic resistance. It was only on July 14 that the powers' combined forces finally occupied Tianjin.

While the imperialist forces and the Boxers were locked in fierce battle in Tianjin, John Hay, on July 3, issued his second circular note to the concerned powers:

In this critical posture of affairs in China it is deemed appropriate to define the attitude of the United States as far as present circumstances permit this to be done. . . . The policy of the government of the United States is to seek a solution which may bring about permanent safety and peace to China, preserve Chinese territorial and administrative entity, protect all rights guaranteed to friendly powers by treaty and international law, and safeguard for the world the principle of equal and impartial trade with all parts of the Chinese Empire. [15]

To protect "all rights" and to safeguard equal trade still remained the ends of American policy. And the means remained the preservation of the "Chinese territorial and administrative entity." It was a practical policy, not an abstract principle, and in 1900 its specific meaning was to preserve the rule of the Qing government in all parts of the Chinese Empire. The Americans knew that the Qing regime was still a tool of the imperialists. During the Boxer affair, the United States struggled on two fronts—on the one hand with the foreign powers and on the other hand with the anti-imperialist movement of the Chinese people. It was frustrating to have to use the Qing regime to cope with these two adversaries.

The United States feared that the other powers might take advantage of the situation in order to partition China openly. In February 1901, John Hay, deeply apprehensive that Russia was planning a coup in Northeast China, reiterated his concern for China's integrity in a strongly worded note to the Chinese Board of Foreign Affairs, warning that it would be "unwise and dangerous in the extreme for China to make any arrangements . . . involving the surrender of territory or financial obligations by Convention with any particular Power." [16] A surrender of Chinese territory to Russia or any other nation would upset the delicate balance of power in the Far East. For America in 1900 the maintenance of that balance had a new significance. From the middle of the nineteenth century, American diplomats in China had talked about how to prevent a foreign state from gaining a preponderant role within the Chinese Empire. In that period, America's policy was directed mainly at protecting its economic interests. But after the seizure of the Philippines in 1898, according to William Rockhill, Hay's advisor and author of the first open door note, the United States became interested in China politically, soon emerging as an active participant in Asian politics. It had to hold the balance of power in China, promote peaceful competition, and expand American interests; [17] the realization of these ambitions required the preservation of the Qing rule.

The American government also feared that the Boxer movement would spread, and consular dispatches constantly warned of the danger of an uprising in the central and southern provinces. The circular note of July 3 announced that it was America's purpose "to prevent a spread of the disorder to the other provinces of the Empire and a recurrence of such disasters." [18] In furthering this purpose, the American government found the Qing provincial rulers highly useful. Li Hongzhang, who in 1899 and 1900 was governor-general of Guangdong and Guangxi, Liu Kunyi, governor-general of Jiangsu, Jiangxi, and Anhui, Zhang Zhidong, governor-general of Hubei and Hunan, and several other governors consistently argued that their primary task was to suppress the rebels and that in no circumstances would they disrupt their relations with the foreign powers. While the imperialist powers combined to attack China in the north, friendly diplomatic and trade relations were to be maintained in the south and east.

On June 21, 1900, Liu Kunyi asked Wu Tingfang, the Chinese minister in Washington, to inform the American President that he, Liu, together with Zhang Zhidong, was confident of keeping the peace and protecting foreigners. President McKinley answered this pledge by ordering the U.S. military forces to refrain from attacking central and southern provinces as long as local authorities maintained order. [19] On June 26, delegates of Liu and Zhang and of the foreign consuls at Shanghai agreed in principle to an arrangement whereby the two governors-general would protect the life and property of foreign merchants and missionaries in their provinces and the foreign troops there would take no action. [20] On July 3, Liu and Zhang sent a joint telegram to the Chinese legations abroad promising to keep the peace in the areas of their jurisdiction. John Hay expressed "appreciation" to these officials, and in his circular note gave them special mention and encouragement. So long as they protected foreigners,

Hay added, "we regard them as representing the Chinese people, with whom we seek to remain in peace and friendship."[21] Referring to the punitive expeditions launched by German forces from Beijing into adjoining areas, Hay complained:

The great viceroys, to secure whose assistance was our first effort and our first success, have been standing by us splendidly for the last four months. How much longer they can hold their turbulent population quiet in the face of these constant incitements to disturbance which Germany and Russia are giving is hard to conjecture.[22]

In Hay's opinion, direct foreign military repression, throughout China, of the Chinese people's resistance would only incite and intensify anti-imperialist sentiments. The best way to "hold the turbulent population quiet" was thus to use the "assistance" of the Qing rulers. This fact provided the major reason why the powers should preserve China's "administrative entity."

To assist the Qings, the American government not only sent troops to reinforce the international expeditionary forces, but it also dispatched William Rockhill to Beijing as a special commissioner. Rockhill's two tasks were, first, to suppress the Boxers in the north and prevent the spread of the insurrection into the south and, second, to bring about a settlement that would preserve the current regime and achieve the ends stated in the note of July 3. Rockhill arrived at Beijing in September. One month before, on August 14, the combined forces of the foreign powers had stormed into the city, and the imperial family, who had fled the capital, had appointed Li Hongzhang and Prince Qing as joint plenipotentiaries and ordered them to sue for peace.

Rockhill called upon Prince Qing. The Prince expressed his "sincere gratification" concerning Hay's circular note. Rockhill urged the reestablishment of complete order, since only through such order could the offensive operations of the foreign forces be checked. The Prince answered that imperial instructions had already been issued for the extermination of the Boxers everywhere and that these orders were being carried out.[23] Rockhill undisguisedly demanded that the Qing government perform in earnest its function of repressing the anti-imperialist movement of the Chinese people.

In October 1900, because of the concern that the Boxer movement might erupt in a new form in the Changjiang Valley, Rockhill made a special trip from Beijing to Shanghai and then to Nanjing and Wuchang. At Nanjing, he called on Liu Kunyi and thanked him for his "statesmanship" in maintaining order. Liu answered that he would continue to his utmost to achieve that goal. In Wuchang, Zhang Zhidong warned the American envoy that an antidynastic and anti-foreign uprising might break out in his provinces and might spread all over the empire. Faced with these dangers, Rockhill told his government that the maintenance of these governors-general in their present offices "is of vital importance to all the Powers and too much cannot be done for them." [24] The author of the open door note, in these reports, had now revealed the fuller meaning of that policy and of its insistence on preserving China's "territorial and administrative entity."

Rockhill also negotiated with the other powers for a settlement of the Boxer affair. It would not be too difficult to secure from the other powers an acceptance of the second note, because, like the first one, it was not opposed to their basic policy. In 1900–1901, the foreign powers, including the United States, were prepared for the eventuality of the partition of China. Hay's note of July 3 did not specifically renounce American territorial desires in China—President McKinley deliberately instructed John Hay not to include any such self-defying pledge. [25] But no country was ready to face a total disintegration of China. Though the powers did distrust each other and did bicker much during both the war and the peace negotiations, they all considered the status quo as more advantageous than a division of Chinese territory.

Even Russia, which was taking the occasion to occupy Northeast China, issued a circular telegram in August 1900 proposing to all the interested states the following principles:

First. The maintenance of the harmony among the powers.
Second. The integrity of the former rule of Government in the Chinese Empire.
Third. The setting aside of all that might lead to a dismemberment of China; and, lastly,
Fourth. The restoration at Peking, through common efforts, of the legally institutional Central Government which would be competent to insure by itself order and tranquility in the country. [26]

After completing the occupation of Northeast China, Russia did not neglect to sign interim agreements with the local Chinese authorities, thus preserving China's nominal jurisdiction over the three northeast provinces.

On August 2, 1900, Britain's under-secretary for foreign affairs,

St. John Broderick, speaking in the British House of Commons, stated that Britain would see to it that war did not spread to the Changjiang Valley. In the event of an emergency in which governors-general proved too weak to handle the situation, Britain would come to their aid. Broderick added that Britain also opposed the carving up of China. [27]

On October 16, 1900, Britain and Germany signed an agreement that declared that the ports on the rivers and coasts of China should remain free and open to the trade and legitimate economic activities of all countries without distinction. The agreement also stipulated that Britain and Germany would not "make use of the present complication to obtain for themselves any territorial advantages in Chinese dominions and [would] direct their policy toward maintaining undiminished the territorial conditions of the Chinese Empire." [28]

The open door policy, initiated by the United States, had finally became the basic program of all the powers. Because forthright division of China would lead to bitter upheavals, upheavals that would be very damaging to the foreign powers, all concerned preferred the status quo. The United States, of course, as a major power, had exerted its weight in bringing the powers into line. But one of the basic factors which prevented the imperialists from carving up China was the Boxer movement itself. The Englishman Robert Hart, inspector general of the Chinese customs, told Rockhill that

he looked upon the Boxer movement as a national and patriotic one for freeing China of the foreigners to whom, rightly or wrongly, it attributed all the country's misfortunes during the last half century. Though crushed at present, he feared that unless the powers would agree to treat the question in a conciliatory spirit which would tend to establish cordial relations with China—a state which had never existed in the past—it might someday come to life again when the world might have to face an armed China, not a rabble carrying spears and tridents. [29]

Hart, for one, realized that the most crucial factor in the situation was the anti-imperialist spirit of the Chinese people.

Alfred Waldersee, a German militarist and commander-in-chief of the joint invading forces, echoed Hart's view in a memorial to his Kaiser:

It cannot be forgotten that the mass of the population cannot count as effeminate or demoralized but still has original power. . . .

The Boxer movement also showed that their martial spirit has not been completely lost. At least 100,000 men of the two provinces of Shandong and Zhili joined the movement and were only beaten because they were badly equipped, to a great degree not even with shotguns.[30]

He therefore held that partition was an unwise move. In the House of Commons, under-secretary for foreign affairs Broderick expressed a similar opinion on the strength of the Chinese people:

I think we have learned by the events of the last few weeks how greatly the defensive power of China has been miscalculated, and that has reacted upon this country and upon this house.[31]

Their experience in dealing with the Boxers had taught the imperialists that partition would only evoke in the Chinese people a spirit of resistance and endless struggle.

The foreign powers, on the basis of the above agreements, imposed on China the "Protocol of 1901." The protocol became an instrument both for sustaining the Qings and for consolidating the imperialists' domination of China. It required the Qing government to extort from its people, as an indemnity to the foreigners, the huge sum of 450 million taels of silver; to pledge itself to suppress all antiforeign activities, societies, and organizations; and to allow the powers both to bring troops to Beijing for "protection" of their legations and to station them along the Beijing-Shanhaiguan line. The Qing rulers professed themselves "moved to tears" by so "magnanimous" a treaty. They also promised that they would forever serve their foreign overlords. From the Protocol of 1901 on, the powers became the direct guardians of the Qing government. Their diplomatic corps actually became the supergovernment of China, directing the Qing court in the Forbidden City. The China "preserved" by the open door policy was not a sovereign China.

Hay's open door policy may have had its origin in Burlingame's policy of cooperation, but Hay's policy was no mere repetition of Burlingame's. In Burlingame's era, when America followed behind the other foreign powers, the policy of cooperation was designed to prevent those powers from crowding out American interests. By the open door policy, however, the United States strove to take the lead in Asian politics and to ask the other powers to follow. Moreover, for America, the young industrial giant of the twentieth century, such a policy would open the way for an American hegemony in the Far East. American policy sought more than the protection of existing interests.

Yet the contradictions inherent in the cooperation policy remained unchanged. That concert of the powers so necessary for the open door policy would not last long. Within three years after the signing of the Protocol of 1901, the clash of colonial interests in Northeast China had driven Russia and Japan to war.

For China, continuance as an "entity" now meant the use of Chinese to curb Chinese, a shrewd reversal of China's policy of using the barbarians to curb the barbarians. When the powers presented the draft protocol to the fugitive Qing government in Xi'an in February 1901, the Qings issued an imperial edict to "all the subjects throughout the Empire," announcing that the government was to "do its utmost to seek the favor of the friendly powers." [32] For the imperialist powers, such a government was naturally worth preserving. But a government of this sort could no longer curb the people. Three years after the signing of the protocol, Dr. Sun Yat-sen founded the first Chinese revolutionary organization. The death knell of the Qing Dynasty had finally been rung.

3

"Open Door" Put to the Test

Even before the signing of the Protocol of 1911, a new round of rivalry among the foreign powers had begun to supplant that unity which was formed during the Boxer insurrection to safeguard their common interests. This rivalry put to the test the recently proclaimed principle of preserving the open door and China's integrity.

Russia had already, in August of 1900, taken the occasion of the Boxer insurrection to invade Northeast China and subject the three northeast provinces of Fengtian, Jilin, and Heilongjiang to a military occupation. The Russian foreign minister, in order to allay the other powers' suspicions, explained that the presence of Russian troops in Northeast and north China was but a temporary measure. Russia, he declared, had no intention whatever of seeking to acquire "a single inch of territory in either China or Manchuria."[1] Nevertheless, five months later Russia revealed its motives for occupying the Northeast. In February 1901, the Russian government handed the Chinese minister in St. Petersburg a set of demands: first, Russia would agree to the restoration of Chinese rule in the Northeast only if Russian troops could assist the railway guards in protecting the Russian-owned Chinese Eastern Railway; second, Chinese troops were to be withdrawn until the completion of the railway, at which time the number of returning troops was to be agreed on by Russia; third, if Russia complained of any official, he would be cashiered; fourth, China must promise not to grant any concession for railroads, mines, or industrial enterprises to foreign powers in Manchuria, Mongolia, and several districts in Xinjiang Province; and finally, China must grant the Chinese Eastern Railway the right to build a railway in the direction of Beijing and right up to the Great Wall.[2] These demands would not only establish a Russian protectorate over the Northeast but would also extend Russia's exclusive control to north and northwest China.

Though in late February, in response to China's objection, the Russians made some modifications, they still persisted in imposing an ultimatum on China: to either accept the demands or face the end of the talks and Russia's free disposal of the three northeast provinces.

Li Hongzhang, who had, from 1896 to 1898, sold out a series of national rights to Russia and who, in 1900 and 1901, conducted the negotiations with the Russian minister in Beijing, now advised the fugitive Qing court to accept the Russian terms. Only through such an acceptance, he said, could the complete loss of the three provinces be avoided. Zhang Zhidong and Liu Kunyi opposed Li's advice. These two influential governors-general in the Changjiang Valley, who had in 1900 maintained a relationship of "mutual protection" with the foreign powers, insisted on rejecting the Russian demands. Such a disgraceful acceptance would not only forfeit these provinces, but it would also invite the other foreign powers to ask for compensations. China would then be partitioned. Zhang and Liu suggested that since China was too weak to repel the Russians, it should enlist the support of the other powers to do so. Such a request was indeed the only way out. "The only chance of China's survival, and it is a slim one," wrote Zhang, "lies in balancing the antagonisms of the foreign powers."[3]

Yet Zhang also knew that without offering the other powers some rewards, they would never "exert their efforts" to help China. He crystallized his ideas into the following scheme:

It will be better to open up, without any reservations, the Three Eastern Provinces to the whole world for commerce than yield to Russia. People from various countries would be allowed to enjoy the benefits of mining, commerce, and free inhabitation while we would remain in the position to collect taxes. In the West such a policy is called "open door to all for commerce."[4]

He urged that the central government immediately inform Britain, Japan, Germany, and the United States of this plan. He was sure that those nations would be glad to accept the offer and to denounce Russia for wishing to bar other nations from sharing the benefits of the Northeast. In this way, "we shall have something with which to requite the foreign powers and at the same time preserve intact the Northeast."[5] It was a scheme, he boasted, which killed two birds with one stone. Wang Zhichuan, governor of Anhui, in putting forward a similar scheme, indulged in still wider fantasy. His plan, he claimed, would bring about three benefits: aside from foiling

Russia's ambitions and counterbalancing the foreign powers, the newly opened area would multiply the government's revenues.[6]

In April 1901, confronted by opposition on all sides, Russia withdrew its demands. In autumn, after Li Hongzhang had resumed the negotiations with the Russians, Zhang Zhidong, in a memorial which reiterated his plan, explained his version of the open door further by saying that, unlike the opening of the treaty ports, his projected opening of the Northeast would

allow men from every country into the interior of that area and allow them to live where they wish, though not to establish concessions. We shall not distinguish between Chinese and foreigners, but allow men from every country to initiate industry, commerce, mining, and railroad-building, and to share the benefits with the Chinese. The authority to govern will still be ours to exercise. . . . Our sovereignty will not be damaged in the slightest.[7]

What a rosy prospect! Zhang and his colleagues dreamed that they could lure the "barbarians" deep into the interior of the Northeast and then watch them either cut one another's throats or checkmate each other, thus saving these provinces for China. But none of the powers rose to Zhang's bait. And as subsequent events will show, even when they did penetrate into this region, the result was not the restoration of China's full sovereignty.

All the major powers except France opposed Russian domination of Northeast China, but not one of them, including the United States, the ardent advocate of the preservation of China's integrity, would "exert their efforts" to repel Russia on China's behalf. In February 1901, when Russia pressed China hard to accept its demands, John Hay issued a circular to China and the powers warning China not to agree to Russian demands without first consulting the other powers. By Hay's action it appeared that the United States would give support to the cause of Zhang Zhidong and Liu Kunyi. However, in a conversation with the Russian ambassador in Washington, Hay said:

We fully recognize Russia's right to adopt such measures as she considers necessary to prevent the repetition of the grievous events of last year. We would even have understood if she had gone further along this path, insofar as it could be acknowledged necessary for her interests and projects, if we have the assurance that our trade would not suffer and that the door would remain open.[8]

As the Sino-Russian talks dragged on into 1902, the Russian government still refused to withdraw its troops unless China granted a monopoly to the Russo-Chinese Bank for the financing of railway and mining enterprises in China's Northeast. On February 2, 1902, John Hay, following Japan and Britain, sent a protest to the Chinese Ministry of Foreign Affairs, saying that such a monopoly would violate the open door policy and would impair China's sovereign rights.[9] But despite his bold words in public, Hay privately admitted: "We are not in any attitude of hostility toward Russia in Manchuria. On the contrary, we recognize her exceptional position in northern China." [10]

In April 1902, Russia promised China that it would withdraw its troops from the Three Eastern Provinces in three stages, six months apart. But in April 1903, when the second stage was due, Russia refused to withdraw; it then perversely reoccupied Shenyang (Mukden) and presented China with seven demands, demands that aimed at turning the whole of north China into an exclusive Russian sphere of influence. During this new crisis, President Theodore Roosevelt said: "In this Manchurian matter we are not striving . . . to prevent Russia from acquiring any political control of the territory in question. . . . We have only insisted upon that freedom of access and of opportunity for commerce which has been guaranteed us." [11]

Within three years, John Hay and Theodore Roosevelt found themselves in full retreat from the policy of the second open door note. They had abandoned the defense of China as a "territorial and administrative entity" and limited their efforts simply to preserving the open door for commerce. This policy once again demonstrates that the preservation of China's integrity was largely a means for the protection of America's own interests. If Russia could guarantee the "freedom of opportunity for commerce" in the Northeast, China's integrity would cease to be an American concern.

In fact, Russia, during this period, had not given America any assurance that it would moderate its monopoly in favor of the open door for commerce. And later Theodore Roosevelt bluntly admitted that the open door policy "completely disappears as soon as a powerful nation determines to disregard it, and is willing to run the risk of war rather than forego its intention." [12] In other words, if Russia determined to squeeze out other nations by force, even the open door policy would be abandoned.

Indeed, when, in 1903, Russia revived the Manchurian crisis, John

Hay had countered by demanding that China open two more ports in the Northeast to American diplomats and businessmen. During the negotiations on this matter, the Chinese promised only that they would, "by themselves," open the ports later on, a promise that reflected their fear of losing their authority to govern these ports. The Americans, on the other hand, insisted on opening the ports on the pattern of other treaty ports, which would allow the foreigners to control the policing and administration of their enclaves themselves. In the end, the two sides agreed that the new Sino-American commercial treaty would designate the ports as self-opened and delay the question of port regulations for a later settlement. This episode produced little effect on Russia's monopolizing position in the Northeast, however; rather, it merely reveals that even had the United States or other powers accepted the "open door" plan designed by Zhang Zhidong, China would still have lost its sovereign rights in the Northeast. In the negotiations, when the Chinese declined to submit, Hay had remarked: "It will never do to let them imagine . . . that the only power they need fear is Russia" [13]—a threat that suggested that America could be just as aggressive as Russia.

In retreating before Russia's advance, Theodore Roosevelt and John Hay found that Japan might save the situation. In February of 1904, Japan, anxious to become the dominant power in Northeast China, declared war on Russia. When stating its reasons for resorting to war, Japan also sang the tune of the open door. It professed that it was seeking "to preserve China's sovereignty and territory" and "the equal opportunity of industry and commerce for the various nations in China." [14] Some Chinese officials thought that now their dream of another foreign power counterbalancing Russia in the Northeast had come true and the region could be saved for China. The United States also intended to use Japan to break Russia's exclusive domination over the area, but not to save China's integrity; on the contrary, all of Theodore Roosevelt's schemes for the Northeast presupposed the sacrifice of China's sovereignty. Roosevelt wanted to bring in Japan in order to create a balance of power, one in which Russia would not be entirely driven out of East Asia but would remain "face to face with Japan as that each may have a moderative action on the other." [15] For both to remain would mean a division between them of China's Northeast. In 1905, with Japan victorious in war but economically exhausted and Russia near revolution, Roosevelt took the occasion to act as mediator and brought the two belligerents to a peace conference at Portsmouth, New Hampshire. By the peace treaty signed in Portsmouth, Russia kept its vested interests in the northern part of Manchuria, while Japan gained the Russian leasehold in Lüshun and Dalian and the south branch of the Russian-owned Chinese Eastern Railway between Harbin and the leasehold. For America, such a balance would serve both to maintain the open door in Northeast China and to keep Japan involved on mainland Asia instead of coveting America's possessions in the Pacific.

Everyone benefited except China. China's role was simply to await the disposal of its territory by the foreign powers and to consent to the final decision. When the Russo-Japanese War broke out, John Hay had asked Tokyo and St. Petersburg to respect China's neutrality and independence. As the war drew to a close, the Chinese government wished to secure full participation in the peace talks in order to guard China's interests. To this end, it looked hopefully to the United States for assistance. But the United States opposed China's request for fear that China's participation would hamper the transfer of the Russian concessions in south Manchuria to Japan. After Japan and Russia had completed the division of Northeast China into their spheres of influence in September 1905, Roosevelt wired William Rockhill, American minister in Beijing, saying:

In my judgment China cannot with propriety question the efficacy of this transfer or hesitate to allow Japanese all the rights the Russians were exercising. If China shall contrive any trouble about the transfer in question, you will at the proper time state this strongly to the Chinese government. [16]

Zhang Zhidong and his colleagues could only see that, although one more power was entering the Northeast, China's sovereignty was still at the free disposal of the imperialist powers.

The humiliations heaped by the imperialist powers upon China since 1900 evoked an upsurge of patriotism from the Chinese people. The continued development of a national capitalism in China also encouraged the demand that the special rights enjoyed by the imperialists be abrogated. This tendency swept many of the bourgeois and petty-bourgeois elements into the anti-imperialist movement, where they associated with the local gentry, students, and lower strata of the masses, and where they called out for the recovery of the rights of railway construction and mining. Their platform stood in stark contrast to that of the high officials like Zhang Zhidong. While the high officials dreamed of enlisting the help of one imperialist power against another by bartering away more and more national rights, the common people initiated a movement for reclaiming the rights lost to the imperialists. The first targets of this struggle were the American financiers who had won the rights to build the Hankou-Guangzhou railroad.

Until 1900, the imperialist powers had built railways in their respective spheres, financed with their own capital and operated under their management. The Chinese Eastern Railway in the Northeast was such an enterprise. The imperialist powers also extended railway loans to the Chinese government and appointed their own men to supervise the management of the lines. Vying for the right to build railways by extending loans to China, the imperialist powers were once again locked in keen competition. The Hankou-Guangzhou railway, which traversed the spheres of influence of Britain and France, was one of the major lines that attracted the powers' attention. Zhang Zhidong, following his policy of involving several foreign powers in these spheres, conceded the Hankou-Guangzhou railway to the American China Development Company. The terms agreed upon in April 1898 were severe: the American company was to provide a loan valued at $20 million, for $18 million cash at an annual interest rate of 5 percent; the railway, after completion, was to be managed by the American company for a period of forty years; and an annual 20 percent of the railway's net profits was to be awarded to the American concessionaires. The company, however, still unsatisfied, soon demanded that construction costs be raised to $40 million and that the deadline for completion of the work be extended from three to five years. The Chinese yielded in July 1900 and signed a supplementary agreement. In pursuance of China's plan to counterbalance the political ambition of other powers in the region, the supplementary agreement stipulated specifically that the Americans "cannot transfer the rights of these agreements to other nations or people of other nationality." [17] The American China Development Company was a speculative venture, though, and only a few months later it violated the agreement by selling two-thirds of the company stock to a syndicate of French and Belgian capitalists. By June 1905, five years after the second contract was signed, the company had completed merely twenty-one miles of the railroad.

In November 1904, the merchants and gentry of the three provinces of Hubei, Hunan, and Guangdong, where the railway was to pass, jointly petitioned the central government to nullify the American concession. At this point another American firm, J. P. Morgan and Company, purchased back a part of the Belgian-controlled shares. The American government also strongly opposed the Chinese wish to annul the concession. But the Chinese people in the three provinces insisted on recovering the railway from foreign domination, whether Belgian or American. Their struggle won the support of Chinese students in Japan and the United States. Zhang Zhidong realized that a revolt in the provinces was possible if people's demands were not met. He was thus forced to arrange a settlement with the Americans in 1905 and to redeem the concession by paying the American company a sum of money. The recovery of the Hankou-Guangzhou railway was the first successful effort made by the Chinese people in the rights reclamation movement.

In the same year, 1905, the Chinese people started another campaign against American imperialism, this time in the form of a boycott of American goods. In the middle of the nineteenth century, when American capitalists needed cheap labor to develop the underpopulated west coast of the United States, they had imported Chinese laborers to build their railways, mine their mines, and reclaim their lands—all under harsh conditions and at low pay. The treaty of 1868 had permitted an unrestricted flow of Chinese to the United States. But after the 1870s, many viewed the Chinese workers as superfluous. Racist antipathy and anxiety for jobs led to the discrimination, persecution, and exclusion of the Chinese. In 1880, in a new treaty, the Chinese government made a concession that allowed the United States to regulate immigration, but not to prohibit it absolutely. Before the ink on the treaty was dry, however, the U.S. Congress decided to deny entrance to all categories of Chinese workers. While repeatedly demanding of the Chinese government that it faithfully fulfill treaty obligations, the American government violated at will the spirit and provisions of the treaties concluded between the two countries. The United States demanded open door treatment from the Chinese: in China, foreign businessmen "could reside in more than ninety treaty ports; Western gunboats patrolled coastal waters and the Yangtze River; military units garrisoned several Chinese cities and foreign capitalists gained treaty rights to exploit and develop economic concessions in the interior of China. Beyond the ports, missionaries enjoyed the right to purchase land anywhere." [18] But in the United States, the American officials responded to mounting racism not only by closing the door to Chinese laborers, but also by applying the process of exclusion and harassment to Chinese merchants, students, and travelers whom American laws designated as exempt. In some areas the racists even inflicted atrocities on the Chinese, including outright slaughter. An American missionary wrote:

There is no particular in which the worst Boxer atrocities in China were not equalled and exceeded by what has been perpetrated in many cities and settlements of Christian America. Great military expeditions and a heavy indemnity avenged the former. Almost all the latter were entirely unpunished. [19]

The extreme injustice stimulated a feeling of deep resentment in China against the American imperialists. On May 10, 1905, the Shanghai Chamber of Commerce passed resolutions urging all Chinese in Shanghai not to buy American goods. It sent telegrams to the chambers of commerce of twenty-two other treaty ports, calling upon Chinese merchants to boycott American products unless the United States modified its immigration policy toward the Chinese. In less than one month, the campaign had spread throughout China. Merchants, students, workers, and overseas Chinese in the United States and its possessions all participated in the movement. The U.S. government lodged a strong protest with the Qing government and staged naval demonstrations, and the American minister in Beijing warned that the Qing government would be held directly responsible for any American losses if the central government failed to halt the organized movement against America. On August 30, 1905, the subservient Qing government issued an imperial decree, threatening severe punishment for those who "foment trouble among the people." [20] But the boycott agitation did not end until 1906.

The boycott failed to moderate the American exclusion policy: all anti-Chinese exclusion laws continued until 1943. Nevertheless, the campaign made clear to the world that the Chinese people could not be bullied. While the Qing government bowed humbly before the imperialists and vainly hoped to enlist America's help to counter other powers, the Chinese people harbored no illusions and dared to take direct action. At the outset of the movement, one of its leaders declared: "When our government proves itself unable to act, then the people must rise up to do so." [21] This was the first boycott of its kind in Chinese history. The Boxers' movement could only take the crude and simple form of peasant revolt, but barely five years later, a modern, disciplined, and organized drive emerged in China. Indicating the new awakening of the Chinese people, it constituted a part of the high tide of the anti-imperialist struggle that led to the Revolution of 1911.

Some Qing high officials continued to work on their plans for securing American assistance, especially in the Northeast. After the Russo-Japanese War, when China recovered a part of its right to govern the Three Eastern Provinces, the Qing officials there found that they were so pressed on both sides by the two penetrating powers that they would soon lack any room for maneuver. The only way they saw to save the three provinces was still the same old project, that is, the opening up of the three provinces to foreign powers other than Japan and Russia. The Qing Dynasty, regarding these provinces as its birthplace, considered them a special region and forbade the Han (native Chinese) people to immigrate into them. But the imperialist iron heels could not be prevented from trampling on the Qing homeland. The old system had to be changed. In early 1907, the government, having decided to replace the military administration with the kind of civil administration prevailing in the provinces within the Great Wall, appointed Xu Shichang as the first governor-general. One of the reasons for doing so was to facilitate the opening up of these provinces to the world.

But before China could "involve" other powers in the Northeast, Japan had already drawn most of the major powers to its side. Apart from the alliance it had concluded with Great Britain in 1902 and renewed in 1905, Japan gradually sought a rapprochement with Russia and friendly relations with France, an ally of Russia. This resulted in the signing, in June 1907, of a Franco-Japanese agreement and, the next month, of a Russo-Japanese agreement. Both agreements contained a secret clause recognizing the special interest of each of the contracting parties in certain specified areas in China. Only the United States had yet to enter into a formal collusion with Japan.

Such was the situation when, in April of 1907, Xu Shichang took office. Xu inherited from his predecessors a project for constructing a competing railway from Xinmintun on the Beijing-Shenyang line northward through eastern Inner Mongolia to Tsitsihar, a line that would link up the southern and northern parts of the three provinces, "sufficient to contend with" the Japanese-run South Manchurian Railway. "The destiny of the three provinces," Xu concluded, "all depends on this measure." [22] But his method of financing the construction of the railway was nothing other than raising a foreign loan. His subordinate, Tang Shaoyi, governor of Fengtian, argued that a foreign loan could elicit both financial and political aid and thus create a balance of power in the Northeast. He looked to the United States for money and diplomatic support, saying:

The great powers of Europe, aside from Germany, openly give to Japan the advantage over us and conclude with her agreements to our detriment; but the United States continues to have in the Far East a national policy independent of all foreign alliance.[23]

Tang approached Willard Straight, the American consul-general at Shenyang. Straight was a careerist. Before coming to Shenyang in 1906, he had been approached by E. H. Harriman, the American railway magnate, about a plan for an intercontinental transportation system, including the construction of new railway lines in China's Northeast. Straight had then dreamed of supplanting the Japanese sphere of influence by injecting into the Northeast the superior financial resources of the United States. He was of course ready to act as an intermediary between Tang and Harriman. However, the financial crisis of 1907 in the United States prevented American participation, so in November Tang contracted with two British firms, the Pauling and Company and the British and Chinese Corporation, to build and finance the projected railroad. Japan repeatedly voiced opposition to the project. From August to November, the Japanese legation in Beijing protested three times to the Chinese government that the route of the new railway would violate the so-called "protocol" of 1905 which prohibited the construction of a railroad parallel or harmful to the South Manchurian Railway. The British government refused to uphold the claims of the British companies.

When all hopes for the success of the railway project had been killed, Xu and Tang turned to another plan, namely, the organization of a Northeast development bank that would include as one of its goals the building of a railway from Jinzhou via Taonan to Aihun. In March 1908 they determined that a bank loan should be floated in the United States and that the excess Boxer indemnity, which the United States was prepared to return to China, should be used to guarantee the loan. In order to win the American government's approval of the bank loan and permission to use the indemnity, the central government sent Tang to Washington as an envoy authorized to thank the United States for the indemnity's remission.

Yet this plan too was doomed, for it ran counter to America's policy toward Japan. Theodore Roosevelt dealt with Japan just as he had with Russia before the Russo-Japanese War: the United States would accept Japan's sphere of influence in south Manchuria in return for Japan's respecting there the rights of American commerce. As long as Japan was expected to preserve a balance of power in Northeast China, Roosevelt could not but follow a policy of accommodation. Furthermore, as the immigration question, in 1907, continued to rouse passion on both sides, Roosevelt realized that he could trade support for the Japanese in Northeast China for their help in stemming the flow of Japanese immigrants to the United States. In 1908 Roosevelt told the Japanese ambassador, Kogoro Takahira, that in matters relating to China's sovereignty he was willing to treat Manchuria differently from the rest of China.[24] All these considerations culminated in the Root-Takahira Agreement of November 30, 1908. In this agreement, both countries subscribed to the maintenance of the status quo in the Pacific,[25] a commitment that implied both U.S. recognition of Japan's ascendancy in China's Northeast and a promise not to support Chinese resistance to Japanese advances.

Tang Shaoyi arrived in Washington on November 30, the day of the Root-Takahira Agreement. He found it difficult even to see Secretary of State Elihu Root to discuss the proposal for using the indemnity remission as security for a loan. Prospects of procuring the State Department's backing for the project remained hopeless.

But Roosevelt's policy of accommodation with Japan did not produce the desired result. It created not a balance of power in Northeast China, but rather the dominance of Japan, a dominance greater than Russia had enjoyed before the war. Japan's rapprochement with Russia in 1907 strengthened its position even further. After the Russo-Japanese War, American exports to China in general, and to the Northeast in particular, fell sharply. Most American diplomats and merchants in China imputed this reverse to Japan's closing of the door in the Northeast to American enterprise. Inside the Great Wall, too, America lagged far behind in the race to invest capital in China. The American government could not turn the tide if it continued to sit back.

Thus, in 1909, the new Taft administration launched a "dollar diplomacy" offensive. The new secretary of state, Philander Knox, believed that the flow of American capital to China, especially if invested in railway development, would neutralize the influence of Japan and the other powers and increase America's trade and political influence. On November 9, 1909, he proposed to Great Britain that the United States and Britain sponsor a project to neutralize all railways in Northeast China either existing or yet unbuilt. Under Knox's plan the powers would lend China the money to purchase the railway from Russia and Japan; the lines would then be under international control during the period of the loan. Knox also proposed that if neutralization proved impracticable, Britain and the United States should support the Jinzhou-Aihun line, the financing of which Willard Straight, now representative of the American banking group organized by the State Department to exploit investment opportunities in China, had in early October approved in a preliminary agreement. The whole plan meant that China would gain nominal ownership of the railways, the powers would exercise joint control over them, and the United States would occupy a predominant position. Japan and Russia would then either withdraw or fall to the position of junior partners.

Knox used the open door principle as a justification for this plan. In the proposal to Britain he explained that his purpose was to

preserve the undisturbed enjoyment by China of all political rights in Manchuria and to promote the development of those Provinces under a practical application of the policy of the open door and equal commercial opportunity. [26]

While Theodore Roosevelt displayed little concern about the open door principle as applied to Northeast China, Knox made ostentatious use of the principle, not merely to guarantee a share in the booty, but also to demand the other powers to give up their vested interests.

The Knox plan, however, was no less wishful than the other projects drawn up by the Chinese officials in the Northeast. Through misinformation from Willard Straight and the American embassies in London and St. Petersburg, Knox assumed that Russia was eager to sell its Chinese Eastern Railway and that Britain would feel free to join America if Japan preserved its interests in its Manchurian railway. But, in actuality, Britain was bound to its Japanese ally. Russia was also Japan's associate as far as their common interests were concerned. After being informed of the Knox plan, Russia and Japan announced on the same day, January 21, 1910, and in similar terms, their decisive veto of the neutralization proposal. On July 4, they went further and signed a new accord, as well as a secret treaty which pledged the two parties to common action in defense of their special interests in Northeast China. [27] They thus erected a joint defense against Knox's plan for shared control of their interests.

On receiving the American proposal, Jutaro Komura, Japanese foreign minister, exclaimed: "They are asking us to internationalize what is our own property, acquired by us at the cost of much treasure and many lives."[28] Knox had to choose between backing down or a costly payment in money and lives for dislodging Japan from its existing position. He chose the abandonment of the whole plan, together with the Jinzhou-Aihun railway project. Taft and Knox were no more inclined to fight over the open door than had been Roosevelt. In the face of Japan's determination, the open door again disappeared. Nevertheless, Knox's action shows that the conflict between the United States and Japan would never disappear; rather, under certain circumstances the rivalry between the two countries might drive the United States to strike back. From 1905 on, the conflict between the United States and Japan became the key factor in the imperialist struggle to dominate China.

As for China, even if the Knox plan had been realized, it would not have helped restore China's sovereignty as the Qing officials wished. Xiliang, who succeeded Xu Shichang as governor-general in 1909, was even more vigorous in advocating the construction of railways using foreign loans. On October 1, the day before he signed the preliminary agreement with Straight on the Jinzhou-Aihun line, he said in a telegram to the Ministry of Foreign Affairs: "Without contracting a foreign loan, we cannot develop Manchuria; without relying upon the strength of foreigners, there is no way to obstruct Japan and Russia."[29] He made this remark from the premise that "whoever borrows money also borrows the strength of the lender." But unfortunately for Xiliang, Knox took the blatantly contrary view that "the borrower is the servant of the lender."[30] As stated above, the Knox plan envisaged a joint control of the railway by the lenders. Knox, like his predecessors in formulating plans concerning China, had not even bothered to consult the Chinese government, which learned of it officially only a month and a half afterward. How ironic that some Qing officials even attempted to expand to the whole country the policy of using foreign loans to balance the foreign powers.

In October 1910, the Qing Ministry of Finance concluded with the American banking group a combined loan for currency reform and for development of the Three Eastern Provinces. The European financiers who were negotiating the loan for the Huguang railway (the Guangzhou-Hankou-Chengdu line) also wished a portion of the above loan. They offered to admit the American group into their financial consortium—to which Knox, by this time, had shifted his interest, hoping to achieve the aims of his dollar diplomacy through cooperation with the other powers. He welcomed the European financiers' offer. In November 1910, the banking groups of Britain, France, Germany, and the United States formed a Four-Power Consortium and agreed to share equally the Huguang railway loan and all future major foreign loans to China. In April and May 1911, the Qing government formally signed with the Consortium a $50 million combined loan and a $30 million loan for the Huguang railway. Within two months the Qing government had gained both a huge amount of money and four powers active in central China to check one another. Knox, for his part, attained what he had failed to achieve a year and a half before. The situation appeared to satisfy all—but it came too late. The Revolution of 1911 broke out in China soon after the two loans were signed, just as the imperialists' ambitious schemes were about to begin operation.

The Huguang railway loan itself was an immediate cause of the 1911 Revolution. The Empress Dowager Cixi, who actually ruled China from 1861 to 1908, concentrated, in her last years, all important administrative powers in the central government. After her death in November 1908, the Prince Regent Zaifeng, the father of the boy-emperor Xuantong, strove to concentrate the power of the Manchu nobles and his own family still further. The Prince Regent increasingly felt the need to control the railways, seeing them as an important link in centralization, and to raise huge foreign loans to relieve his exhausted financial resources. The covetous Manchu nobles were also delighted at the prospect of being able to divert much of the incoming foreign capital into their own pockets. As early as 1898 Sheng Xuanhuai, a protégé of Li Hongzhang, and notorious for his graft and embezzlement, had asserted that China should beg foreign powers for "joint protection" by surrendering the railways and mines of the whole country to foreign investors.[31] Now, in 1911, Sheng, as minister of post and transportation, sought to satisfy the prevailing desire to concentrate power in the hands of the imperial family by suggesting a policy of nationalization for all the Chinese-run railroads. On May 13, 1911, an imperial decree declared the railroads nationalized. A few days later, on May 20, Sheng signed with the Four-Power Consortium the above loan for the building of the Guang-zhou-Hankou-Chengdu line. The people, however, seeing through this "nationalization," regarded it as nothing but a sellout of the country's railways to foreign powers.

When, in 1905, the rights recovery movement had regained from the American concessionaires the right of building the Guangzhou-Hankou railway, the merchants and gentry of the three provinces Guangdong, Hunan, and Hubei had formed a private company to build the railway, with another company, the Sichuan-Hankou Railway Company, set up in Sichuan Province for the same purpose. In reality, though, these companies were under the control of provincial officials who, by selling railway shares, extorted money from the people. When the greater part of the money had been collected, these officials appropriated it for other uses and never seriously began to build the railways. The anger of the people had thus already been aroused. Now suddenly the railways fell into the hands of foreigners, under the name of "nationalization." Moreover, the government actually confiscated the companies' funds, because the companies had failed to give the government fair reparation. A storm of opposition burst out in the four provinces. In Sichuan, the members of the radical Chinese Revolutionary League, or Tong Meng Hui, turned the storm of opposition into swarms of armed risings. The people now turned their spearheads against the Qing Dynasty, a dynasty that for seventy years had sold out China's national rights. The risings heralded the Wuchang Insurrection of October 10, 1911. Four months later, the Qing emperor abdicated.

The path of history has twists and turns. It was not until 1949 that the Chinese people succeeded definitely and permanently in driving out the imperialist powers. But the 1911 Revolution had indicated that the Chinese people had the ability decisively to defeat the imperialists, by toppling their instrument, the Chinese feudal monarchy.

4

Yuan Shikai, an old bureaucrat of the Qing Dynasty and chief of the Beiyang warlords, usurped the fruits of the 1911 Revolution and secured the Provisional Presidency of the Republic.

The imperialists had long sought to establish and maintain a regime in China which could both serve them and be strong enough to rule the country. Since the Chinese people, through the 1911 Revolution, had forced the imperialists to acknowledge the downfall of the Qing Dynasty, the imperialists had discovered Yuan Shikai and had helped him become the new ruler of China. For the imperialists, Yuan, in control of the army and experienced in affairs, was the ideal "strong man," and his government, while as servile as the Qing regime, was far more powerful and stable. They thus gave him full support. In February of 1912, following the establishment of the Yuan government, the International Consortium loaned it an immediate advance of 310,000 taels of silver and planned loans on a large scale for the future.

The American government also felt that Yuan was a strong man and "the best hope for Chinese stability."[1] In May 1913, the United States recognized Yuan as Provisional President of the Chinese Republic. President Woodrow Wilson's message of recognition closed with the hope that China would respect and fulfill its "legal obligations."[2] Yuan, of course, never hesitated to meet this hope. Time and again he pledged that he would observe both written treaties and unwritten "precedents."[3] He would do all that the Qing had done to fulfill treaty provisions and more.

After having secured the support of the foreign powers, Yuan attempted to liquidate the revolutionary and democratic elements. In July 1913, he attacked the Nationalist Party in the south and wiped out part of its armed forces. Before that struggle had become a full-blown war, both Yuan and the Nationalists had applied to the American chargé, Edward Williams, to act as a peacemaker. Williams, who believed that Yuan could restore "order," advised Washington to refuse. The State Department readily approved his recommendation and adopted a policy of noninterference, which meant that Yuan had a free hand to suppress the democratic forces.

The defeat of the south further strengthened the imperialists' confidence in Yuan. He was indeed the "strong man" they sought. The United States thus took the lead in October of 1913 in recognizing him as China's formal President.

Outside support only encouraged Yuan to pursue more power. In a speech in December 1913, he complained that his government was still not strong enough "to put our own house in order," and asserted that "the success of its domestic and foreign policies depends in its turn, on the strength of the government. It matters little whether the regime is monarchical or republican."[4] He not only demanded more power, but also hinted that he would restore the monarchy with himself as emperor.

The Americans knew that Yuan was an autocrat at heart. But what counted for them was that Yuan was a "stable factor in Chinese politics." Though "aware of the false nature of the current republican institutions in China," Wilson "constantly sought to foster the force of order and stability regardless as to whether these forces were democratic or even republic in nature."[5] It is ironic that the liberal president of a democratic republic agreed with the autocratic Yuan Shikai on the problem and manner of governing China.

In 1914, Yuan promulgated a "Constitutional Compact," which conferred on him dictatorial power. But he was still not satisfied. One year later, he openly launched the movement for the restoration of the monarchy.

In the planning of the monarchical movement, the American Frank Goodnow, formerly a professor at Columbia University, played a considerable role. As Yuan's constitutional advisor, he had a large influence in forming the Constitutional Compact. An August 1915 article, "On Republic and Monarchy," provided a theoretical basis for the monarchical movement. In it he asserted that "under modern conditions countries must devise some method of government under which peace will be maintained or they will have to submit to foreign control." Proceeding from this theory, Goodnow argued that "a monarchy is better suited than a republic to China."[6] Though what he wrote represented only his private opinion, it was an opinion that found support within the American government. This was not mere coincidence. The American government had also stressed the maintenance of internal peace and was ready to recognize Yuan as the Emperor of China if there was "no serious organized opposition" and if Yuan had the "ability to preserve order."[7]

America's support of a subservient ruler willing to fulfill "treaty obligations" and strong enough to control the country was not at variance with the view of the other powers. The only difference was that the Wilson administration wished to pursue this policy independently of the other powers. In April 1913, Yuan signed an agreement with the International Consortium for a 25 million pound loan. On the eve of its signature, however, the United States withdrew from the Consortium. This action did not mean that America would not render Yuan financial aid, but merely that it intended to follow an independent course, hoping to open the Chinese market and resources to competitive business and finance.

Less than one year after Wilson sent a telegram congratulating Yuan on becoming China's "duly-elected" President, the outbreak of World War I altered the whole situation, upsetting the balance of power in the Far East. The war involved almost all the Western powers; and although the United States was still officially neutral, it could not pay much attention to the East either. Consequently, Japan became the only major power free to impose its will on China.

Japan desired anything but the free competition envisaged by America. Seeking sole dominance over China, Japan regarded the European war as a golden opportunity to achieve it. Furthermore, neither Yuan Shikai nor his successors were actually "strong men." As warlords, despots, and traitors to the Republic, they enjoyed no popular support, nor could they take any important action without the assistance of their imperialist masters. Japan quickly won decisive power in China. Thus America, shortly after deciding to enhance its interests in China by upholding Yuan, faced a formidable challenge from Japan. Having "strong men" serve one's interest was not so easy after all. In the face of the Japanese offensive, America retreated.

China, when war broke out in Europe, declared its neutrality. To forestall Japanese plans for expansion, China asked the United States to assist in preventing the spread of hostilities to Chinese soil. China proposed that the latter "endeavor to obtain the consent of the belligerent European nations to an undertaking not to engage in hostilities either in Chinese territory or marginal waters in adjacent leased territories."[8] The American government attempted merely to "sound out" opinion on such an arrangement. Except for Germany, no powers interested in China gave their consent.

On August 14, the Japanese government presented an ultimatum to Germany, demanding that the latter withdraw all naval vessels from Japanese and Chinese waters, and that it turn over to Japan the leased territory of Jiaozhou "with a view to eventual restoration of the same to China."[9] No reply came from the German government, and on August 23, Japan declared war on Germany. On September 3rd, the Japanese invaded Shandong at Longkou on the north coast, far from their objective at Qingdao, the city which dominated the Jiaozhou region. The Japanese forces then took over the Jiaozhou-Jinan railway as far as Jinan, two hundred miles in the interior, and occupied most of Shandong Province. On November 6, the Germans in Qingdao surrendered.

Five days after the Japanese presented their ultimatum, the U.S. State Department informed the Japanese government that the United States "notes with satisfaction that Japan, in demanding the surrender by Germany of the entire leased territory of Jiaozhou does so with the purpose of restoring that territory to China, and that Japan is seeking no territorial aggrandizement in China."[10] Later, though before the German surrender, the State Department instructed its minister in Beijing to inform the Chinese government that "the Department realizes that it would be quixotic in the extreme to allow the question of China's territorial integrity to entangle the United States in international difficulties."[11] This statement reflected the United States' satisfaction with Japan's alleged "purpose" and its acquiescence to Japan's military occupation of Chinese territory.

Having gained Shandong, Japan continued aggressive action in accordance with its plan of converting China into a vassal state. At this time, Yuan Shikai, who had set his heart on becoming Emperor, realized that if he were indeed to effect such a fundamental reversal, it was essential to get Japanese aid. Japan also knew this truth. On January 18, 1915, the Japanese minister in Beijing presented his government's Twenty-one Demands directly to Yuan. It was clear that acceptance of these demands was a condition for Japan's recognition of Yuan's monarchy. The demands were divided into five groups. The first group, dealing with Shandong, required China to assent to any agreement which Japan made with Germany over the rights in the province after the war; it also granted Japan railway-building rights and opened additional ports in the province to foreign commerce. Group two established Japan's paramount interest in south Manchuria and eastern Inner Mongolia. The third group required China to recognize the Hanyeping Coal and Iron Company as a joint Sino-Japanese enterprise with monopoly mining rights in the Changjiang Valley, and the fourth demanded that China cede no harbor or bay along the coast of Fujian to another power. The fifth group required China to accept influential Japanese as political, financial, and military advisors and to allow Japanese to help police important points in China. China was also required to purchase half its arms in Japan (or establish joint arsenals in China) and permit Japan to build railroads around Nanchang, and Fujian Province, if it needed foreign capital, was to consult Japan first. The news of these imperious demands aroused the Chinese people and brought a storm of protest down on Yuan's head. He hesitated for some time, but, bent on winning Japan's assistance, he finally, on May 9, accepted the humiliating demands.

The demands deeply disturbed the American government. All of them, though especially the fifth group, were designed to reduce China to a Japanese protectorate and to deny all other powers any influence. But the American government also feared that if it objected too strenuously, it would excite the hostility of Japan. It thus chose to make a deal with Japan. On March 13, the State Department dispatched a note to Tokyo, pointing out that certain Japanese demands, mostly found in the fifth group, were in violation of American interests and of the open door principle. The State Department expressed the hope that Japan would not force China to accept the fifth group. Two important concessions, however, were made: first, the United States would raise no objection to the demands relative to Shandong, south Manchuria, and east Mongolia; second, the United States would recognize "that territorial contiguity creates special relations between Japan and these districts." [12] The hope expressed and the concessions made in the note indicated that America was willing to surrender its "treaty rights" in these districts in return for Japan's respect for U.S. interests in the rest of China.

Even on the fifth group, the American government later suggested that China and Japan should make some compromise. On the subject of advisors and armaments, China should not discriminate against Japan, but should give it a share along with the other leading nations. In the matter of police, "Japan's rights of supervision should be limited to places in Manchuria and Eastern Mongolia which have a considerable percentage of Japanese subjects." [13]

The Japanese immediately published these concessions in order to show that the American government had already acquiesced in all the demands. The American people were, by now, greatly excited and shocked. Not only was there a marked tone of irritation in public discussion of the matter, but a profound distrust arose concerning Japan's intentions in the Far East as well. These developments made the American government uneasy, and, turning away from any suggestion of compromise, it urged Japan to drop all of its group-five demands. America, to make its position clear, issued a circular note reiterating its adherence to the open door policy. The British government also warned Japan that public opinion in Britain would consider a Sino-Japanese break over group five a violation of the spirit of the Anglo-Japanese Alliance. On May 7, Japan delivered its ultimatum to China, but now it reserved group five for future discussion. Although in winning the temporary withdrawal of group five the pressure exerted by the American government had had considerable influence, it was largely the righteous indignation and strong protest of the Chinese and foreign people that caused Japan to weaken its demands.

But whatever role America finally played, it had not only made concessions to Japan, but it had also recognized Japan's special position in China—and all on its own initiative. Though some would contend that, because America had to center its attention on Europe, and because it lacked the ability to intervene in the Far East, it had to acquiesce in the Japanese action, it is still far from clear that the United States had to recognize Japan's special position. Nor did Japan press for such a concession at this time. The reason why America took this step should be sought elsewhere. Twelve days before the dispatch of the note of March 13, Robert Lansing, then counselor of the State Department, had made a suggestion to Secretary of State Bryan. It was this suggestion that revealed the basic thought of the American policy makers:

I would suggest for your consideration whether it would not be well for this government to state that if it refrains from urging its undoubted treaty rights relative to Southern Manchuria and Shandong, it would do so as a friend of Japan, who is solicitous for her welfare, recognizing her economic situation and the relief which would doubtless result from an opportunity to develop Southern Manchuria through Japanese emigrants into that region.

It could be further stated that, if this government adopted such a policy out of friendship for Japan and with an earnest desire to see her wishes accomplished, it may justly expect reciprocal friendly treatment on the part of the Japanese government, and similar evidence of good will on their part.

. . . The Japanese government:

(1) will make no further complaint in regard to legislation affecting land tenures in the United States unless such legislation is confiscatory in character, or materially affects vested rights;

(2) will reaffirm explicitly the principle of the "Open Door" making it particularly applicable to the territories affected by the demands;

(3) and will prevent any monopolization by Japanese subjects of particular trades in these territories, and any preferential rates or treatment by Japanese railways or other transportation concerns for the benefits of Japanese subjects or their merchandise.[14]

In short, America would grant Japan certain territories in China that would act as a safety valve and would divert the tide of Japanese expansion elsewhere. It would be a gift to the Japanese that would bring America rewards in other places. It was this thought that led to the note of March 13. The exigencies of wartime only made it more desirable to complete a deal already seen as useful.

But the Japanese were not ready, as Lansing had expected, to give America "reciprocal friendly treatment." They simply became China's overlords and employed Yuan Shikai as their exclusive servant.

Yuan Shikai's treasonous foreign policy and monarchical aspirations incurred such powerful nationwide opposition that in March of 1916 he had to cancel the monarchy. Soon thereafter he died. Vice-President Li Yuanhong became President, and Duan Qirui Premier, into whose busy hands the real power of government soon fell. As one of Yuan's chief subordinates, Duan inherited both Yuan's power and his policy of maintaining that power by resorting to foreign support.

In February 1917, the United States severed diplomatic relations with Germany and sent a note to China, as to all neutral states, suggesting that they follow suit. On March 14, China broke off diplomatic relations with Germany and Austria-Hungary. This step, however, was taken amid a domestic factional struggle between Li Yuanhong and Duan Qirui. When the United States declared war on Germany in April, and the issue of China's entry into the war was debated in Beijing, the struggle between Li and Duan came to a head. In order to secure foreign financial assistance, Duan and the northern military governors strongly advocated China's participation in the war. Fearing that foreign aid would augment the political and military strength of Duan's faction, Li insisted on continued neutrality and dismissed Duan. Duan refused to give way. He conspired with the warlord Zhangxun to restore the Manchu boy-emperor to the throne and thereby drive Li from office. Duan, under the banner of "saving the republic," then threw Zhang and the boy-emperor out and reinstated himself as Premier. There was now little opposition to his decision to take part in the war. On August 14, 1917, China declared war on Germany and Austria-Hungary.

The discord between Li and Duan reflected the rivalry between America and Japan over China. When the American government suggested to China that it break relations with Germany, the American minister in China, Paul Reinsch, lost no time in urging the Beijing government to take concerted action with the United States. But the American government feared that if China received American aid in preparation for war, it would provoke Japanese opposition; and even if it did not, Japan would probably take the occasion to demand control of China's arsenals and troops. The American government thus concluded that it would be wiser to urge China to remain quiet. Accordingly, it instructed Reinsch to inform Beijing that China, if it took action, should do no more than break diplomatic relations. It was this advice that led to Li Yuanhong's assertion of continued neutrality.

But Japan did not allow China to remain quiet. In 1915 and 1916, Japan had worked to prevent China from joining the Allies for fear that China would be entitled to an independent voice at the peace conference and so a say in the disposal of German rights in Shandong. When America's severance of relations with Germany and the Reinsch activities in Beijing seemed likely to bring China into war as a protégé of the United States, Japan was determined to recover the lead. In February and March of 1917, it had already approached the Allies one by one and received their assurance of support for Japanese claims in Shandong and the German Pacific islands. Then suddenly Japan changed its attitude diametrically, not only approving China's rupture of relations with Germany, but also inciting China to enter the war. It made use of the Duan clique, telling them, "If you borrow American money, you cannot spend it for any other purpose than sending an expedition to Europe; if you accept Japanese loans, you will not be hampered to use them for liquidating internal disorder under the name of training an army for participation in the European war." [15] This offer fitted exactly into the plot of Duan, who wished to use foreign aid in a civil war against his opponents. And so Duan insisted on war participation.

At the high tide of the controversy between Li and Duan, the American government, on June 6, 1917, had sent a message to the Chinese Foreign Office advising that the question of China's entry into the war was secondary to the need for restoring internal harmony. This was an effort to help Li resist the Japanese-backed Duan. But, without active measures to reinforce it, the American step was too weak to be effective. It only served to provoke Japan's opposition, which America had been endeavoring to avoid. The Japanese protested and asked whether or not America had, in March 1915, recognized Japan's special position in China. Furthermore, they made clear that the United States should not interfere in Chinese politics without first consulting Japan. It was but a small step when, after the downfall of Li and the reinstatement of Duan as Premier, Japan brought China into the war as its protégé.

Japan then turned to America for formal recognition of its paramount position in China, sending a special mission to the United States headed by the former foreign minister, Kikujiro Ishii. Reinsch, in the meantime, recommended repeatedly that his government win over Duan with "adequate loans." [16] But the American government reverted to the policy it had adopted in the spring of 1915, and thus, with the arrival of the Ishii mission, it saw an opportunity to reach an understanding with Japan. During the negotiations from September 6 to November 2, 1917, between Ishii and Robert Lansing, now secretary of state, Lansing suggested that the cobelligerents should redeclare the open door policy in a joint statement. Ishii replied that Japan had a special interest because of its unique position in regard to China. While Japan desired to have China open and free to all countries, he added, a bare declaration of the "open door policy without some mention of Japan's special interest" would arouse adverse criticism. [17]

The result was an agreement which was embodied in an exchange of notes on November 2, 1917. Although both governments agreed not to infringe on the independence and territorial integrity of China and to adhere to the principle of an "open door," the crucial part came in the statement that

the Governments of the United States and Japan recognize that territorial propinquity creates special relations between countries, and consequently, the Government of the United States recognizes that

Japan has special interests in China, particularly in the part to which her possessions are contiguous. [18]

It is obvious that America had fully acceded to Japan's aggressive claims. Even the American minister in Beijing, when he learned of the agreement, complained, "This naturally struck me in the face with stunning force. . . . I knew nothing of the motives which had animated the President and Secretary of State when they agreed to the paper." [19]

What were the motives? To discover them demands a deeper look at Lansing's role. After the exchange of the notes, Japan immediately published the agreement in Chinese, translating the original "special interests" into characters which meant "paramount interests." Confronted with this interpretation, Lansing explained that the interests referred to were of an economic, not a political nature, and that it was a geographic axiom that territorial propinquity created special interests. [20] If it was merely an axiom, then why did it necessitate a declaration? During the negotiations, Lansing himself had said, "We recognized the fact that Japan, from her geographic position, had a peculiar interest in China, but . . . to make a declaration to that effect seemed to me needless as it was the result of natural causes and not political; . . . any such declaration might be interpreted as a peculiar political interest, and I was very doubtful whether it would be wise to include it in a reaffirmation of the Open Door policy." [21] He not only knew the needlessness of making the declaration, but also foresaw its consequence. Yet still he did what he deemed unwise.

In explaining why he did so, Lansing told Gu Weijun (V. K. Wellington Koo), China's minister in Washington, that by conceding this axiom the United States had obtained "a declaration of policy which restrained the other party." [22] But during the negotiations, he had admitted that Ishii "seemed desirous to avoid a discussion of the application of the principle of the 'Open Door.'" [23] He knew that what the United States obtained was merely an empty formality, a mere reiteration in the abstract of the open door policy. Yet he was still content with such a declaration and thought it would restrain Japan.

Perhaps he meant to say that this declaration would restrain Japan from creating spheres of influence. In explaining why he wanted to reaffirm the open door policy at this time, Lansing had told Ishii that if the creation of new spheres of influence in China were allowed to continue, the Allies would claim that Japan and the United States were using the war to monopolize opportunities in China.[24] But in the end, the concessions he made in the agreement with Ishii merely turned all of the Chinese provinces to which Japan's possessions were contiguous into Japanese spheres of influence.

Although these inconsistencies appear puzzling, they are not beyond comprehension if one remembers the underlying thought of the note of March 15, 1915. Shortly after the opening of the Lansing-Ishii negotiations, Edward House, Wilson's personal advisor, restated this aim very plainly in a letter to the President: "We cannot meet Japan in her desires as to land immigration, and unless we make some concessions in regard to her sphere of influence in the East, trouble is sure, sooner or later, to come."[25]

What was the American reward for conceding Japan a larger sphere of influence? Besides the published exchange of notes, there was an accompanying secret protocol: the two governments "will not take advantage of the present conditions to seek special rights or privileges in China which could abridge the rights of the subjects or citizens of other friendly states."[26] The Americans believed that they could still gain something: by providing Japan with spheres of influence, they could divert the tide of Japanese immigration away from America. Japan also formally promised not to abridge American rights in China. Thus, the Unites States was pursuing a policy which would both satisfy Japan and keep the door open.

Unhappily, Japan was no longer satisfied with spheres of influence. Under the guise of helping China's war efforts, it advanced to Duan Qirui's government a multitude of loans, which in less than two years, totaled more than 500 million yen. In return for these loans, Duan bartered away China's national rights and put his "War Participation Army" under Japanese control. In a 1918 exchange of notes with Japan concerning Shandong, he even ordered his minister in Tokyo to state that "the Chinese government is glad to agree" to all the Japanese terms, which were calculated to take over and further extend Germany's previous privileges in that province.[27] Through the Duan faction, Japan succeeded in dominating China.

Toward the end of the world war, America attempted to break the monopoly that Japan had achieved over Chinese finance and politics. On July 10, 1918, the United States sent identical notes to the British, French, and Japanese governments proposing the organization of a new Four-Power Consortium and inviting their participation. The Americans proposed that the participating powers should relinquish to the Consortium all their preferences and options for both existing and future loans to China. It was a shrewd project, one designed to drag Japan into the group and to restrain it from within. The United States, supported by France and Britain, would have a determining position in the new Consortium which, after prolonged negotiations, came into existence in October 1920. But the clash of interests among the four powers made it impossible for the Consortium to take action.

At the Paris Peace Conference of 1919, America launched another offensive for restoring to China the former German rights in Shandong. America wished to prevent Japan from keeping its stranglehold on that key province. Thus, no sooner had the conference opened than the State Department put forward the opinion that "with respect to Shandong the German rights there lapsed with all Sino-German treaties upon the declaration of War. A succession of treaty rights from Germany to Japan is therefore not possible." [28]

This was also the position taken by the Chinese. Woodrow Wilson's public utterances, particularly those relating to self-determination and the rights of weak nations, had left a deep impression in intellectual circles in China. Many Chinese people, both official and lay, not only maintained that China's participation in the war made the old treaties with Germany and Austria-Hungary invalid, but they also hoped that the peace conference would work a change in the international position of their country. In October 1918, Duan Qirui resigned his premiership. The new government, pressured by national public opinion, sought in the peace conference the abolition of all special rights enjoyed in China by foreign powers in general and the liquidation of German privileges in particular.

On November 26, 1918, the Chinese minister, Gu Weijun, had an audience with Wilson in the White House. In broad terms, Gu asked the President to support China at the conference, and the latter agreed.

After the opening of the conference in January 1919, Japan brought its claims to the German rights in Shandong to the Council of Ten, on which Japan had two representatives and China had none. The Japanese delegate Nobuaki Makino sought to address these claims to Germany alone, that is, to make Shandong a bilateral issue between Germany and Japan. He asserted that "Japanese relations with China on these questions were on a different footing" and he "did not wish to discuss in the presence of the Chinese delegates Japanese relations with Germany." [29] Wilson, however, quickly replied that he "did not understand Makino to contend that the disposition of Jiaozhou did not affect China."[30] The Council of Ten then agreed to allow the Chinese delegates to attend its meeting on January 27, 1919, when Makino put forward the Japanese claims. Wilson had foiled the Japanese strategy of keeping the issues in Sino-Japanese relations outside the peace conference.

In the meeting of January 27, Makino said that his government claimed from the German government the unconditional cession of the leased territory of Jiaozhou along with the railways and other rights that Germany possessed in Shandong. After the Japanese presented their case, the Chinese delegate Wang Zhenting asked the Council to reserve their decision on matters so vital to China until the Chinese had presented their viewpoint. The delegates agreed to this request.

Immediately after the meeting, Gu Weijun called on Wilson. Gu expressed the hope that Wilson might see fit to say something on China's behalf when the Shandong question was brought up, and Wilson assured him that he felt deeply sympathetic toward China and would do his best to help.

In the next meeting, Gu declared that China looked to the conference to guarantee that justice was done by restoring to China all former German rights in Shandong. Makino, in reply, claimed that Japan had been in possession of the area and had entered into an understanding with China under the Twenty-one Demands and the 1918 agreements, understandings and demands that now governed the question. Wilson interrupted to ask that the notes constituting the understanding be laid before the Council. Makino stated that he would have to seek the permission of his government. Gu, however, readily agreed to submit them. By interrupting, Wilson called into question the agreements that had grown out of those Twenty-one Demands and 1918 treaties, upon which Japan based her commanding position in Asia.

Makino emphasized the point that since Japan had taken this territory by conquest from Germany, it must first obtain from Germany the right of free disposal. Until that was done, Japan could not carry out the promise of eventual restoration of the territory to China. Wilson rose to the occasion, asserting that the "Council was dealing with territories and cessions previously German without consulting Germany at all."[31] He insisted that if Japan intended to restore the territory to China, it could do so forthwith without having to wait for permission from Germany.

Makino insisted on his point and stressed the fact that the matter had already been made the subject of an interchange of notes between China and Japan. Gu argued that China's entrance into war had canceled all existing treaties with Germany. As for the Sino-Japanese agreements, they were extorted from China under duress and should be revised in the light of the conference's new principles.

Rebuffed in Paris, the Japanese exerted pressure on the Beijing government to withhold the wartime agreements from the conference, unless Japan gave consent to their release. On learning of these moves on the part of Japan, Wilson instructed his subordinates to advise the Chinese government to stand firm and tell Gu "to follow the course that he thinks right."[32]

In the early phase of the peace conference, Wilson, taking clear action against the Japanese claims to Shandong, had forced Makino to retreat from one trench to another. All the Japanese delegation had to validate their claims was the wartime agreements, here they were far from invulnerable given the Wilsonian principle that, in the adjustment of colonial claims, "the interest of the population concerned must have equal weight with the equitable claims of the government whose title is to be determined."[33]

Nevertheless, later in the conference, Wilson changed his attitude, betraying both his promise to support China and his own principle of respecting the rights of weak nations.

Makino, on April 21, called on Wilson to approve the justice of Japanese claims in Shandong. Wilson proposed that the German rights be ceded to five big powers, which would include Japan as a trustee for the disposition. But Makino would listen to no compromise. Wilson now retreated before the Japanese demands.

Makino appeared the next day before the Council of Four and maintained that Japan must obtain from Germany the rights in Shandong if the provisions of the 1915 and 1918 treaties were to be carried out. He defended the legality of these treaties and claimed the support of the secret 1917 treaties with Japan's allies. In the afternoon, the Council met with the Chinese delegation. Wilson echoed the Japanese assertions of the morning session by telling the delegates that, although Gu had claimed that the war had canceled the agreements with Germany, it had not canceled the Sino-Japanese agreements made before and after China's entry into the war. He said quite emphatically, that Britain, France, China, and Japan were all bound by treaties and that they were obliged to keep them "because the war has been fought largely for the purpose of showing that treaties cannot be violated."[34]

In his Fourteen Points, Wilson had declared to the world that "there shall be no private international understandings of any kind,"[35] and in the peace conference, he had fiercely opposed the secret Treaty of London, by which Fiume had been allotted to Italy. Yet now, in the case of China, Wilson, the denouncer of secret diplomacy, suddenly changed his views and became the champion of the sanctity of secret treaties.

The Japanese delegation repeatedly threatened that Japan would not sign the treaty with Germany unless their terms were met. On April 28, Wilson surrendered. He announced that if the Japanese would yield their military rights in Shandong and retain only their economic ones, he would agree to what they desired. This formula was accepted as the terms of the Council and handed to the Japanese. The Allies had, in 1917, already pledged their support of the Japanese claims, and they stated at the peace conference that they would fulfill these commitments; all that was left for the Japanese to do was to secure an American agreement. They had now won. Of Japan's victory, Tasker Bliss, one of the American delegates, had correctly warned that, "stripped of all words that befog the issue, would we not, under the guise of making a treaty with Germany, really be making a treaty with Japan by which we compel one of our allies (China) to cede against her will these things to Japan?"[36]

Indeed, to preserve Wilson's honor, the Japanese in late April gave an oral guarantee that they would "hand back the Shandong Peninsula in full sovereignty to China, retaining only the economic privileges granted to Germany."[37] But this statement was made behind the closed door of the Council of Three, in the absence of the Chinese delegation, and it was never mentioned in the Treaty of Versailles, in which the Japanese right to the leasehold and other German privileges in Shandong was included. Furthermore, and as the subsequent events showed, the oral guarantee counted for nothing, since Japan persisted in basing the solution of the Shandong problem on nothing but the 1915 and 1918 treaties with China. Such treaties, despite a clause or two on genuine economic privileges, were again examples of colonial exploitation backed by superior political power. The privileges Japan gained would render China's "full sovereignty" an empty shell while granting the substance to Japan.

The term "economic privileges" is reminiscent of the Lansing-Ishii Agreement, and the impression it made was that, under certain conditions, the American government would sacrifice both China's sovereignty and its territories. In the spring of 1919, the conditions which forced Wilson to yield to the Japanese demands were a hundred times more critical than the situation motivating the Lansing-Ishii Agreement. The Russian Revolution was spreading to Central Europe and threatening to sweep the West. Wilson himself explained his final decision to his press secretary, Ray Stannard Baker: he must keep the world together and establish a League of Nations that included Japan. If Japan went home angry there would be danger of a Japanese-Russian-German alliance. He "must work for world order and organization against anarchy and a return to old militarism."[38] No doubt, when Wilson said "to keep the world together," he never meant to include Soviet Russia in the League. Wilson wished to retain Japan as an anti-Bolshevik power which would stem the revolutionary forces. In 1917, the purpose of the Lansing-Ishii Agreement was to provide a safety valve which would control the tide of Japanese expansion; in 1919 the settlement on Shandong was adopted in order to win Japan over to opposing world revolution. The 1919 settlement came at a heavier price. Why was China ordered to pay it?

Yet despite the imperialists' expectation, the Chinese people did not obey the order. Although Wilson's public utterances had at first engendered illusions in the hearts of many people, the reality of the peace settlement showed that the great powers were dividing up the spoils at China's expense. Events also showed that neither the warlords nor the imperialists could be relied upon.

The powers pressed China to agree. The Beijing warlord regime, especially Duan's faction, long accustomed to selling out the country, was ready to sign. On May 4, 1919, some three thousand students demonstrated in Beijing against the Paris decision. They demanded that the government denounce the clauses concerning Shandong and that it punish the internal traitors. They then declared a general strike to carry forward their protest. The strike drew support from every corner of the country, not only from students but also from workers and merchants. Paralysis threatened the nation. On June 10, the Beijing government was compelled to ask three notorious traitors to resign. The treaty was due for signature on June 28. More than ten thousand students of Beijing and Tianjin besieged the President's residence and pressed him to cable the Chinese delegates in Paris not to sign the treaty. Once again he yielded.

The American minister who witnessed the affair commented: "For the first time in her history China had roused herself and wrung from her government a specific surrender."[39] For the whole May Fourth Movement, his evaluation was that "for the first time in thousands of years public opinion was aroused and organized in China."[40]

This movement was unprecedented both in scope and in character. By it the people, especially the progressive intellectuals, acquired a new awareness of the true nature of imperialism. Said one of them:

"Let us see the decision of the Paris Conference. Which one of them has the slightest shadow of humanity, justice, or brightness, and which one of them is not built on the sacrifice of freedom and rights of the weaker peoples!"[41] They also realized that since China's reactionary forces were the puppets of foreign imperialists, opposition to them also meant opposition to the imperialists. Their slogan was thus "to win back national rights from without, and to eliminate traitors from within."[42] This twofold aim determined the content of the May Fourth Movement.

The movement distinguished itself from former movements by its thorough and uncompromising opposition to imperialists. In the 1911 Revolution, the revolutionaries, in order to secure the aid of the imperialists, vied with the reactionaries in respecting the rights that foreigners had gained through treaties. The May Fourth Movement put an end to such a situation.

The decision of the Paris Conference also aroused bitterness among Americans. The American Chamber of Commerce of China and the Anglo-American Association sent protests to Washington. In the United States, a storm of protest swept the country. The press teemed with such phrases as "the crime of Shandong," "the conspiracy to rob," "a damnable enterprise," and "the rape of Shandong."[43] The high point of Americans' anger came in a speech by Senator Borah. He bitterly observed that the Shandong decision

is one of those things so immoral and unrighteous that we wish to approach with deaf ears and closed eyes. We dread even to think about it. We loathe to be forced to attempt to define it. It will dishonor and degrade any people who seek to uphold it. War will inevitably follow as the result of an attempt to perpetrate it. It is founded on immorality and revolting injustice. It is outside the pale of respectability even according to ancient standards. It shocks the conscience even of European diplomacy. Naked, hideous, and revolting it looms up before us as a monster from that cruel and shameless world which all had hoped and prayed was forever behind us.[44]

The Shandong decision became one of the main reasons why the Senate rejected the Treaty of Versailles and one of the reasons for the Democratic failure in the presidential election of 1920. The people's anger at the treaty for granting Japan dominance in Shandong and their sympathy with China were no small factor in the politics of 1920. The American government could not ignore their voice.

The deal made by America and Japan in the peace conference only portended an even more intense rivalry in the postwar years.

5

The Western powers during World War I, as stated earlier, were in no position to meddle in the affairs of the East. As a result, the war presented China's industries with an opportunity for rapid development since it loosened, for a moment, the West's economic aggression. But the war also gave Japan a better opportunity to intensify its aggression against China and to collude with the corrupt elements of the Beijing government. Japan, taking advantage of this situation, intensified aggression against China on all fronts, with the aim of reducing China to a colony, even if it meant using ruthless means. This aggression and collusion with reactionary forces formed a serious impediment to the development of China's productive forces. It was a contradiction that welded together the social basis of the May Fourth Movement. Japan's aggression and the warlords' bartering away of national rights provoked vehement opposition from the whole people, including the national bourgeoisie. The Russian Revolution also enhanced China's national awakening as the emancipation of the Russian people stirred and stimulated the Chinese people to work for their own emancipation.

Under these circumstances, China's warlord government could no longer pursue an openly traitorous policy. On January 24, 1920, Japan approached the Foreign Ministry of the Beijing government with a proposal that the two governments start direct negotiations on the Shandong issue on the basis of the 1915 and 1918 agreements and the Versailles treaty. To negotiate on such a basis meant China's outright capitulation. Waves of mass protest spread throughout the country. The Beijing government dared neither to reject the Japanese proposal nor to negotiate directly with Japan. On May 22, after lengthy deliberation, Beijing sent Japan a reply: it refused to negotiate. Among the reasons for the refusal was that "the whole people of China have assumed a strongly antagonistic attitude in regard to the question in hand." [1] Clearly, then, but for public opinion, the Chinese ruling group would have agreed to negotiate directly with Japan. For two years the Chinese people stoutly resisted any attempt at direct negotiations and insisted on unconditional restoration. However venal some of the Beijing cabinets might have been, they still did not dare run counter to the wishes of the people.

America too had to face the issue of Japan's actions in China. Paul Reinsch, American minister in Beijing, after describing "Japanese imperialist politics with its unconscionably ruthless and underhanded actions," concluded:

They will not be stopped by any consideration of fairness and justice but only by the definite knowledge that such action will not be tolerated.

Now at last, when the pressure has been released, America as well as the European countries must face the issue which has been created. [2]

After the Paris conference, the American government pressed Japan to fulfill its pledge to the Council of Four to hand back to China the Shandong Peninsula in full sovereignty, retaining only economic privileges. Wilson meanwhile informed the Japanese that "negotiation with China on the basis of the agreements of 1915 and 1918 would not be tolerated." [3]

Following Versailles, the victors continued to struggle for their colonial rights and self-interests. The Western powers turned their attention to the Far East once more, and China again became the object of their scramble. America contested Japan for influence in China, eastern Siberia, and the Pacific. It was also engaged in a struggle with Britain for supremacy at sea. Complicating affairs was the Anglo-Japanese Alliance, which some Americans insisted was now aimed solely at the United States. All these controversies found their manifestation in a naval race among the three powers. The march of events in the Pacific pointed toward war.

The American people, however, who were opposed to further participation in the naval race, soon raised a clamor for disarmament. In these circumstances, the American government had to resort to other tactics in order to win the upper hand in its struggle with Japan. It sought to undermine Japan's relations with third powers. At the same time, there existed the possibility of bringing the British into a tacit partnership for the purpose of checking Japan.

In 1919, the British foreign minister, Lord Curzon, had expressed the opinion that "the days had gone by when China could be cut up into spheres of influence nor did her future lie in the assumption by Japan of the overlordship of the Far East. The future of China lay rather in international assistance and cooperation than in rival groups of interests or the ascendancy of individual powers."[4] In America, it was also believed that Britain and the United States should cooperate "to resist the trend toward extending to China policies of special interest."[5] In 1921, the Anglo-Japanese Alliance was due to expire. In a debate over the renewal of the Alliance, the Canadian prime minister convinced British statesmen that it should not be renewed in its existing form. Something else, of course, would have to be put in its place. The American government, realizing this fact, proposed in July 1921 that a conference be held in Washington on armament limitations and Pacific and Far Eastern affairs. Britain assented.

The principal participants at the Washington Conference were the United States, Britain, Japan, France, and Italy, which had emerged from World War I as the "Big Five." Since their discussions on Pacific and Far Eastern affairs involved problems relevant to China, it was decided to invite China and the governments of Holland, Portugal, and Belgium, which had interests in China, as well.

According to the plan of American secretary of state Charles Evans Hughes, the agenda should be broad enough to embrace the open door, equality of commercial opportunity, the integrity of China, and other Far Eastern questions. In his invitations, the President of the United States expressed his trust that "the spirit of friendship and a cordial appreciation of the importance of the elimination of sources of controversy [would] govern the final decision."[6] The Chinese thus entertained the hope not only that the conference would solve the Shandong problem in the interest of justice to China, but also that it would do something to remove existing limitations and infringements on China's sovereign rights. Accordingly, the Chinese delegation to the conference presented a long list of grievances for settlement, a list which ranged from such topics as the abolition of foreign postal agencies and radio stations to the problems of restoring tariff autonomy and relinquishing extraterritorial rights. And of course, there was the all-important question of Shandong.

On July 21, 1921, after it was decided to convene the Washington Conference, secretary of state Hughes had a conversation with the Japanese ambassador, Kijuro Shidehara. During the conversation Shidehara suggested that the secretary try to influence China to enter into direct negotiations with Japan on the Shandong issue. Hughes replied that the possibility of his employing good offices depended upon the specific terms Japan might propose. A few weeks later, he informed the ambassador that Japan would have to present a satisfactory offer. On September 7, Japan presented to China its terms for the settlement of the Shandong controversy; the following day, it communicated these terms to Hughes.

The 1915 and 1918 agreements had demanded, first, that a concession in the Jiaozhou leased area be under the exclusive jurisdiction of Japan; second, that Japanese be employed at the headquarters of the railway police force; and third, that the Jiaozhou-Jinan railway be made a Sino-Japanese enterprise. In its new proposals, Japan no longer demanded a concession or the employment of Japanese in the police force, but it still insisted that the railway be a joint enterprise. Secretary Hughes told Shidehara that he believed that China would not consent to joint ownership of the railway; he could therefore make no hopeful suggestion to China on this basis. He suggested that it might be possible for Japan to offer a solution under which China could obtain complete ownership and control of the railway by making compensation. He also told the Japanese ambassador that the latter "must understand . . . there was a general conviction that there should be a restoration to China of what Germany formerly had in Shandong."[7] Hughes's reference to "a general conviction" indicated that he was aware of American opinion and of the attitude of the Chinese people. The pressure of public opinion had already brought about some progress in solving the Shandong question.

The Chinese delegation at the Washington Conference wished to bring up the Shandong issue; Japan, on the other hand, wished to exclude it from the agenda. Through the efforts of Charles Evans Hughes and Arthur Balfour, the British chief delegate, a compromise was reached: "informal" conversations were to be held between the Chinese and Japanese representatives during, though technically outside of, the conference. American and British "observers" would be present, and no argument should be based upon treaty commitments.

In the talks, the railway question proved to be at the core of the entire Shandong controversy. At the beginning, the Japanese reiterated their original proposal to operate the Jiaozhou-Jinan railway as a joint Sino-Japanese enterprise. They sought permanent control of a railway that reached from a first-class port into the heart of China. The Chinese delegates strenuously objected to such control. The Japanese then proposed that China seek a long-term loan from Japanese bankers for the purchase of the railway and that, during the term of the loan, China engage a chief engineer, a traffic manager, and a chief accountant—all to be of Japanese nationality and recommended by the Japanese financiers. The Japanese delegates were moving toward Hughes's suggestion for restoring the railroad to China in return for payments. But because the payments would last a long time, the plan was calculated to secure actual control for an equally long time.

Early in January, the conversations reached a deadlock. The Japanese insisted on their plan for a Japanese loan. The Chinese countered with two alternative plans: either a cash payment with a single deposit in a bank of a third power at a specified date, or else a deferred payment in treasury notes or in notes of the Chinese Bankers Union over a period of twelve years with an option of redemption after three. China was also to select and employ a Japanese district engineer.

An incident in China's internal politics, however, led to an impasse over the railway. On December 24, 1921, Liang Shiyi, a member of the pro-Japanese faction, supported by the warlord Zhang Zuolin, became the new Premier. On the 29th, he was called on by the Japanese minister to Beijing, Torikichi Obata. Replying to Obata's anxious inquiry concerning a solution to the Shandong railway issue, Liang told the minister that "a loan would be sought and the railway operated under Chinese management."[8]

The Japanese delegate to the Washington Conference used this occasion to tell Hughes that Liang had made a proposal to Obata which was very similar to the Japanese plan. Later, Liang repeatedly denied having talked with anybody in favor of a Japanese loan for the redemption of the railway. But it was clear that the word "loan" did not rule out an arrangement with Japanese financiers. The affair put the Chinese delegation in an extremely difficult position. When the conversations were resumed on January 4, 1922, the Japanese attitude had hardened and they stuck more tenaciously than ever to their plan.

In the meantime two powerful agencies were at work outside the confines of the conference table. Public opinion began to stir in both China and the United States. In China, Liang's action brought on mass meetings and demonstrations. In the face of violent protests, the Beijing government immediately issued declarations denying the alleged plan for the redemption of the railway through a Japanese loan. The Chinese delegation in Washington also decided to adhere to the original course of action. Liang was overthrown, barely one month after taking office.

In America, the people were resolved to allow no repetition of the Versailles fiasco, and they made this resolve clear to congress. Senator Walsh brought up the Shandong issue in the Senate in direct connection with the Four-Power Pact. The impression gained from the remarks of Walsh and their reception in the Senate was that the entire set of treaties and agreements from the Conference might not meet the approval of the Senate if the Shandong dispute were not ended. Senator Walsh's action reflected the temper of the American people. "In fact, as the Conference sagged on toward the end of its third month it became increasingly evident that it was the pressure of public opinion in the United States that was China's strongest advocate at the conference table." [9]

Secretary of State Hughes was well aware that the success or failure of the Washington Conference depended upon a just settlement of the Shandong case. But what he sought was only a quick settlement, one that would satisfy public opinion. On January 18, Hughes and Balfour, the two "mediators," agreed to Japan's "minimum" demands, namely: (1) deferred payment by Chinese treasury notes running for fifteen years, but redeemable at any time after five years; (2) appointment of a Japanese chief accountant and a Chinese chief accountant, of equal powers, both to be under the control of the Chinese director-general of the railway; and (3) appointment of a Japanese traffic manager subject to the control of the Chinese director-general. Hughes then exerted heavy pressure on the Chinese to accept this formula, telling their delegation and the Beijing government that if they chose to break off negotiations over trivialities and thus bring disaster upon themselves, they could not "count on any support either from public sentiment in the United States or from this government." [10] Under this threat, the Chinese yielded. On February 4, the agreement on the whole Shandong issue was signed by the Chinese and Japanese representatives.

Pursuant to the agreement, Japan was to restore Jiaozhou to China, the area previously leased by Germany and occupied by Japan since 1914. China was of her own volition to open Jiaozhou to foreign residence, industry, and trade. Japanese troops were to be withdrawn. Japan would transfer the railway to China, which China would pay for over a period of five to fifteen years. In addition, Japan agreed to withdraw the fifth group of its Twenty-one Demands, which would have converted China into a Japanese protectorate (see chapter 4). This settlement, of course was still not a fair one. But it would have been even less just had not the people of China and America forced a corrupt Beijing government, and a Hughes quite indifferent to China's interests, to reduce Japan's demands.

The Western powers at the conference were also prepared to make some concessions. Britain was prepared to surrender the lease of Wei-haiwei and France agreed to enter into negotiations with China for the return of Guangzhou Bay. In addition, the tariff schedule would be revised from the actual rate of 3.5 percent to the effective rate of 5 percent. A special commission would be convened, that would, among other things, authorize the levying of surtaxes.

Although the powers at the Washington Conference did not treat China as an equal, the above decisions mark the first time since 1839 that China, in dealing with the foreign powers, did not lose national rights but rather gained something back. The restoration of the rights in Shandong was, to be sure, still conditional, but the conditions were much less harsh than those the Japanese had originally demanded.

Certainly, America was attempting to put a brake on the Japanese advance into China. But this policy meant only to regulate future conduct, not to redress past grievances. Hughes told the principal members of the American delegation on December 17 that "he had gone along the theory always that this country would never go to war over any aggression on the part of Japan in China, and that conse-quently the most that could be done would be to stay Japan's hand." [11]

Within China, changes had taken place in the power struggle among the warlords. In July 1920, the Zhili clique backed by Britain and America had defeated Duan's pro-Japanese Anhui clique in a civil war. The Zhili clique's victory, however, did not mean the ultimate defeat of Japan, since Japan had found a new tool in Zhang Zuolin, a warlord of the Fengtian clique. Under the aegis of Zhang's armed forces, pro-Japanese elements remained active in the government.

Therefore, neither the policy of the American government nor the temporary triumph of its clients in China were decisive in pro-ducing the above-stated results. The vigor of the May Fourth Move-ment of 1919 was unabated at the time of the Washington Con-ference. In September 1921, the new American minister Jacob Schurman found that "a strong national consciousness is in existence and an aggressive patriotism is actuating the leaders of China and the rising generation." [12] John Dewey, who came to China to lecture in the period, said in October: "the most impressive single feature of my stay in China was witnessing the sure and rapid growth of an enlight-ened and progressive public opinion." [13] Thus, the Chinese people's struggle and the American people's aid were the decisive factors in the Washington Conference.

The treatment of other matters presented by the Chinese delegation was much less favorable to China. America's main concern was with the so-called Nine-Power Treaty, "A Treaty Between All Nine Powers Relating to Principles and Policies to Be Followed in Matters Concerning China." After the war, America, in order to safeguard its own interests, was determined to end Japan's dominant position in China. But a second and different phase of American policy involved cooperation with Japan to protect their common interests. Furthermore, though America wished to restrain Japan's advance into China, it was not anxious to end its vested interests. All these features were reflected in the Nine-Power Treaty.

The central idea pervading the treaty was the so-called "open door and equal opportunity" doctrine. Though the doctrine was not a novelty, America now sought to convert it into a covenant, a covenant that all foreign powers would observe and that would serve as America's postwar policy for China.

The first article of the treaty involved four principles:

(1) Respect for the sovereignty, the independence, and the territorial and administrative integrity of China;

(2) Provision of the fullest and most unembarrassed opportunity for China to develop and maintain an effective and stable government;

(3) Use of foreign powers' influence to establish the principle of equal opportunity for commerce and industry of all nations throughout China;

(4) Refusal of these powers to take advantage of conditions in China in order to seek special rights or privileges which would abridge the rights of subjects or citizens of friendly States and from countenancing action inimical to the security of such States.[14]

These four points were directed against the policies which Japan had pursued since the outbreak of World War I. They also provided some conditions under which China could present her grievances and demand redress.

According to Elihu Root, the American delegate to the Washington Conference and author of this treaty, these principles would neither be retroactive nor modify existing treaties or agreements.[15]

In other words, these principles were designed to freeze rather than to modify the status quo.

But, what status quo? This article required a respect both for China's sovereignty and for those "rights of subjects or citizens of friendly States" that infringed that sovereignty. This was merely a repetition of the thesis of the open door policy made by the American government in 1900, namely, "to preserve China's territorial and administrative entity, protect all rights guaranteed to friendly powers by treaty and international laws." [16] The two points were, of course, self-contradictory. The rights were "guaranteed by" unequal treaties, built upon a violation of China's sovereignty and territorial and administrative integrity. If the foreigners' rights were to be protected, China's sovereignty would have to be sacrificed. But in the Washington Conference, Elihu Root tried to reconcile the two. Upon inquiry from Japan's Komei Kato, Root said that the words "administrative integrity" "did not affect any privileges accorded by valid or effective grants, that, on the contrary, respect for the administrative integrity of a country required respect for the things that are done in the exercise of its full sovereignty by an independent State." [17] This argument involved a strange logic. Later, when refusing to abrogate the 1915 treaties which were intended to destroy China's sovereignty, the Japanese delegate Shidehara said: "It has, however, been held by the conference on more than one occasion that concessions made by China ex contractu, in the exercise of her own sovereign rights, cannot be regarded as inconsistent with her sovereignty and independence." [18] Except for a colony or semicolony, no country would have such "full sovereignty" for granting concessions or for respecting the concessions which had injured its sovereignty. The arguments for respecting China's integrity and at the same time preserving the status quo meant only that the powers were determined to keep China in a semicolonial status.

The settlement of specific issues also shows that America and other powers had little inclination to modify the status quo, whether such was established by treaties or by other means. The conference refused the Chinese delegation's request for the restoration of China's right to determine its own tariff rates. One of the principal "reasons" why the powers opposed any increase in China's customs revenue was that, owing to the lack of a parliamentary government, the increased revenue might be absorbed by the provincial military governors and thus might be used to cause further disturbances in China. The American delegate Underwood said: "I hope that the day may not be far distant when China will have established a parliamentary government representing her people, and that thus an opportunity will be given her to exercise in every respect her full sovereignty and regulate her own customs tariff." [19] Lord Balfour expressed a similar opinion.

These reasons, however, were but pretext for denying to China the right of tariff autonomy. The powers did not really fear that the warlords would absorb the revenue and so cause further disturbances. On the contrary, they had furnished the warlords' factions with huge sums of money and fanned the flame of civil war. Dr. Sun Yat-sen was, in 1921, the only national figure who had devoted his life to the establishment of a parliamentary government. Yet no foreign power had ever given him any aid. In May 1921, he established a revolutionary government in Guangzhou and appealed to President Warren Harding for recognition. Harding refused. The Washington Conference also refused to allow his government to send an independent delegation. The British imperialists even adopted a hostile stance toward Sun's government, supporting the warlords in Guangdong in order to gain mining concessions in that province.

The treaties of extraterritoriality constituted the most flagrant violation of China's sovereign rights. The Chinese delegate Wang Chonghui asked the powers to pick a date for the surrender of all extraterritorial rights. Secretary of State Hughes responded with a call for an inquiry into existing conditions in China. The removal of these humiliating treaties was thus postponed to a distant future.

The Chinese delegation proposed the reconsideration of the treaties and notes resulting from the Twenty-one Demands of 1915, which granted to Japan special rights in Northeast China and eastern Inner Mongolia, but with no success. Only Hughes made a statement:

With respect to this grant, the government of the United States
will, of course, regard it as not intended to be exclusive, and, as in
the past, will claim from the Chinese government for American citizens the benefits accruing to them by virtue of the most favored
nation clauses in the treaties between the United States and China. [20]

What concerned Hughes was to share the "benefits." The real meaning of the phrase "equal opportunity" was now revealed. It was "Disgorge what you have swallowed and let each of us enjoy the takings equally."

China's chief delegate, Shi Shaoji, declared that the maintenance, without China's consent and despite its protests, of Japanese troops upon Chinese territory constituted a standing violation of the country's sovereignty and territorial and administrative integrity. But Hughes reduced this problem of principle into a problem of "whether [the existence of] adequate protection for life and property . . . would warrant Japan in withdrawing from China her troops and police."[21] In other words, the allegation that China could not offer adequate protection for life and property became a pretext for acquiescing to the presence of foreign troops in China.

The actions of America and other powers at the Washington Conference reveal that the alleged respect for China's integrity meant only respect for its "integrity" as a semicolony. They also reveal that, on many practical issues, the United States did not hesitate to accommodate Japan. Why? One reason was that cooperation with Japan would help preserve their common interests. "Open door" meant the preservation of "the common interests of all powers in China,"[22] which in turn presupposed a partnership or cooperation among the imperialist powers.

In 1919 Lord Curzon had talked glowingly about international cooperation. On the eve of the conference his successor at the foreign office, Lord Balfour, prepared and informally presented to Secretary of State Hughes a draft treaty which would be agreed to by Britain, France, Japan, the United States, and China. The objectives of this treaty were the application of the principle of the open door and the substitution of international cooperation for international rivalry in China. It proposed, among other things, that the five governments would, whenever any of these principles was in jeopardy, communicate with one another, fully and frankly. They would then consider measures to be taken to safeguard their menaced rights and interests.

Although this draft was never laid before the conference, most of the underlying ideas were incorporated into the Nine-Power Treaty, as well as the Four-Power Pact, which Britain, the United States, France, and Japan concluded concerning their possessions in the Pacific. The Four-Power Pact provided that the powers agreed to respect one another's rights in relation to their insular possessions and dominions in the Pacific, and to refer future disputes in that area to a joint conference. It further stipulated that if other powers threatened the rights of the four signatories, they should "communicate with one another fully and frankly in order to arrive at an understanding as to the most efficient measures to be taken, jointly or separately, to meet the exigencies of the particular situation."[23] The Four-Power Pact also embodied the two sides of American policy. It ended the Anglo-Japanese Alliance, detached Britain from tacit support of Japan in the Far East, and, in effect, aligned Britain with America against Japanese expansion. The pact also confirmed the powers' mutual respect for their respective rights and their willingness to cooperate in safeguarding their common interests.

The Nine-Power Treaty had the same results. It denied Japan exclusive rights and a monopolistic position in China. On the other hand, it did involve the idea of partnership. Although the treaty did not openly require joint consideration in the event of a crisis, it still provided that

whenever a situation arises which in the opinion of any one of [the signatories] involves the application of the stipulation of the present Treaty, and renders desirable discussion of such application, there shall be full and frank communication between the Contracting Powers concerned.[24]

This provision implied that no signatory would take action in China without consulting the others.

In 1928, the United States and the Nationalist government of China signed an agreement that nullified all treaty provisions between the two countries concerning tariffs and related matters. It restored tariff autonomy to China, subject to the restrictions of the most-favored-nation clause. Of this affair, American historian Merlo Pusey said: "Breaking away from the cooperative policy that had been established in Washington, the State Department suddenly negotiated a separate customs treaty with Chiang's Nationalists and began yielding to Chinese pressure for ending extraterritoriality," actions that Pusey regarded as "deviations from the Hughesian policy of cooperation."[25] Pusey's conclusion displays two truths: first, that the "Hughesian policy" involved cooperation with Japan, and second, that the purpose of that cooperation was the preservation of colonial rights. If America took separate steps to modify China's semicolonial status, it would be a "deviation" from that policy.

On the eve of the Washington Conference, a Chinese progressive warned that "if China does not strive to launch a vigorous resistance, the fate of divided control or joint control by the powers will inevitably befall her sooner or later."[26] The Washington Conference brought to China neither divided control nor outright joint control.

China remained a semicolony, but was confronted with a new situation: the imperialist powers had transformed competitive aggression into concerted aggression.

Aggression, however, cannot really be concerted. As the American minister, Jacob Schurman said at the time, "China offers incalculable commercial prizes to those who can win them. But under the established policy of the United States, Americans must win them, if at all, in a free, fair, and open struggle with competitors from all the world."[27] Perhaps the Americans imagined that, under the open door doctrine, and through the use of their vast financial power, they might make profitable gains in China. But history has time and again shown that colonialist interests are seldom free or fair.

As we have seen, toward the end of World War I, the United States, in proposing a Four-Power Consortium, had tried to substitute a concerted approach in place of Japan's dominance, but the clash of interests among the four powers made it impossible for the newly formed Consortium to act. In 1919, John Earl Baker, an American advisor to the Railway Department of the Beijing government, put forward a plan for joint management of Chinese railways by the United States, Japan, Britain, France, and China. But the plan fell through as a result of strong opposition by Japan.

The Washington Conference did not mitigate the conflict between the United States and Japan. The fight for special privilege in China continued to rage. Barely two months after the conclusion of the conference, war broke out on a still larger scale between the warlord factions, with each of them enjoying the support of the imperialist powers. Contradictions and struggles among the various warlords in China reflected the contradictions and struggles among the various imperialist powers. Since the imperialists still cooperated on the surface, they did not attack one another with arms. But because their rivalry in China continued unabated, each tried to use one or more warlords, against the others. Both Duan Qirui's Anhui clique and Zhang Zuolin's Fengtian clique were tools of Japan, whereas the Zhili cliques of Cao Kun and Wu Peifu were supported by America and Britain. War broke out in April 1922, and the Zhili faction defeated the Fengtian faction and won control of the Beijing government. In order to turn the tables on the Zhili warlords, Japan gave unremitting support to the Fengtian warlord Zhang Zuolin. The United States, on the other hand, spared no efforts to strengthen the Zhili clique so as to prevent the Fengtian forces from staging a comeback. To help Wu Peifu implement his policy of "unification by armed force," the

United States lavished both munitions and money on him (a single delivery of which in 1923, for instance, was valued at $3 million). In 1924, the Fengtian-Zhili war broke out again.

The fact that America continued to use the warlords in its struggle with Japan in China proves that the policy of restraint plus cooperation embodied in the Nine-Power Treaty was impracticable. Some historians have suggested that the treaty failed because there was no force to defend it. But the problem is more complex: American threats to use force would have undermined its desire to achieve its goals through cooperation, but threats of force were the only means to restrain Japan. The basic cause of the failure was the impracticability of the treaty itself.

6

The United States, after the Zhili-Fengtian war of 1922, supported the Zhili warlord clique with ever greater intensity until its destruction by the Nationalist revolution in 1927. The Zhili warlords, after their victory over the Fengtian clique in May 1922, ousted Xu Shichang, who had been elected president by the Anhui-controlled parliament, revoked the parliament of 1912, and installed Li Yuanhong as the legitimate president. Dr. Sun Yat-sen, after the fall of Xu, had asked the United States for aid in the establishment of a unified and democratic China. But the American government turned him down. Since the death of Yuan Shikai, the American government had hoped "for the emergence of some strong man in the north to pull the country together under a conservative government which would restore order and safeguard foreign rights."[1] During the war between the Zhili and Anhui cliques in 1920, the Zhili forces, with Wu Peifu's army as the nucleus, overthrew the Anhui clique's pro-Japanese regime. From then on, the Anglo-American imperialists thought that Wu Peifu was precisely the strong man they had long sought to rule China. In March 1923, Wu called a council of war at his Luoyang headquarters, raising the slogan of "unification of China by armed force." At the same time, Cao Kun, the leader of the Zhili clique, sought the Presidency. The United States encouraged all of Wu's and Cao's ambitions. In May 1923, when Cao wished to ascertain the attitude of the foreign powers, the American minister, Jacob Schurman, quickly journeyed to Baoding for a personal talk with him. In June, President Harding of the United States said that American banking groups would be willing to help China achieve "unification."[2] Cao Kun, by bribing members of parliament, was, on October 5, "elected" President. On the day of the "election," Schurman made a special visit to the parliament—the "only foreign Minister present."[3] He also showed concern for the new president and said that "it seems to me very desirable that he and his party should have the good will of the powers in their attempt to govern China."[4]

While sustaining the Zhili warlords, the Americans and British sought to undermine the revolutionary cause led by Sun Yat-sen in Guangzhou. They combined other powers to exert both financial and military pressure on the Guangzhou government. It was at that time the practice for the foreign commissioners of customs to have direct control of Chinese customs revenue collection, to deduct the sums required for the payment of the indemnities under the Protocol of 1901 and other loans and obligations, and to hand over the remainder, known as customs surplus, to the Beijing government. After the Guangzhou government was formed in 1917, the foreign powers, in an attempt to buy it over, gave it a share of the customs surplus. By 1923, however, the powers had become disappointed in the Guangzhou government—they now considered it unworthy of receiving a single penny, even though all the money was Chinese.

In September 1923, the Guangzhou government requested the customs surplus collected in the areas under its jurisdiction. The diplomatic corps in Beijing rejected the request. U.S Secretary of State Charles Evans Hughes instructed his minister in Beijing to insist that "the Diplomatic Body deals with customs surplus only as trustees for the recognized Government of China."[5] The powers had decided that they would give the money only to their client, the Beijing warlord government. Later Schurman bluntly told the foreign minister of the Beijing government that the powers "were doing a kind and friendly act for the Chinese government in assisting it to keep its principal source of revenue intact."[6] In December, when the Guangzhou government attempted to take matters into its own hands and retain the revenues of the Guangzhou customs, the United States and Britain each sent seventeen warships to Baietan, near Guangzhou. Schurman predicted, "[Sun Yat-sen] may collapse within a few weeks if he fails to get the customs revenues."[7] This prediction revealed the imperialists' intent to strangle the Guangzhou government by denying it its rightful share of the customs surplus. But, contrary to Schurman's expectation, the action of the imperialists only aroused mass indignation in Guangzhou. A boycott of American and British goods was declared. Thanks to popular support, the Guangzhou government did not "collapse" but grew more stable than ever before.

The affair of the customs surplus shows that the imperialists used their control over China's maritime customs as a means both to exploit the Chinese economically and to interfere in China's internal politics. The imperialists were adamant that they would never renounce their special rights as such. Although the Chinese people vehemently demanded the end of unequal treaties and although many Americans expressed sympathy for the Chinese and urged that the United States give up extraterritoriality and tariff controls, the American government still refused to make any concession that would disturb the treaty system. It was even reluctant to execute the pledges it had made with other powers at the Washington Conference. That conference had provided for an increase in existing customs duties and called for a future conference to consider further possible adjustments. The powers had also promised to authorize a commission to inquire into the present exercise of extraterritorial jurisdiction.

In September 1922, the commission on the tariff worked out a revised schedule of tariff rates that would yield no more than the effective 5 percent that previous treaties had stipulated. The foreign powers did not consider an increase in tariffs until October 1925. In a tariff conference, held at the Beijing government's urging, the powers only authorized China to levy a customs surtax, which had already been agreed upon at the Washington Conference. China's right to tariff autonomy was still a goal within sight but beyond reach. The extraterritoriality commission did not start its work until January 1926, and it took another nine months to trot out a report, which merely outlined a program of reform for China's judicial system. After China had carried out this program, the powers might then consider the relinquishment of their rights of extraterritoriality!

So the imperialists remained, still riding roughshod over the Chinese people. And the warlords, backed by their foreign masters, continued to wage civil wars to oppress the people. It appeared that the "status quo" in China, which the Washington Conference sought to preserve, would remain unchanged forever. But this state of affairs shows only one aspect of the trend. During the five years after the Washington Conference, the struggle of the Chinese people made such great headway that the imperialists and warlords soon had to confront an entirely new situation.

Vigorous patriotic forces, unleashed in China after the May Fourth Movement, persisted throughout the postwar era. Underlying the domestic struggles against the warlords, and continually reappearing in one form or another, was a powerful drive for emancipation from the semicolonial status imposed by the unequal treaties. But this drive was not a simple continuation of the May Fourth Movement. After May 4, 1919, the Chinese working class became an independent force in the people's patriotic movement and proved themselves stalwart fighters in the struggle against imperialism. Many revolutionary intellectuals realized the formidable strength of the working class and saw the necessity of integrating Marxism-Leninism with the workers' movement, and intellectuals with the workers. On this basis, on July 1, 1921, the Communist Party of China was founded. After this event, the Chinese people enjoyed the leadership of a party that guided them in the correct direction and fought unflinchingly in the forefront of their struggle against the powerful imperialists and their lackeys in China. Three months after the end of the Washington Conference, the Communist Party of China held its Second Congress. That congress pointed out in its manifesto that the feudal regime of warlords and bureaucrats in China was in league with imperialist forces. Accordingly, the congress set forth as the Party program the overthrow of the warlords and liquidation of international imperialist oppression.

The Third Congress of the Communist Party, held in June of 1923, gave the stamp of approval to the anti-imperialist and antifeudal convictions of Kuomintang (Nationalist Party) leader Sun Yat-sen, and decided to establish a revolutionary united front, based on Kuomintang-Communist cooperation, so as jointly to promote the democratic revolution against imperialism and feudalism. Although Sun Yat-sen, at times, had had illusions about the Western powers and even tended to compromise with the warlords, his illusions and compromises had led only to disappointment and frustration. One lesson he had learned from his failures was to ally himself with the political party of the working class. In January 1924, he convened the First National Congress of the Kuomintang, formally established the united front with the Communist Party, and planned a northern drive to overthrow the warlords' regime.

On March 12, 1925, Sun Yat-sen died before he could carry out his revolutionary plans. But his death did not keep the movement against imperialism and warlords from going forward and from demanding the nullification of the unequal treaties. This demand arose from the conclusion in May 1924 of an agreement between China and the Soviet Union in which the Soviet Union voluntarily annulled all the unequal treaties concluded between Tsarist Russia and China, renounced extraterritorial rights, restored Tsarist concessions in Chinese ports to China, relinquished the Russian share of the indemnities under the Protocol of 1901, and recognized China's tariff autonomy.

This treaty, the first equal one China had signed since the Opium War, encouraged the Chinese people to demand that the other powers follow the example of the Soviet Union. After the massacre of May 30, 1925, when the Japanese and British imperialists killed and wounded Chinese workers and students, the anti-imperialist movement reached its peak. While the foreign powers and the Beijing government attempted to deceive the people by arguing over tariff rates and extraterritoriality, the Chinese people demanded the immediate and unqualified abolition of all unequal treaties.

In July 1926, in the storm raised by mass protests against imperialism, the Kuomintang and their Communist allies launched the Northern Expedition. Supported by workers and peasants, in less than six months the Northern Expeditionary Army had fought its way through the Changjiang River basin and liberated half of China. In early January 1927, British soldiers killed and wounded Chinese civilians in Hankou and Jiujiang, whereupon, on January 5 and 6, enraged workers occupied the British concessions in the two ports. On March 21–23, the workers in Shanghai staged an armed insurrection and liberated the whole Shanghai municipality except for the international settlement and the French concession. The British imperialists, who had a large stake in the Changjiang Valley, fell in a flurry of violent protests. On December 18, 1926, the British government circulated a memorandum to each of the governments which had participated in the Washington Conference, stating Britain's intention of noninterference in China's internal affairs and proposing progressive abandonment of foreign treaty privileges in China. In February 1927, the British government formally returned the Hankou and Jiujiang concessions to China, signing two agreements with the Nationalist government.

This was no surrender, however, for at the same time they were preparing for armed intervention. In January 1927, they assembled twenty-seven warships and twelve thousand troops in Shanghai, planning to repeat that massacre with which allied foreign troops had crushed the Boxers. After the Northern Expeditionary troops captured Nanjing on March 24, 1927, the warships of the Anglo-American imperialists in the Changjiang River beside Nanjing, on the pretext of protecting foreign nationals from the "outrages" by the Northern Expeditionary soldiers, bombarded the city, producing two thousand Chinese military and civilian casualties. The imperialists were wielding a dual tactic: first, divide the revolutionary movement by making concessions, second threaten armed intervention.

The combination of concession with threat was also the policy of the United States toward the Chinese Revolution of 1924–1927. The American people sympathized with the aspirations of the Chinese people. They had no desire to uphold the corrupt, reactionary regime which had for so long held sway at Beijing. It was popularly felt that the time had come to break away entirely from any concert of powers, and to aid the Chinese revolutionaries by surrendering at once all special rights. But the American government was hostile to the Nationalist revolution, even more hostile than it had been in dealing with the previous revolutionary movement in China. Besides the United States' traditional desire not to lose any privileges enjoyed by other powers, its leaders now had a latent fear of Communist influence within the Nationalist regime. Like other major powers, America sent naval and military forces to Shanghai, drew up plans for armed intervention, and participated in the bombardment of Nanjing. Yet it knew that the Chinese revolutionary regime was a coalition between the Nationalists and Communists, and hoped that by stressing the soft phase of its dual policy it could allay the anti-imperialist feeling of the Chinese people and thus both split off the rightist element from the revolutionary camp and undermine the revolution from within.

Secretary of State Frank Kellogg issued a statement on American policy toward China on January 27, 1927, declaring that

the United States is now and has been ever since the negotiation of the Washington Treaty, prepared to enter into negotiations with any Government of China or delegates who can represent or speak for China not only for the putting into force of the surtaxes of the Washington Treaty, but entirely releasing tariff control and restoring complete tariff autonomy to China.

The United States would expect, however, that it be granted most favored nation treatment . . . and that the open door with equal opportunity for trade in China shall be maintained, and, further, that China should afford every protection to American citizens and to their property and rights. . . .

The Government of the United States was ready then, and is ready now, to continue the negotiations on the entire subject of tariff duties and extraterritoriality, or to take up negotiations on behalf of the United States alone.[8]

The United States was willing to negotiate "with any Government of China or delegates who [could] represent or speak for China." Moreover, it was ready to deal directly with China irrespective of the actions of other nations. Kellogg was working on two lines: first, win over the bourgeois in the coalition by a willingness to negotiate with them, and second, outmaneuver other powers by preparing to take independent action.

American hopes for splitting the revolutionary front were not without foundation. Only a few months after starting the Northern Expedition, Chiang Kai-shek, commander-in-chief of the Northern Expeditionary Army, prepared to betray the revolution. When his army approached Shanghai, the economic and political base of compradorism and the stronghold of foreign and Chinese capitalism, Chiang turned his headquarters at Nanjing, the capital of Jiangxi Province, into a marketplace from which to auction off a revolution. Reactionary politicians of all factions haunted the city. In the early winter of 1926, British and American business interests and Chinese banking groups in Shanghai dispatched Yu Qiaqing to negotiate with Chiang. They made a deal: Yu promised to provide Chiang with a huge fund of 60 million Shanghai dollars; in return, Chiang pledged to "oppose and exterminate communists" in China.[9] Two months before Kellogg's statement, Chiang had already, in a November 21, 1926 interview with foreign correspondents, "expressed friendship toward the United States."[10] From February 1927 on, Chiang embarked on the fulfillment of his pledge to his foreign and domestic masters.

Chiang arrived at Shanghai on March 26, 1927. In a series of interviews with foreign journalists, he repeatedly stated that "the Nationalist leaders have always wished to maintain friendly relations with the foreign powers." He then promised that "in spite of the present obstacles to a clearer and better understanding, we hope to remove these so that there will be a clearer and better relationship between China and the foreign powers which will be based upon a mutual friendship and understanding."[11] By "obstacles" he meant the workers who had controlled Shanghai since the March 21 insurrection. On April 12, 1927, Chiang put his promise into practice by ordering a surprise attack on the workers. He massacred large numbers of workers and Communist Party members in Shanghai and other areas under his rule. The Revolution of 1924–1927, symbolic of Kuomintang-Communist cooperation, ended in tragedy. But the Revolution proper did not end: the Communist Party continued to lead the Chinese people in their fight for the cause of national liberation.

Four days after the Shanghai coup, on April 18, Chiang Kai-shek set up an anti-Communist, dicatatorial government in Nanjing.

Chiang's regime, like the reactionary regimes before it, became a tool of imperialists, rich landlords, and the bourgeoisie. After the establishment of the government, Chiang's foreign minister, Wu Chaoshu (C. C. Wu), lost no time in announcing:

The Nationalist Government addresses itself to the task of the abrogation of the unequal treaties, and will employ for that purpose all legitimate means. . . . With every confidence in the good intentions of the foreign governments, this government earnestly hopes that negotiations with a view to the conclusion of new treaties will immediately be opened. [12]

Six months earlier, Chiang Kai-shek had boasted: "It is just as great a part of the revolutionary movement to abolish extraterritoriality and Foreign Concessions as it is to stamp out the northern militarists, and this Revolution will not come to an end until that has been done." He had even added that this would be done "at once." [13] But now rather than "stamping out" the unequal treaties "at once," his government would abolish them through negotiations and by "all legitimate means." In January 1928, Chiang repeated in person that the abrogation of unequal treaties would be achieved "by peaceful negotiation." [14] One month later, his new foreign minister, Huang Fu, a politician formerly in the service of the Beijing warlord government, simply struck out the term "abrogation" and replaced it with the word "revision." Huang added that pending the conclusion of new agreements, his government was prepared to maintain and develop friendly relations with the foreign powers with a view to removing all sources of difficulties and misunderstandings between Chinese and foreigners. [15]

One of Huang's first acts for the removal of misunderstandings was to settle with the United States the Nanjing Incident of the previous year. The U.S. government found Chiang's behavior since April 1927 so satisfactory that it gave Chiang moral support by negotiating separately with the Nanjing government instead of working jointly with the other powers. On March 30, 1928, Huang Fu exchanged notes with John MacMurray, the U.S. minister in China. Although it was the imperialist powers who had killed and wounded two thousand Chinese people, the Nanjing government still accepted responsibility for the incident. In order to please the American imperialists, Chiang's regime was without scruple in alleging that the incident was "entirely instigated by the Communists" prior to the establishment of the Nationalist government at Nanjing. With the extermination of the Communists and their influence, argued Huang, the Nationalist government felt confident that the protection of foreigners would be easier, and it would also undertake specifically to see that there would be no similar violence or agitation against American lives or legitimate interests. Effective steps, Huang asserted, had been taken for the punishment of the soldiers and other persons implicated in the incident. The Nationalist government was, moreover, willing to compensate in full for all personal injuries and material damages done to the Americans.[16]

Chiang's government was no less subservient to foreigners than the Qing Dynasty and Yuan Shikai. Small wonder Secretary of State Kellogg, on seeing the text of the note, answered that the State Department was "very much gratified."[17] Concerning the bombardment of Nanjing, the American government stated that it felt "that its vessels had no alternative to the action taken, however deeply it deplores that circumstances beyond its control should have necessitated the adoption of such measures for the protection of the lives of its citizens at Nanking."[18] The slaughter of Chinese people seemed always to be justifiable.

On July 7, 1928, the Nanjing government requested that the foreign powers "negotiate—in accordance with diplomatic procedure—new treaties on a basis of equality."[19] But in actuality it was begging the foreign powers to grant it some concession, if only as a fig leaf to cover up its betrayal of the revolution. It weakened the demand for the abrogation of unequal treaties by requesting revisions on merely two items: tariff control and extraterritoriality. The United States was the first country to respond positively to the request, but it confined the negotiations to tariff autonomy, aiming at a simple tariff treaty. Such a treaty was signed on July 25, 1928, by John MacMurray and Song Ziwen (T. V. Soong), minister of finance of the Nationalist government. It provided that

the principle of complete national tariff autonomy shall apply subject, however, to the condition that each of the High Contracting Parties shall enjoy in the territories of the other with respect to the above specified and any related matters treatment in no way discriminatory as compared with the treatment accorded to any other country.[20]

This stipulation meant that the United States would not restore to China complete tariff autonomy unless and until such was done by other foreign powers. Before concluding the treaty, Secretary Kellogg had already assured President Coolidge that "if China guarantees us equal treatment under a treaty I do not think we can suffer."[21] That was why the American government strove to limit the revision of treaties to tariffs. Limited as the treaty was, it was, nevertheless, the Nationalists' first treaty, and it was the Americans who had broken the ice. Kellogg informed the Chinese minister in Washington that, in the opinion of the State Department, the signing of the tariff treaty constituted recognition of the Nationalist government.[22] He also candidly stated the reason for signing the treaty. He told a representative from the Japanese government that he felt one of the greatest dangers confronting the powers in China at this time was "Communist activities inspired from Russia" and that he believed the powers should cooperate to strengthen the efforts of the Nationalist govenment to create a stable administration in China. The best way to achieve this was "by going as far as each country could go, considering its own interests, towards solving these questions of the treaties."[23]

The American capitalists found in Chiang Kai-shek another Yuan Shikai or Cao Kun and sought, as they had with Yuan and Cao, to strengthen him as an instrument for the suppression of revolution in China.

As in 1913, great changes took place in the world shortly after America's recognition of the Nationalist regime. Japan decided to conquer China, and the United States lost the diplomatic dominance it had gained between 1927 and 1931 and had to retreat before Japan's advance, losing almost all of its interests in China.

About two years after the outbreak of the Great Depression, on September 18, 1931, Japan, without any provocation, invaded Northeast China (Manchuria). Although the warlord Zhang Xueliang had a mammoth army of three hundred thousand soldiers stationed in the Northeast's three provinces, to the great surprise of the whole country and the world, Chiang Kai-shek's Nanjing government adopted and persisted in a policy of nonresistance. Chiang repeatedly ordered Zhang not to resist: "Absolutely no resistance is allowed," one note commanded; "if the Japanese demand your troops to disarm," said another note, "then lay down your weapons; if they wish to occupy our barracks, let them in."[24] Chiang's stated "reason" for this policy was to prevent the affair from expanding, but in fact it did just the opposite. The policy, which could find no analogy in China's past, led the Nanjing government, in less than four months, to offer to Japan 1,300,000 square kilometers of territory, thirty million people, and countless natural resources.

Along with the policy of nonresistance, the Nanjing government relied on the League of Nations and the signatories to the Kellogg-Briand Antiwar Treaty and the Nine-Power Treaty for justice. It argued that by resorting to pacific means, China would be in a better position to appeal to the League for assistance. But, though after several months no relief came from the League or from any other powers, Nanjing still persisted in its policy of nonresistance. In dealing with the Japanese aggressors, the Nationalist Party decided to "make concessions," "endure humiliation," and "resign itself to adversity." [25] Yet, it continued to regard the Communists as implacable foes "who endanger the very existence of the nation and must therefore be ruthlessly stamped out." [26] This attitude revealed that the real reason for the Nationalist government's pursuance of a nonresistance policy was to preserve its military strength for "stamping out" the Communists, who were now conducting an armed struggle in the countryside.

The League of Nations and the United States followed a policy similar to that of the Nanjing government, namely, nonresistance to Japan and hostility to the Communists. After the outbreak of the affair on September 18, 1931, China at once appealed to both the League and the United States for support. The League first advised Japan to withdraw its troops by October 13, and then by November 16. But Japan went blithely ahead on its predetermined course of conquest. In the face of Japan's defiance, the League made no move to restrain it, not even daring to utter a moral censure.

The American government was at first unwilling to take any action except to express the hope that both Japan and China would refrain from "further application of force." [27] Such a hope showed only that the American government deliberately declined to distinguish between the aggressor and the victim, between right and wrong in the case. At the same time, U.S. Secretary of State Henry Stimson frequently urged the League not to be too severe against Japan. Not until October 8, when the Japanese bombed Jinzhou, did Stimson indicate that the United States might join the League powers in invoking the Kellogg Pact. But this invocation did little more than remind both China and Japan of their obligations under the pact and express the hope that "the two nations would refrain from measures which might lead to war." [28] For Stimson, Japan had not yet unleashed a war! Sanctions or any direct pressure upon Japan were, of course, out of the question. President Herbert Hoover was reported to have told his cabinet, "We will not go along on war, or any of the sanctions either economic or military, for these are the roads to war." [29]

After the Japanese army had brought all three of the provincial capitals of Northeast China under its control and turned its attention southwest toward Jinzhou, Foreign Minister Shidehara, on November 24, 1931, assured Secretary Stimson that there would be no movement of Japanese troops in the direction of Jinzhou. On the 25th, the League Council released the draft of another resolution, one in the composition of which the United States had played a considerable part. During the discussion of the draft, the Chinese representative had demanded the immediate evacuation of Japan from the occupied areas. But the American representative turned him down. As a result, the draft only invited the Japanese troops to withdraw "as soon as possible"; [30] there was no mention of a date for the withdrawal and no demand for an immediate cessation of hostilities. Yet Stimson, relying on Shidehara's promise that Jinzhou would not be attacked, urged the Chinese government to take conciliatory steps and accept the proposal of the League Council.

On January 3, 1932, the Japanese army attacked and captured Jinzhou. Four days later, on January 7, Stimson announced his Doctrine of Nonrecognition. He notified the Chinese and Japanese governments that

with the recent military operations about Chinchow [Jinzhou], the last remaining administrative authority of the Government of the Chinese Republic in South Manchuria, as it existed prior to September 18th, 1931, has been destroyed, . . . in view of the present situation and of its own rights and obligations therein, the American government deems it to be its duty to notify both the Imperial Japanese Government and the Government of the Chinese Republic that it cannot admit the legality of any situation de facto nor does it intend to recognize any treaty or agreement entered into between those Governments, or agent thereof, which may impair the treaty rights of the United States or its citizens in China. [31]

Nonrecognition did nothing to deter Japan, however, nor did it have any significance on future events. But Stimson's note to the Chinese and Japanese, and the measures already adopted by the American government, were illustrative of the true essence of America's policy. They showed that the American government quickly supported the Japanese occupation of Northeast China, and that

America's real concern was to safeguard its own interests, not China's territorial integrity. On the same day that Stimson issued the Doctrine of Nonrecognition, he called in the Japanese ambassador and told him that he, Stimson, was going to explain to the press

(1) that we had no quarrel with any of Japan's rights in Manchuria, (2) that we had no desire to intrude into the terms of any settlement which might be made in the future between China and Japan except (a) such settlement should not impair our own rights in China and (b) there should not be any violation of the Kellogg Pact.[32]

The doctrine also showed that the United States attached special importance to Jinzhou. America's reaction to Japanese military operations there indicated that America actually regarded the Jinzhou area as a line of demarcation. America's policy, in essence, was that it would acquiesce in Japan's occupation of Northeast China but would not approve of its continuous expansion to the southwest of Jinzhou, which would impair American interests inside the Great Wall. The Japanese conquest of the Northeast was less detrimental than advantageous to the Western powers. In the early years of the twentieth century, Theodore Roosevelt had contemplated a Japanese counterweight against Russia in the northeastern Asian mainland. Now, in the 1930s, Japan was playing an even more important role in opposing the Soviet Union, a fact that impressed itself on the American envoys in China and Japan. Nelson Johnson, American minister in China, saw the occupation of Jinzhou as the last in a series of acts aimed at the Soviet Union. "More and more," he stated to a friend, "am I convinced that Japan's moves in Manchuria are to be interpreted in the light of Japan's position vis-à-vis Russia."[33] Joseph Grew, American ambassador to Japan, felt there was much to be said in favor of the occupation of China's Northeast by the Japanese. Properly administered, Manchukuo, the puppet state set up by Japan in March 1932, would serve as a buffer to stop the spread of Bolshevism eastward.[34]

The League's Commission of Inquiry held some views similar to those of Johnson and Grew. In December 1931, the League Council had adopted a resolution creating a neutral commission—to be headed by the Englishman Victor Lytton, and with an American, Frank McCoy, as an informal member—to study the Manchurian issue on the spot. In February 1933, the League Assembly finally adopted the report prepared by the Commission. The only result was

Japan's withdrawal from the League. But some parts of the report still merit attention. The report considered "the dissemination of communism from the U.S.S.R." as of fundamental importance in bringing about the Japanese invasion of Northeast China. The official summary of the report states:

The possibility of a danger from across the north Manchurian border became a matter of concern to Japan. The likelihood of an alliance between the communist doctrines in the north and the anti-Japanese propaganda of the Kuomintang in the south made the desire increasingly felt to impose between the two a Manchuria which would be free from both. Japanese misgivings have been still further increased in the last few years by the predominant influence acquired by the U.S.S.R in Outer Mongolia, and the growth of communism in China.[35]

The Japanese aggression, in short, had as one of its purposes the elimination of the Red danger. The Commission recommended that international control of Northeast China would provide the solution of the problem.

The report was released on October 2, 1932, by which time Japan had already created its puppet state. The Commission knew that its recommendations were fanciful, and the League had made no attempt to institute them following adoption of the report. These attitudes and acts revealed that the United States and the powers who controlled the League preferred to let Japan go its own way, and did so in part so that it could use the Northeast as a base from which to battle the "danger from across the north Manchurian border."

But, contrary to the wishes of the Western powers, the Japanese militarists did not direct their spearhead to the north, but rather pressed on southward. In January of 1932 they launched an attack on Shanghai, the center of Western imperialist rule in China. In February 1933 they swallowed up Jehol and later forced on the Nanjing government a truce that compelled the withdrawal of all Chinese troops from east Chahar and east Hebei. The Japanese thus paved the way for encroachments on north China whenever they wished.

Chiang Kai-shek, in the face of Japan's steady forward movement, followed a traitorous policy called "pacification of internal disorder before resistance to foreign aggression." It was a policy requiring China to yield to whatever the Japanese demanded so that Chiang could concentrate his own efforts on the suppression of the Communists, the anti-Japanese mass movement, and opposition factions inside the Kuomintang. From June 1932 to October 1934, Chiang assembled a million troops in order to encircle and suppress the revolutionary base area of the Communist Party in central China. At the same time, the Nanjing government asked the Western powers for assistance in its "construction and unification."

The League of Nations responded to this request by giving China technical assistance. In May 1933 the U.S.-based Reconstruction Finance Corporation granted a $50 million wheat and cotton credit to the Chinese government. Early in 1934 the American Curtiss-Wright Corporation set up at Hangzhou an airplane assembly plant. In 1932–1933, the Aeronautics Trade Division of the U.S. Department of Commerce cooperated with American aircraft firms in the selection of a number of American aviation officers, who assisted in establishing training schools for Chinese pilots at Hangzhou and Guangzhou. Sales of American aircraft and accessories to China, including military planes, rose from $157,515 in 1932 to $1,762,247 in 1933.[36] Chiang Kai-shek used these airplanes and pilots to reinforce his military campaigns against the Red Army. Although the Nationalist government repeatedly professed that the funds derived from the wheat and cotton credit were spent on peaceful production, they were actually used to purchase munitions and warplanes. Chiang was not strengthening China's national defense against Japan; rather, he was carrying out his policy of "pacification of internal disorder"—in which, through foreign aid, the Western powers were in fact cooperating.

Nevertheless, the Japanese militarists, could still not tolerate the Western powers' intervention. By 1934, they regarded not only the Northeast but also the whole of China as their exclusive colony. On April 17, 1934, Eiji Amau, a spokesman for the Japanese Foreign Office, proclaimed in a press conference that, owing to the special position Japan had with China, its attitudes respecting China might not agree in every point with those of foreign nations; but it must be realized that Japan was called upon to carry out its mission and to fulfill its special responsibilities in East Asia. It must often act alone and must oppose any attempt by China to use other countries to resist. Japan would also oppose any joint operations undertaken by foreign powers, even if only in the form of technical or financial assistance.[37] Japan undisguisedly denied the Western powers their open door policy in China.

Neither the League of Nations nor the American government made any effort to oppose this doctrine. In response to the Amau statement, the American government delivered to Japan on April 29 an aide-mémoire saying that "in the opinion of the American people and the American Government, no nation can, without the assent of the nations concerned, rightfully endeavor to make conclusive its will in situations where there are involved the rights, obligations, and the legitimate interests of other sovereign states."[38] But actually the American government accepted the Amau doctrine as conclusive, deferring to it at once and bearing it in mind whenever the State Department deliberated on its China policy. The Roosevelt administration, coming to power in 1933, had decided that it must avoid friction with Japan. Secretary of State Cordell Hull was more willing than his predecessor to explore every possibility of reconciling conflicting American-Japanese aims in order to reach a more friendly accord. Now, shortly after the issuance of the Amau statement, the State Department decided that the American government should render no further financial aid to China. From 1934 until late 1938, the United States gave Japan free rein in its forward push into China.

Chiang Kai-shek also continued to placate the Japanese. But the Chinese people could never allow such a humiliating policy to go on. Chiang's policy of nonresistance to Japanese aggression and his anti-Communist civil war not only enraged the people but also spurred the centrifugal forces inside the Kuomintang. The Communist Party, assessing the situation, concluded that the national contradiction between China and Japan, and not the contradictions among the classes at home, had become the greatest and most overriding of problems. The Party thus worked out a political line for National Anti-Japanese United Front, which called for the formation of as extensive a front as possible, comprising all those who were willing to resist Japan.

Zhang Xueliang and Yang Hucheng, commanders of the armies deployed against the Communists in northern Shaanxi, accepted the Communist Party's policy for a united front. On December 12, 1936, the two generals detained Chiang, who had come in person to Xi'an, capital of Shaanxi Province, to press them for more enthusiasm in the fight against the Communists. As soon as they had Chiang arrested, Zhang and Yang cabled the Communist Party to send a delegation to Xi'an so that measures could be jointly worked out in the interests of national salvation. The Communist Party insisted that if the matter were not handled properly, a large-scale civil war could break out and jeopardize the cause of national liberation. Because of these considerations, the Communist Party urged a peaceful settlement on the basis of united resistance to Japan. Finally, after Chiang agreed to rescind his policy of Communist annihilation and to unite with the Red Army to resist Japan, the two generals released him. The peaceful settlement of the Xi'an Incident ended that civil war, which had raged for the ten years following Chiang's 1927 betrayal of the first united front between the Kuomintang and the Communist Party. The Communist Party's proposal of a National Anti-Japanese United Front won support nationwide.

Six months after the Xi'an Incident, the Japanese militarists launched an all-out assault upon China, starting the offensive in north China on July 7, 1937, and in Shanghai on August 13. The whole of China was united in resistance, for the first time in one hundred years. Though the Nationalist government was obliged to wage a war of resistance, it still did not abandon its policy of compromising with Japan in the hope that further concessions might prevent the expansion of hostilities. On July 12, four days after the outbreak of the armed conflict, the Chinese government asked the Americans and British whether they would help mediate the crisis. Secretary of State Hull refused.

The United States continued its policy of ingratiating itself with Japan. It regarded the retention of Japan's goodwill as necessary for the maintenance of American interests in the Far East. Some business interests even urged that Japanese control in eastern Asia, enforcing a new measure of law and stability, would increase America's trade with China and therefore be to the interests of the United States.[39] On July 12, the State Department told both the Japanese ambassador and the counselor of the Chinese embassy that "an armed conflict between Japan and China would be a great blow to the cause of peace and world progress."[40] It lumped together Japan's unjust war of aggression and China's just war against aggression without bothering about Japan's guilt. Because Japan abhorred any meddling in China by third nations, Secretary Hull lost no time in telling the Japanese ambassador that he would not enter into the Sino-Japanese dispute by acting as a mediator.[41] He also rejected four different British proposals for a joint Anglo-American attempt at settlement of the conflict. He did not even mention Japan's assault on China in his long statement, issued on July 16, declaring American policy.

In accordance with the League of Nation's resolution of October 6, 1937, the signatories of the Nine-Power Treaty and interested states held a conference in Brussels in order to find a solution. On November 3, nineteen countries sat down to seek an agreement. The declared purposes of the conference were "to provide a forum for constructive discussion . . . and to endeavor to bring the parties together through peaceful negotiation."[42] But Japan refused a twice-repeated invitation to attend the conference, on the grounds that the action which Japan had taken did not come within the scope of the Nine-Power Treaty. In view of this situation, the delegates declared that they would reconsider what their common attitude should be. Secretary Hull then cabled the American delegate that "questions of methods of pressure against Japan are outside the scope of the present conference."[43] He resolutely opposed the Chinese delegate's request for economic sanctions against Japan. Nothing was left for the conference to do but declare, on November 24, that discussions would be suspended indefinitely.

One of the major reasons for U.S. opposition to economic sanctions was that American businessmen were making fortunes by supplying Japan with war materiel. As T. A. Bisson pointed out in 1940,

During the past three years, taking the first eleven months in each case, the ratio of war materials to total American exports to Japan was 58 percent in 1937, 67 percent in 1938, and 70 percent in 1939. Of the war materials supplied to Japan during these years by the United States, approximately 97 percent was accounted for by petroleum and petroleum products, iron and steel scrap. . . . Since 1937 the American market has thus been the single most important adjunct of Japan's war machine, enabling the destructive military operations in China to be continued on an increasingly extensive scale.[44]

On the other hand, the American government, before late 1938, rejected all of China's requests for economic aid. Cordell Hull wrote in his memoirs that he did not want America to become "a kind of silent partner in Japan's aggressions"[45] and thought that he was conducting a policy of noninvolvement with respect to the Sino-Japanese war. But in fact, by lending Japan both political and economic support, the United States not only became involved but also acted as a partner. Small wonder the Japanese took "every little opportunity to show their appreciation" at the friendly attitude the United States had consistently maintained toward them.[46]

But the Japanese did not always appreciate the United States. On December 12 1937, Japanese planes bombed and sank the American gunboat *Panay*, along with three merchant vessels, near Nanjing.

After the "friendly settlement" of this affair, the Japanese militarists intensified their atrocities against American nationals' lives, property, and establishments, and introduced various measures to lessen American rights and interests in China. On October 6, 1938, the American ambassador delivered to the Japanese government a detailed summary of Japan's continuing violations of the open door principle in China, combined with an implication of retaliatory action. The Japanese reply, while denying such violations, tacitly indicated that the principles of the open door policy were no longer applicable to the "new order" which Japan was constructing in East Asia. On December 5, Japanese Foreign Minister Arita told Ambassador Grew that since a reconciliation of the principle of an open door with the actualities was impossible, he proposed to call a spade a spade. He therefore declined to confirm the assurances given by his predecessors that American interests and rights in China would be respected and that the open door would stay open;[47] instead, Japan shut the door completely.

America strove to conciliate the Japanese militarists, but it could never reconcile its yielding to Japanese aggression with the preservation of American interests. The very purpose of Japanese conquest and the gist of the "new order" was the elimination of Western interests from East Asia. The harder America tried to appease Japan, the more acute became the contradictions between the two countries. Now, finally, America began to consider assisting China.

7

From December 1938 to November 1940 the American government extended $170 million in credit to the Chinese government. Soon after the passage of the Lend-Lease Act in 1941, President Roosevelt included China among those nations entitled to such aid. He declared: "China likewise expressed the magnificent will of millions of plain people to resist the dismemberment of their nation. . . . China, through the Generalissimo, Chiang Kai-shek, asks our help. America has said that China shall have our help."[1]

But for seven long years, from 1931 to 1938, America had looked on coldly as Japan dismembered China. As far as ambassador Nelson Johnson was concerned during that time Sino-Japanese relations were of only academic interest for the United States.[2] As late as 1941, Secretary of State Hull held the way clear for a possible understanding with Tokyo. A mere two weeks before Pearl Harbor, he still sought to achieve a temporary modus vivendi with Japan, some arrangement by which, in setting aside the question of dividing China and Japan, a crisis could be avoided. America's concern was its own interests in East Asia and the Pacific. Johnson had predicted:

[if the Japanese] threaten America's right to sail her ships freely and without handicap in the Pacific, and the right of American citizens to trade freely . . . in Asia, or threaten policies which we have undertaken in good faith to fulfill in regard to the future of the Philippines, then American interests are vitally concerned, and we must be as ready to defend our interests as the other man is to attack them.[3]

Yet before the conclusion of the Nazi-Soviet Pact in August 1939, and even before the German blitz of May 1940, most American officials presumed that European powers in Asia would augment

American forces, and hoped that Tokyo might press northward toward Siberia rather than southward toward Indo-China. Not until the fall of France in May 1940 was the United States confronted with the fact that Japan had supplanted the European colonial powers in Asia and established there its long-heralded "new order." America's security and interests in all East Asia and the Pacific were now threatened. At this moment, the Americans also discovered that China formed one of the few remaining bulwarks against these new predators. They concluded that Chinese resistance to Japan, if maintained by American aid, would prove useful in the containment of Japan's southward advance.

Of the $170 million in loans, $145 million was provided in 1940. America viewed the use of Chinese resistance to deter Japan as a first line of defense. American aid to China was given largely to serve the United States' own national self-interest, which now included a firm resistance to Japanese aggression. In the period from late 1938 to late 1944, the American policy toward China aimed at bolstering the Nationalist government in order to stop Japan. Because America's war effort against the Axis powers also constituted a part of the world people's anti-Fascist struggle, its aid to China against Japan was thus in keeping with the aspirations of the Chinese people.

After the United States began to assist the Chinese government, drastic changes unfortunately took place within China. In the first year and a half of the War of Resistance, though the Nationalist government fought the invaders relatively actively, it still continued to repress the people's movements for national salvation. Divorced from the masses, the Kuomintang troops were routed and large expanses of land fell into enemy hands. In contrast, the Eighth Route and New Fourth armies, led by the Communist Party, persistently plagued the Japanese forces by penetrating deep into their rear, opening up vast anti-Japanese base areas where the armies dispersed themselves among the villages and towns to instruct the people as to the why's and how's of resistance. With the help of the army, people who refused to be slaves of a foreign nation quickly set up local organizations of national salvation and irregular armed forces. The mobilization of the common people behind the enemy lines eventually created a vast sea in which many of the aggressors drowned.

The Japanese realized this danger. At the end of 1938, after they had occupied Wuhan in central China, they halted their advance on the Kuomintang and instead gradually shifted their main forces to the rear in order to launch a mopping-up operation against the

Communist-led base areas. Meanwhile, the Japanese tried to tempt the Kuomintang into surrendering. In response to this inducement, in December of 1938 the pro-Japanese faction within the Kuomintang, headed by Wang Jingwei, openly defected to the enemy. Chiang Kai-shek's faction, though still remaining in the anti-Japanese camp, adopted a passive attitude toward the War of Resistance against Japan and an active one against the Communists: in January 1939, the Fifth Plenary Session of the Kuomintang Fifth Central Executive Committee, in accordance with Chiang's report, formally adopted a policy of Communist repression. Kuomintang troops then launched, in coordination with the Japanese aggressors, a military encirclement and economic blockade against the base areas. From 1939 to 1943, they mounted three successive anti-Communist assaults. In the meantime, the fighting against the Japanese had resolved into a stalemate. Chiang Kai-shek confessed in his diary on March 9, 1940: "The military situation as usual remains unchanged. Only the Communist Party, which is doing evil, is active, and that disgusts me."[4]

Such was the situation when America began to assist China. On October 18, 1940, Chiang Kai-shek, in a message which he personally asked Ambassador Johnson to communicate to the American government, stated:

I trust that for further bolstering the morale of the Chinese people, America will see fit to grant a single big loan rather than small piecemeal credits. As I have declared above, it is not the Japanese Army which we fear, because our army is able to deal with it, but the defiant Communist. American economic assistance plus the aid of the American Air Force can stabilize our unsteady economic and social conditions, thus making it impossible for the Communists to carry out their schemes.[5]

Chiang himself declared in unequivocal terms that his request for large-scale American economic and military aid was for the purpose of dealing with the Chinese Communists rather than with Japan. The next day, October 19, Chiang, through his chief of staff, ordered the Communist-led Eighth Route and New Fourth Armies to move within one month to the north of the Huanghe (Yellow) River. The Communist Party rejected this order but did agree to move the New Fourth Army's troops in south Anhui to the north of the Changjiang River. On November 30, Washington decided to grant a $100 million loan to China, giving Chiang the financial reassurance which he desired from the United States. Fearful that increasing American aid would embolden the Kuomintang, Communist representatives in Chongqing appealed to the American embassy for mediation. Ambassador Johnson, with Hull's approval, refused to interfere with what he called problems of an internal character.[6] In early January 1941, Kuomintang troops, acting on a predetermined plan, ambushed the New Fourth Army, which was on its way north, and destroyed the New Fourth Army's headquarters and most of its troops to the south of the Changjiang River. This South Anhui Incident shocked the country and the world.

As early as the summer of 1939, Kuomintang troops had made surprise attacks on units of the Eighth Route Army in north China. In October that year, Peng Xuepei, vice-minister of communications of the Nationalist government, declared to American diplomats that the Communist Party was "receiving material support from the Soviet Government and [was] subservient to Stalin."[7] In the first years of the War of Resistance, the Soviet Union was the only country that provided China with substantial assistance. From 1938 to 1940, it had extended $500 million in military credits to the Nationalist government and successively dispatched a thousand warplanes and over two thousand volunteer airmen to China, many of whom laid down their lives for the cause of China's national liberation. Johnson admitted that "the Soviet Union government had never, so far as I can learn, shown any tendency or desire to support the so-called communist force as against the Chinese National Government. On the contrary, Soviet support, which has been considerable and which has been of material assistance to China's war economy, has been given exclusively to the Kuomintang Government."[8]

But the Kuomintang officials did not hesitate to lie blatantly in order to win American support for operations against the Chinese Communists. Before they secured new suppliers of money and arms, however, they still did not dare an all-out attack against the Communists. By 1940, they felt assured of American patronage. When Washington announced the $100 million loan to China, a Kuomintang spokesman told an American embassy official that Chongqing no longer needed to appease the Communists.[9] One month later, they perpetrated the South Anhui Incident. On January 25, 1941, the Soviet ambassador visited Chiang Kai-shek and inquired about the causes of the incident. Chiang replied: "This is merely a matter of strengthening military discipline. It is nothing political, still less partisan. It is necessary to maintain in the armies stern discipline and unified command." When the Soviet ambassador asked about the future disposal of the New Fourth Army's troops north of the Chang-jiang River, Chiang answered in still stronger terms: "The New Fourth Army has been disbanded. There will no longer be a question of that Army." [10] Chiang and his adherents complacently thought that thenceforth they would enjoy a free hand in striking against the Communists.

American aid thus played a role in encouraging the Kuomintang to resist Japan passively and attack the Communists actively. After the United States entered the war in December 1941, the Kuomin-tang, now persuaded that the Americans would win the war for them, were ever more determined to use the American alliance as a means of accumulating reserves of money, weapons, and influence for a full-scale civil war, following the defeat of Japan. America's original inten-tion was to bolster the Nationalist regime in its fight with Japan and thereby to tie down a considerable portion of Japanese forces on the mainland and so abate the pressure on other areas. Chiang's policy ran counter to this objective since his preoccupation with the Commu-nists would bar the taking of any effective military action against the Japanese. John Magruder, head of the American Military Mission in China, predicted that the Nationalists would conclude a de facto truce with Japan, leaving the Americans to carry on the war. They in-tended, he claimed, to hoard American aid for postwar military ac-tion. To expect the Kuomintang to launch an offensive was only an alluring fiction. In Magruder's opinion, one reason for the failure to inaugurate an offensive on a large scale lay

in the age-long practice of Chinese commanding officers of regarding their soldiers as static assets, to be conserved for assistance in fight-ing against their fellow countrymen for economic and political supremacy. [11]

In view of the true state of affairs in China, some American officials and private observers, such as Evans Carlson and Edgar Snow, had advocated that aid be granted directly to armies in the field which were fighting Japan, regardless of their political affiliations.

However, though the American government knew that its alliance with Chiang would not yield the results it hoped for, it neither revised its policy of dealing exclusively with the Kuomintang nor took any effective measures to change the situation. It became clear that oppo-sition to Fascism was but one of America's war aims. Another aim was American "leadership" in the Far East. Nelson Johnson, as early as

February 1939, had urged that the United States, as heir to the British Empire in Asia, must assume the mantle of world leadership. "The frontiers of the United States are the world," he told President Roosevelt.[12] America sought not only to defeat Japan but also to supersede the old colonialist powers and forge its own new order in East Asia. In attaining this goal, the Americans reckoned that they would probably encounter three obstructions: the revolutionary and nationalist movements of the former colonial countries, enhanced by the anti-Fascist struggle; the Soviet Union's influence in the Far East, which certainly would grow in the postwar period; and the remaining forces of the old colonialist powers. President Roosevelt found that a China unified under Chiang's Kuomintang would be useful in coping with all these obstacles.

Walter LaFeber, in an article entitled "Roosevelt, Churchill, and Indochina," discusses Roosevelt's plans:

Roosevelt viewed Chiang's government as fundamental in America's Pacific plans. . . . The United States and China "would police Asia," Africa would be stabilized by Great Britain and Brazil, and Europe by the British and Russians. Presiding over these regional arrangements, the president told Eden in March 1943, would be the big four of the United States, Russia, Great Britain, and China who would make "the real decisions." Eden demurred, arguing that China would be unstable after the war. But FDR, in Eden's words, "maintained that China was at least a potential world Power and anarchy in China would be so grave a misfortune that Chiang Kai-shek must be given the fullest support." . . . He also felt that "China, in any serious conflict of policy with Russia, would undoubtedly line up on our side." Then Roosevelt revealed the other side of his plan. Since China would be so crucial the British should give up Hong Kong as a gesture of "good will."[13]

To "police Asia" meant that China would undertake to quell revolutionary movements in this region and to bring Asian nationalism into the orbit of America's new order. Roosevelt also felt it necessary to have China "as a buffer state between Russia and America."[14] In the attempt to liquidate the old colonial empires, he hoped that China would line up on the side of the United States.[15] It followed that, in order to perform such formidable tasks, China must be elevated to world power status. It seemed to Roosevelt that, within China, Chiang's regime was the stabilizing force that could transform that country into a great power. Chiang must therefore be given "the fullest support." But at the same time, this "great power" must remain under the thumb of its patron. Roosevelt's game was to "develop a China strong enough to police Asia but weak enough to be dependent upon the United States" [16]—nothing more than an amplification of what America had earlier expected of the Qing Dynasty and the northern warlords for maintaining order outside China. But Chiang and his regime were just as corrupt as the earlier rulers. The American patron hoped that American aid would induce Chiang to vigorously reform his government.

So even when assisting Chinese resistance to Japan, America's policy already looked forward to employing the Kuomintang as a means of extending its influence. With the approach of victory over Japan, moreover, the considerations about Chiang's postwar role prevailed over the demand that he reform his regime. America's policy leaned more and more toward outright support of the Nationalists.

In 1942, the American government, in order to strengthen China's war efforts, sent General Joseph Stilwell to China to serve as commander of the American troops in the China-Burma-India theater, administrator of lend-lease, and Chiang Kai-shek's chief of staff. As front commander, Stilwell gave top priority to the war against Japan. Naturally this required a reorganization of Chiang's corrupt military structure; Stilwell planned to select thirty divisions to be reformed, retrained, re-equipped, and put under new command. His proposals of military reform, however, came in direct conflict with Chiang's entire political and military system.

Chiang's dictatorship rested on a private army, a secret police, and a bureaucratic capitalism, in which the capital, land, and tools of production were concentrated in the hands of a handful of bureaucrats and financial magnates. Chiang Kai-shek embodied a mixture of warlord, stockbroker, and underworld boss. Before becoming a warlord in the 1920s, he had joined the underworld gangs in Shanghai and engaged in stock market speculation. His dictatorship relied above all on military power. The regional warlords, of course, also had their private armies, but Chiang ruled because he possessed more troops than the others. He also relied on the secret police to trample on the rights of the people and to ferret out opposition. And finally, he relied on bureaucrat-capitalists to control the economy. In wartime, under the pretext of concentrating economic power in order to better prosecute the war, these bureaucat-capitalists, drawing on their political and military power, cruelly plundered the people. Their banks issued unlimited amounts of paper money, raised prices of commodities, and by this inflation reduced the people's means of livelihood.

In dealing with both internal and external politics, Chiang followed the tactics he had learned as a warlord, stockbroker, and underworld boss. Toward the Chinese Communist Party, his attitude varied from soft to tough. But the soft tactic was only a temporary expedient; at the very same time that he used it he was preparing the next tough move. When toughness did not work, he could momentarily soften his moves. Though at the start of the War of Resistance he had ostentatiously turned to unity, he soon engaged first in veiled strife, then in open struggle. By 1941, he had changed his tactic from restricting and checking the Communist Party to attempting its liquidation. Chiang manipulated his own troop commanders, especially the regional militarists, by making vital funds and supplies dependent on their obedience. Toward Japan he pursued a policy of alternating fighting with cajoling in the hope of entering into an advantageous compromise, and the United States he alternatively coaxed and threatened in the hope of procuring aid with which to pursue the civil war.

Pearl Harbor and the American entry into the Pacific war set the stage for an unprecedented request for aid. On December 30, 1941, Chiang Kai-shek sent for Ambassador Gauss and appealed for a loan of $500 million. As Gauss reported to the Secretary of State, Chiang stated that

the initial Japanese successes and Japanese exploitation thereof for propaganda purposes have affected morale. [Chiang] specifically mentioned the recent radio appeal made to him by the Prime Minister of Thailand for Asiatic solidarity against westerners. China can help the common cause with fighting manpower but America and Britain must help China financially in order to prevent further deterioration of the economic foundation, confidence in Chinese currency, et cetera. Such help would go far to strengthen morale and silence the doubtful and critical elements. [17]

Chiang implied that without a huge loan his government could not surmount further economic deterioration and the rise of defeatism, and he might have to join with Japan in an "Asiatic solidarity." He thus accompanied his request with a threat, making it at the very time that the United States faced disaster in the Pacific. Half a year later, Chiang made three new demands of the United States: the dispatch to China of three American combat divisions; the immediate creation of a combat air force of five hundred planes; and five thousand tons of supplies by air transport monthly. Stilwell told Gauss that Chiang insisted upon the three demands, otherwise he would have "to make other arrangements"—which implied peace with Japan. [18] From then on, whenever Chiang felt the American delivery of aid to be unsatisfactory, he threatened that he would surrender to the Japanese.

The United States formally granted the $500 million loan in March of 1942. Although Chiang had told Gauss that the loan would be used partially in a domestic bond issue designed to curb inflation, in the end this design had the opposite result. Chiang's wife and relatives, as well as powerful officials, bankers, and landlords, monopolized the purchase of the bonds and, through a fixed exchange rate which was many times lower than the real rate, transferred the American money into their pockets.

Chiang's Kuomintang thus persisted in corruption and gangster politics, calling all attempts to purge it of these traits mere efforts to pull the rug from under its feet. Stilwell's demand for the reorganization of the Kuomintang army only aroused Chiang's suspicion that the American general wished to assert his power over major military and political issues. [19] In July 1942, barely four months after the general's arrival in China, Chiang instructed his foreign minister, Song Ziwen (T. V. Soong), who was then in Washington, to press American officials for the possible recall of Stilwell. Stilwell, on his part, knew Chiang feared that any reorganization of the army would undercut his own position. Yet, without reform Stilwell could not create a military force capable of driving back the Japanese. And the massive aid which Chiang demanded would be hoarded and eventually turned against the Communists and other domestic enemies. Therefore, both General Stilwell and Ambassador Gauss urged Washington to concede nothing to Chiang in the light of his threats. Rather, Gauss suggested:

A decision should be reached as to what can be supplied to and used in China—and it is important that we consider not what China wants but what China can use—and Chiang should then be told that he will be given that support. If he persists in demanding more and threatens peace with Japan, I am of the opinion that he should be told, with authority of Washington, that when he undertakes to negotiate a peace with Japan the American military and diplomatic missions will immediately be withdrawn without further ado from

China, and that finishes all American assistance to China—now and for the future.[20]

Indeed, the United States may yet have put forth a counterthreat and used its aid as a lever to compel Chinese reform and thus spur the war effort against Japan. But the fact was, Stilwell's views were not only in conflict with Chiang's vital interests but also at variance with the perspectives of some in the American government. While Stilwell laid stress on preparations for defeating Japan, many American government representatives attached more importance to Chiang's usefulness in postwar Asia. Responding to Chiang's demands and threats, Roosevelt sent his administrative assistant, Lauchlin Currie, to China on a special mission from July 21 to August 7, 1942. In his report to the President, Currie said:

We have a unique opportunity to exert a profound influence on the development of China and hence Asia. It appears to me to be profoundly in our national interest to give full support to the Generalissimo, both military and diplomatic. I do not think we need to lay down any conditions nor tie any strings to this support. . . . We can rely on him so far as it lies within his power to go in the direction of our wishes in prosecuting a vigorous war policy and in creating a modern democratic and powerful state.[21]

Currie recommended almost unconditional support for Chiang. His first concern was Roosevelt's "moral leadership in Asia and therefore America's ability to exert its influence for acceptable and just settlements in postwar Asia."[22] America's influence should be paramount. His recommendations, which were in striking contrast with those of Stilwell and Gauss, were more congenial with Roosevelt's inclination. Roosevelt decided to meet Chiang's demands with no strings attached, and on October 22 he replied by promising to raise monthly air transport supplies to five thousand tons and to send five hundred combat aircraft to China. Only determined opposition from Marshall and Stimson dissuaded Roosevelt from removing Stilwell.

Lauchlin Currie and some other officials in Washington, whenever they talked about America's policy of assisting China, did not forget to express their "wishes" that Chiang's Kuomintang should take measures to achieve unity and reform. But what they meant by "unity" was a unity under Chiang Kai-shek. Chiang's government not only repressed the Chinese Communist Party but also clamped down on the activities of the minor political parties and the people's organizations. After 1941, the Kuomintang went so far as to follow a policy of "saving the nation through curvilinear course," that is, to order some of its armies to defect to the Japanese, join the puppet army, and then attack the Communist-led forces in coordination with the Japanese mopping-up operations. By August 1943, five hundred thousand troops had defected, constituting 62 percent of the puppet army. "Unity under Chiang" could only mean unity under Chiang's corrupt dictatorship.

The Americans wished not only that Chiang would reform but also that he would long remain in power as the instrument of American influence. If vigorous demands for reform threatened the loss of Chiang's goodwill, they must be abandoned. In a letter to George Marshall on March 8, 1943, President Roosevelt stated:

All of us must remember that the Generalissimo came up the hard way to become the undisputed leader of four hundred million people.

Besides that, the Generalissimo finds it necessary to maintain his position of supremacy. . . . He is the Chief Executive as well as the Commander-in-Chief, and one cannot speak sternly to a man like that or exact commitments from him the way we might do from the Sultan of Morocco. [23]

But Chiang Kai-shek was not really an "undisputed leader." On the contrary, he was an autocrat without popular support. That Roosevelt considered his leadership "undisputed" was actually because no other "strong man" was available. American policymakers had contemplated supporting a substitute leader but could find none, basically because the liberal bourgeois of this semicolonial and semifeudal China were so few, weak, and vacillating. They could not constitute a force sufficient to challenge either the comprador-feudal classes represented by the Kuomintang or the proletariat and peasantry behind the Communist Party vanguard. America's plan of acting through Chiang's China as the guardian of postwar Asia was counter-revolutionary in nature because it precluded the enlistment of China's revolutionary or progressive force. Therefore, only Chiang and his faction remained the "undisputed" choice.

For the sake of maintaining Chiang's position and treating China as a great power, the United States and Great Britain, in February 1943, each signed a new and separate treaty with China. These treaties relinquished all unilateral privileges written into earlier treaties, including consular jurisdiction, the right to maintain troops or gunboats in China, the control of international settlements, and special rights in inland trade or navigation. This recognition of China's complete independence was the fruit of the Chinese people's struggle and sacrifice in the past hundred years, particularly in the bloody War of Resistance. As the American leaders saw it, it was a step toward raising China's status, although what America and Britain surrendered, was largely privileges that had been lost to Japan and could hardly be re-established after Japan's defeat. In December 1943, the U.S. Congress repealed the old exclusion law and adopted a new law admitting some 105 Chinese a year. In November 1943, Roosevelt formally made China one of the Big Four by nominally including her in the Four-Power Declaration issued from Moscow by the foreign ministers of the United States, Great Britain, and the Soviet Union. The declaration stated that the four powers would continue their cooperation in preserving peace and security after the war.

The most striking demonstration of the international acceptance of China as a great power came when Roosevelt invited Chiang Kai-shek to attend a three-power summit conference at Cairo. Thus on November 23–26, 1943, Chiang sat with President Roosevelt and Prime Minister Churchill and discussed plans by which China would be propped up until it could replace Japan as the leading nation in eastern Asia. On the eve of the Cairo conference, to arrange for Chiang's presence, Roosevelt dispatched a personal emissary, Patrick Hurley, to China. In a cable to the President, Hurley wrote:

In evaluating the Generalissimo's conversation it is advisable to consider with some skepticism the Chinese capacity, or readiness, to contribute materially to offensive warfare. It is advisable likewise to give consideration to the relative importance placed by the Chinese Central Government upon conserving its strength for maintenance of its postwar internal supremacy as against the more immediate objective of defeating Japan.[24]

Hurley even advised Roosevelt to endorse Chiang's basic policy of conserving his strength for civil war and leaving his American ally to fight the Japanese. Chiang Kai-shek, elated that he had become the acknowledged leader of one of the Big Four and aware that he was indispensable to America's longterm plans, became less inclined than ever to reform.

The ineptness, perversities, and weaknesses of the Kuomintang culminated in the catastrophe of 1944. China suddenly faced economic collapse: corruption, unprecedented in scale and openness, permeated and demoralized the governmental and military structure; workers, peasants, soldiers, and the intellectual and salaried classes struggled to stave off starvation. Resentment and unrest grew. At this juncture the Japanese launched a furious offensive "to open up the mainland traffic arteries" for the rescue of their isolated forces in Southeast Asia. They started the attack in Henan on April 18, 1944. The demoralized Kuomintang armies fled pell-mell before the enemy with the Japanese making inroads through Hunan and Guangxi up to Guizhou. The Kuomintang government in Chongqing was too scared even to prepare for flight. In barely eight months, from April to December, the Kuomintang lost six hundred thousand troops, four provincial capitals, 145 large cities, seven air bases, and thirty-six aerodromes. This disaster manifested in the most stark manner the consequence of the Kuomintang's incompetent and reactionary policies.

In contrast, by early 1945 the Communists had emerged as a tremendous force, powerful, dynamic, and heralding a new order. Nineteen base areas were now under Communist Party leadership, as opposed to only one base area at the outbreak of the war in 1937 (the Shaanxi-Gansu-Ningxia border region). The population of the base area had grown from 1.5 million to over 100 million, and the people's armed forces from 40,000 to 1.2 million. The army and people led by the Communist Party had put 520,000 Japanese troops out of action.

Under these circumstances, General Stilwell and his political advisors not only continued to press for fundamental political and military reforms in China, but also repeatedly urged Washington, as they had since 1943, to enlist Communist-led forces for a joint attack on the Japanese. They also urged that American observers should visit the Communist headquarters in Yan'an, Shaanxi Province. On February 9, 1944, President Roosevelt sent a message to Chiang Kai-shek, requesting that Chiang permit an American team to go to Communist-led areas in order to increase the flow of intelligence about the Japanese in north China and Manchuria. Chiang refused. Vice-President Henry Wallace, during his visit to China in June 1944, pressed Chiang directly on the matter of a mission to Yan'an. This time Chiang reluctantly agreed.

On July 22, 1944, the first contingent of the U.S. Army Observer Group arrived at Yan'an. The leaders of the Communist Party and the Eighth Route Army personally held talks with the group, expressing their willingness to cooperate with the Allied powers in fighting Japan and in building a postwar peace. But the primary task of the mission, according to the instructions to group leader David Barrett, was to discover the conditions of the Japanese in north China and of the Communist-led forces.[25] The sending of the mission never meant that the United States itself had committed itself to aiding or supporting the Chinese Communists.

To save the serious situation which resulted from Japanese advances in central China, Stilwell took another, even bolder step. He asked General George Marshall to allow him the command of all Chinese forces, including those under Communist leadership. On July 6, 1944, President Roosevelt, acting in accordance with Marshall's recommendation, sent a message to Chiang Kai-shek, stating:

> The critical situation which now exists in my opinion calls for the delegation to one individual of the power to coordinate all the Allied military resources in China, including the Communist forces.
>   . . . I am promoting Stilwell to the rank of full general and I recommend for your most urgent consideration that you call him from Burma and place him directly under you in command of all Chinese and American forces.[26]

One of the chief characteristics of warlordism was that the warlord's army was private and the warlord's only means of survival. To deprive Chiang of the command of his army was tantamount to dethroning him. Moreover, enlistment of the Communist-led forces under Stilwell's command meant that these forces would share American aid. This was more than Chiang could tolerate. There were, he thought, only three ways to cope with this pressure: "refusal, acceptance, and temporization. Finally I decided to temporize."[27] He asked Roosevelt to send a special emissary to China to discuss details of the arrangement for Stilwell's command. Roosevelt selected Patrick Hurley for the mission.

With the military situation in China further deteriorating, Roosevelt, at the request of Stilwell and Marshall, sent on September 19, 1944, a pressing message to Chiang. The message blamed Chiang for courting "catastrophic consequences," urged that he at once place Stilwell "in unrestricted command" of all forces, and implied that otherwise American aid would be terminated.[28] Chiang was infuriated, and noted in his diary: "This is the most galling humiliation I have ever been subjected to in my life."[29] He knew that he could not stall any longer. On September 24, he asked Hurley to forward an aide-mémoire to Roosevelt, stating that while he agreed on the choice of an American officer as field commander, he could never accept Stilwell in this position, because

General Stilwell had no intention of cooperating with me, but believed that he was in fact being appointed to command me. . . . If, ignoring reason and experience, I were to appoint General Stilwell as Field Commander, I would knowingly court inevitable disaster.[30]

Hurley supported Chiang, advised the recall of Stilwell, and told Roosevelt that Chiang was the leader best qualified to execute a policy of Sino-American cooperation. Roosevelt must choose between an expendable general and the "indispensable" leader of China. "My opinion," Hurley wrote Roosevelt, "is that if you sustain Stilwell in this controversy you will lose Chiang Kai-shek and possibly you will lose China with him."[31] On October 18, Roosevelt decided to recall Stilwell, appointing his successor Albert Wedemeyer—who, however, would not be expected to command any Chinese forces.

Roosevelt accepted Hurley's advice because the President himself also regarded Chiang as "indispensable." About a year before, he had asked his son, "Who is there in China who could take Chiang's place? There's just no other leader. With all their shortcomings, we've got to depend on the Chiangs."[32] Vice-President Wallace held the same viewpoint. He reported to Roosevelt that "at this time, there seems to be no alternative to support of Chiang. There is no Chinese leader or group now apparent of sufficient strength to take over the government."[33] The campaign for the appointment of Stilwell as commander of all forces fighting in China was merely a measure to meet the critical situation. In the face of Chiang's rebuff, it was only natural that Roosevelt had to fall back to considerations of America's long-term goals. As long as the American leaders strove to control China and hence to extend their influence to the rest of East Asia, they could not abandon such a suitable agent as Chiang Kai-shek. They knew that "there is widespread popular dislike for the Kuomintang government,"[34] but they still felt that there was no other alternative. This was the tragedy of America's China policy.

Hurley, with great ardor, carried out the doomed policy. Shortly after the recall of Stilwell, Hurley was appointed to succeed Gauss as American ambassador to China. On December 24, 1944, he declared that, as he understood it, the policy of the United States in China was to "sustain Chiang Kai-shek as President of the Republic and Generalissimo of the Armies." It was also America's aim, he added, to achieve the unification of all Chinese military and political groups under Chiang's rule.[35] Such a policy, of course, inevitably meant aiding Chiang against the Chinese Communist Party and the Chinese people at large, and thus entangled the United States in China's internal affairs. That entanglement would last a long time and leave vestiges still present today.

8

Aid to Chiang Against the Chinese Communist Party

In a speech of August 13, 1945, entitled "The Situation and Our Policy After the Victory in the War of Resistance Against Japan," Mao Zedong, Chairman of the Chinese Communist Party, emphasized that Chiang Kai-shek's policy was well established and inflexible, and it was the policy of civil war. "Our policy," added Mao, "is to give him tit for tat and to fight for every inch of the land." According to Mao, Chiang Kai-shek relied entirely on an imperialistic United States as his mainstay, using U.S. aid to preserve his dictatorship and to wage the civil war. Mao also felt that the United States planned to support Chiang and his civil war in order to turn China into an American dependency, and that "this policy, too, was set long ago."[1]

The policies of both Chiang and the United States were indeed well established. Chiang's policy during the latter phase of the war against Japan had been to wait for victory, conserve his forces, and prepare for civil war. President Roosevelt had envisaged a strong Nationalist China capable of serving as a "stabilizing force" in the Far East. In the last stage of the war with Japan, Roosevelt still insisted that if China could not become a great power, it should at least control its region and help further American interests by checking Communism. The American ruling circles knew that the Chinese Communists were a threat. But, according to Hurley's estimate, once the war with Japan was over, Chiang's "well-equipped divisions will have a walkover in their fight with the Communists."[2] Both Hurley and Wedemeyer believed that the Chinese Communists "could be put down by comparatively small assistance to Chiang's central government."[3]

For America to have assisted Chiang in waging a large civil war before the end of the Japanese war would have jeopardized the war effort against Japan. Hurley, because he considered the Chinese Communists militarily too weak to gain power, fancied that he could place the Communists under Chiang's control simply by promoting negotiations between the two parties. Moreover, many of the politically conscious people in the Kuomintang area opposed civil war and demanded democracy. In September 1944, the Communist representatives in the People's Political Council (a purely advisory body to the government) proposed the convocation of a conference of all anti-Japanese political parties and nonparty personalities. The aim of that conference would be to organize the Nationalist government into a coalition government on a democratic basis. Members of various parties and many eminent figures in Chongqing, including Madame Sun Yat-sen, held meetings, and all made the same demand. These appeals soon developed into a nationwide movement for democracy, which Chiang Kai-shek could not ignore. During the months before and after Japan's surrender, then, Chiang and the American government were forced to adopt dual tactics: to prepare actively for civil war and to negotiate intermittently with the Communist Party.

In order to stem the tide of popular demand for democracy, Patrick Hurley, after consulting with the Kuomintang officials who attended the negotiation, flew to Yan'an on November 7, 1944, and presented Chairman Mao with a five-point proposal as the basis for a settlement between the two parties. Mao revised all five points. His first point called on the two parties to work together for the unification of all military forces in China. The second point really included two demands: that the present Nationalist government be reorganized into a coalition government, embracing representatives of all anti-Japanese parties and nonpartisan political bodies, and that the National Military Council be reorganized into a United National Military Council that would include representatives of all anti-Japanese armies. Mao's third point called for the coalition government to pursue policies designed to promote progress and democracy; his fourth requested that all anti-Japanese forces not only observe and carry out the orders of the coalition government and its united military council, but also be reorganized, with all supplies acquired from foreign powers being equitably distributed. Mao's fifth and final point demanded that the coalition government recognize all anti-Japanese parties.[4] Hurley told Mao that these amendments were "entirely fair,"[5] and both signed it in duplicate. Hurley then took the copy back to Chongqing on November 10 to present to Chiang for his approval.

These terms were minimum demands and fell far short of satisfying the basic desires of the people. Yet even such a proposal encountered Chiang's flat refusal. Hurley had agreed to these terms because he thought that they might induce the Communists to subscribe to a "military unification" under the Nationalist government.[6] But Chiang would not tolerate the Kuomintang to enter a coalition government. As one "who always tries to wrest every ounce of power and every ounce of gain from the people,"[7] Chiang would never accommodate himself to anyone who intended to "disrupt" his monopoly of political power.[8]

Chiang's government, through Hurley, countered on November 21, 1944, with a three-point proposal: first, the government would agree to incorporate, after reorganization, the Communist-led forces into the National Army and to recognize the Chinese Communist Party as a legal political party; second, the Communist Party would yield control of its troops to the government's National Military Council, in return for which the government would designate some high-ranking officer from among the Communist forces to membership in that council; and third, the government would pursue policies designed to promote democracy.[9]

For Chiang, of course, a coalition government was out of the question. His proposals were devised to absorb the Communist-led forces into the "National Army" at the price of granting the Communists some representation in the military council. The paramount issue in Chiang's mind was control of the Communist army. He made no attempt to conceal his desire to make the Communists submit unconditionally to the principle of unified military command. But given the nature of his military dictatorship, for the Communists to put their troops under Chiang's military council would mean extinction. His promise to promote democracy and his offer of representation on the council signified nothing. The Communist Party naturally rejected these proposals. They could not accept the unification of military command unless a coalition government was realized. From November 1944 on, in all subsequent negotiations, Chiang never changed his formula: "Surrender your army first, and then I shall give you 'democracy.'"[10]

It is evident that Chiang wished to use all negotiations for unity, negotiations pursued as he feverishly prepared for civil war, as a means eventually to quell the Chinese Communists. It is also evident that the United States supported him in this policy.

In the winter of 1944–1945, another problem arose that would make curbing the Communists more difficult: the Soviet Union's probable declaration of war on Japan. The United States had long expected the Soviets' eventual entry and welcomed their help in invading Japan. But it also feared that once Soviet troops entered the Asian war they would intervene in China. It apprehended that the Soviets would "back the Communists in the north and turn over to them the administration of the Chinese territory liberated by the Red Army. Then the situation will be progressively difficult for Chiang." [11] On the one hand, the Americans hoped that Soviet entry into the war would accelerate the defeat of Japan; on the other hand, they dreaded a resulting expansion of the Chinese Communists. The best way to forestall this effect, they thought, was to work out a settlement between the two parties as soon as possible. Soon after Hurley became ambassador to China on November 17, 1944, President Roosevelt personally sent him a note, stressing the need for "a working arrangement between the Generalissimo and the North China forces." [12]

This desire for a working arrangement proceeded not from the concern for a fair solution of the KMT-CCP dispute, but from an open desire for a stronger Chinese effort against Japan and a less openly expressed fear of an increase in Communist strength. This latter fear both helped determine the method used to tackle the problem and precluded any success at its solution. The American leaders found it inconceivable that they should assist the Communists and use such assistance as a lever with which to compel Chiang to compromise with Yan'an. Patrick Hurley, on the contrary, pressed the Communists to accept the Kuomintang terms, an act that contradicted the very five-point proposal he had signed. He announced that his mission was to sustain Chiang Kai-shek and that his every move was taken "with the consent, advice, and direction of the Generalissimo and members of his Cabinet." [13] He repeatedly informed the Communists that they would receive no American aid, military cooperation, or political support until they had reached a political compromise acceptable to Chiang. [14] Roosevelt, in accordance with Hurley's recommendation, ordered all American military officers to support the existing Chinese government, and not to aid any elements in China which Chiang did not specifically approve. [15] Actions were also taken to reinforce these words. American military aid to the Kuomintang grew rapidly after January 1945, despite the fact that little of it was being used against the Japanese. Hurley believed that such measures would scare the Communists into submission. But no submission resulted. Mao Zedong had answers to every threat and was confident that the day would come when the Americans would find aid to Chiang a mere waste. "The imperialists think that all people in the colonial countries can be scared," wrote Mao, "but they do not realize that in China there are people who are not afraid of that sort of stuff." [16]

Besides bolstering Chiang from within, Hurley also sought to enlist Soviet cooperation for the American policy and to ask the Soviets to pressure the Chinese Communists to come to terms with Chiang. When Hurley returned to China in April 1945 after a short trip to the United States, Roosevelt had him stop off first in Moscow. From there Hurley returned to Chongqing in high spirits, claiming that he had obtained the desired assurance that the Soviet Union would persuade the Chinese Communists to accept "reasonable Kuomintang proposals" and would not support "Chinese units except those which are incorporated into the unified Chinese army after it is formed." [17] In July 1945, Hurley still asserted that "without the support of the Soviets the Chinese Communist Party will eventually participate as a political party in the National Government." [18] Again Hurley placed his strategy on mistaken assumptions. The Chinese Communists rested their policy on their own strength, not on foreign aid. They had always stressed "regeneration through our own efforts": "Relying on the forces we ourselves organize," Mao said, "we can defeat all Chinese and foreign reactionaries." [19] The KMT-CCP negotiations, with Hurley as a "broker," had actually broken down in mid-February.

Hurley's activities achieved nothing beyond increasing Chiang's intrasigence. On March 1, 1945, Chiang made a radio speech in which he announced that he had decided to convoke his Kuomintang-dominated "National Assembly," the representatives of which had already been handpicked eight years before, the following November. Chiang's speech indicated that he not only flagrantly rejected the proposal for a coalition government, but promised to make no compromise whatsoever.

Though American and Kuomintang schemes failed to curb the Communists, they are nevertheless revealing. They show, for one thing, that Chiang and the United States might vary their tactics in certain circumstances but they displayed no sign of changing their basic policies. A few American foreign service officers did realize that the Chinese Communists were strong, dynamic, and would, with or without Soviet aid, eventually overcome the Nationalists. They had suggested in February 1945 that the American government should supply and cooperate with the Chinese Communists, win them over to America's side, and use that alliance to force Chiang to share power with them. But their superiors at the State Department and in the White House brushed aside their suggestions. Such a plan ran counter to the American government's basic fear of Communism and the desire of some to use Chiang as an instrument for keeping China in America's sphere of interest. In March the American government again reaffirmed its commitment to sustain and work with Chiang, and on April 2 Hurley very bluntly declared, "We do recognize the National Government of China and not any armed warlords or armed political parties in China." [20] This position could not but render large-scale civil war in China inevitable and thus doomed the American government, in Mao's words, to "fall irretrievably into the deep stinking cesspool of Chinese reaction." [21]

As soon as the War of Resistance against Japan came to a victorious end, Chiang began to deploy his forces for civil war. But such troop dispositions took time. Chiang thus again resorted to peace talks with the Communists. He cabled Chairman Mao three times, inviting him to Chongqing to "hold consultations over state affairs." After careful consideration, the Communist Party decided that Mao should go to Chongqing for negotiations with the Kuomintang authorities; this would expose the falseness of the Kuomintang claims that the Communist Party did not want peace or unity. On August 28, 1945, Hurley, after making a special trip to Yan'an, accompanied Mao on his flight to Chongqing. After protracted talks, the two parties reached an agreement on October 10 and Mao returned to Yan'an. The Kuomintang agreed to convene a political consultation conference, accord equality and legal status to all political parties, release all political prisoners, and abolish the repressive secret services. But it refused to establish a coalition government or to recognize the legal status of the Communist-led army and the governments in the liberated areas.

The negotiations that led to the agreement of October 10 lasted forty-three days. Chiang and Wedemeyer made use of this interim to reoccupy the key areas held by the Japanese in central and north China. Immediately upon Japan's surrender, on August 15, 1945, President Truman issued General Order Number One, designating Chiang as the only authority permitted to accept the surrender in China. On August 17, General Marshall advised General MacArthur to stipulate that the Japanese commanders in China be instructed to surrender only to Chiang's commanding officers. On August 11,

Chiang issued an "order" to Zhu De, commander-in-chief of the Communist-led Eighth Route Army, to stay, pending further order, where it was.

During the War of Resistance, while Chiang had abandoned vast territories to the Japanese, the Communist-led forces had recovered much lost land, especially in the countryside, with the result that the Japanese-occupied territories in north China formed only a bare skeleton. Now the Communists were to be excluded from sharing in the fruits of a victory for which they had so long struggled and with such heavy sacrifices. But, since Chiang's main forces were hidden in the western provinces without assistance from his allies, he could not prevent the Communists from regaining the Japanese-held areas. In July 1945, Chiang had already conferred with Wedemeyer for assistance in the seizure of strategic locations. While Mao was in Chongqing, American planes and ships transported Kuomintang troops and officials into the vital ports and cities of east and central China. From these points the Americans began a massive airlift of Kuomintang armies to North China and planned to ferry troops to Manchuria. These were the forces Chiang used in his campaign against the Communists. In addition, during September and October Wedemeyer landed fifty-three thousand American marines and secured for Chiang ports and airfields on the northern coasts, thus releasing Chiang's forces for penetration into the interior.

These crucial measures were adopted under the guise of carrying out the Japanese surrender. But the Japanese invaders, even after surrender, continued to hold for Chiang the principal cities and lines of communication in north China, thus suddenly becoming, not enemies, but allies of the Kuomintang. Meanwhile, the Nationalists incorporated as many as five hundred thousand Chinese soldiers—Japan's former puppet troops—into their own forces, dubbing them their "advance force." America, by putting Chiang in a position to subdue the Communists, had become his ally in a civil war. In such a vital port as Tianjin, the three allies—the U.S. Marines, the Japanese army, and the former puppet troops—fought side by side against the surrounding Eighth Route Army units. On August 10, 1945, the American Joint Chiefs of Staff ordered Wedemeyer to "assist in the rapid transport of Chinese Central Government forces to key areas in China." [22] By "key areas" the Joint Chiefs meant territory occupied or claimed by Yan'an. When Secretary of State James Byrnes wondered how the United States could justify ferrying additional armies to north and Northeast China, the War Department's John McCloy argued that such aid was vital if Chiang were to defeat the Communists and discourage Soviet intervention. [23] Barely a few days after the war with Japan had ended, Washington began discussion of continued military aid to Chiang. On September 5, Truman granted a six-month extension on lend-lease support for China, to be supplemented by a program granting China, as "surplus," large amounts of American materiel in China and the Pacific. On September 14, at Chiang's request, Truman agreed to expand Chiang's military power through completion of the wartime program for training and equipping thirty-nine divisions and 8 1/3 air groups. Chiang and his allies thus possessed a formidable battle force. No wonder Chiang complacently concluded that "deployment at the major strongpoints has been settled; the primary basis of unification has been laid." [24]

Before the ink of the KMT-CCP agreement of October 10 was dry, Chiang ordered attacks on the base areas that the Eighth Route Army had opened up during the war with Japan in north China. After only one month of fighting, however, the Eighth Route Army had wiped out more than a hundred thousand invading troops. Among the senior enemy officers captured were army and divisional commanders. The victory was a head-on blow for Chiang and his American supporters.

General Wedemeyer now recognized that the Chinese Communists were no inconsequential force. He concluded that if America wished the unification of China under Chiang, then "involvement in fratricidal warfare and possibly in a war with the Soviet Union must be accepted." He added, most ominously, that such an acceptance would require more American forces than were present in China. [25] After supporting the Nationalist forces' advance to the front in the civil war, America's leaders had to consider their next move carefully. The heads of the military establishments urged direct American military intervention on behalf of Chiang. But such a move would require the employment of substantial American forces for an indefinite period of time, a prospect unpalatable to an American public that was "particularly unanimous in opposing United States participation in the Chinese civil war." [26]

Should America, to please that public, end all support for Chiang? Should America leave north and Northeast China, and even the whole country, to Communist domination? Such an abandonment the American leaders could never accept. The United States had defeated Japan, its aggressive rival in the Far East; the other colonialist powers in this region, too, had been greatly weakened. Nationalist China had become ever more dependent on America, a position that furthered America's desire and ability to dominate the market for goods and investment in China. But more important than these economic gains was the fact that north and Northeast China would constitute a strategic base against the rising Soviet influence in the Far East. General Marshall told President Truman that if the United States abandoned its support of Chiang, the tragic consequences would be a divided China and a probable Soviet reassumption of power in Manchuria, the combined effect of which would result "in the defeat or loss of the major purpose of our war in the Pacific." [27] Those occupying the highest positions in the American government were never willing to see American hegemony fall before an expanding Communism.

The American government by late November of 1945 had decided to keep the U.S. Marines in north China, to furnish military supplies to Chiang, to assist Chiang in taking over Manchuria, and to prepare for shipping more Nationalist troops into north China. Simultaneously, President Truman designated Marshall as a special envoy to help broaden the Nationalist government base to include some Communist Party representatives.

Thus the Marshall mission came into being. Shortly before its birth, in talking about China, President Truman had warned that "unless we took a strong stand in China, Russia would take the place of Japan in the Far East." [28] To take a strong stand against Communism was the basic attitude of the American government in its support of Chiang's seizure of north and Northeast China. Marshall, after his appointment, reviewed the advice which Truman and Byrnes had given him: he was to induce the Communists and the Nationalists to make reasonable concessions to "desirable political unification," and if the Communists refused to make concessions, he was authorized to transport more Kuomintang troops into north China. If, on the other hand, Chiang refused to cooperate, it would still be necessary for the U.S. government "to continue to back the National Government of the Republic of China—through the Generalissimo within the terms of the announced policy of the U.S. government." [29] Truman twice concurred on this view of the matter, which echoed Hurley's unconditional support for Chiang. The so-called "political unification" was also a reiteration of Chiang's persistent demand for "unifying the military command" and for "unifying government administration." Truman, in a statement issued at the time of Marshall's departure for China, said even more explicitly that "the existence of autonomous armies such as that of the Communist army is inconsistent with, and

actually makes impossible, political unity in China. With the insti-
tution of broadly representative government, autonomous armies
should be eliminated as such and all armed forces in China integrated
effectively into the Chinese National Army." [30] Marshall was to help
realize the elimination of the Communist-led army by giving the
Communists some representation in the Nationalist government.

Hurley, who had resigned on November 28, 1945, had failed in
this task. Marshall would also fail. The difference was that he enjoyed
the prestige of a wartime chief of staff and a national hero, whereas
Hurley did not. For the purpose of subduing the Chinese Communists, the American government employed every possible means short
of direct military intervention. Yet, Marshall's fate, despite his prestige, would be no better than Hurley's.

Marshall arrived at Chongqing on December 23, 1945. Chiang
had just suffered a defeat in an offensive in the liberated areas and was
forced to use peace talks to disguise his preparation for a new push.
He therefore agreed that the Political Consultation Conference provided for in the two parties' agreement of October 10, 1945, should
meet in January of 1946. In early January, a preliminary meeting of
representatives of the two parties was held, with Marshall attending
as a mediator. On January 10, this Committee of Three reached
agreements on the cessation of hostilities, to go into effect on January
13 and to be implemented by an Executive Headquarters in Beijing.

The Political Consultation Conference, which met January 10–13,
included not only representatives from the Nationalist and Communist parties but also from two other parties. Some nonpartisan personalities also participated. The conference passed, among other resolutions, one that required that the Nationalist government, pending
the convocation of the National Assembly, reorganize itself into a
provisional coalition government that would be called the State Council. There would be forty State Councillors, whom the President of
the national government would choose from among both the Kuomintang and non-Kuomintang parties. The State Council would be the
supreme organ of the government and would be in charge of national
affairs. If a resolution before the State Council should involve changes
in administrative policy, it must be passed by a two-thirds vote of the
State Councillors present. This resolution thus overruled the Kuomintang demand that the integration of the Communist-led forces into
a national army should precede the establishment of a coalition government. Only a little more than a month later, in early March, the

Second Plenary Session of the Kuomintang Sixth Central Executive Committee actually negated the decisions of the Political Consultation Conference and retained for the Nationalist Party supreme power over the government. The Kuomintang also persisted later in demanding revision of important decisions that the conference had reached.

Chiang then turned to war. Once again he hoped to win by battle what he had failed to win by negotiations. He started his campaign in Manchuria. His strategy was first to mount large-scale battles in Manchuria while limiting battles inside the Great Wall to a smaller scale, and then, after victories in Manchuria, to spread the war to all other regions.

For fourteen years, the Nationalist government, through its policy of nonresistance, had forfeited Manchuria to the Japanese. Only the Communist Party, by organizing the people in a United Anti-Japanese Army, had kept up the struggle for these provinces. Before the victory over Japan and in the three months that followed, there was not a single Nationalist soldier, or any armed hostilities, in Manchuria.

But Chiang and his American supporters made peaceful Manchuria their principal target. Its seizure by force was a crucial part of their anti-Communist strategy. At Marshall's first meeting with Truman and Byrnes on December 11, 1945, Byrnes took the position that Nationalist forces must be assisted in taking over Manchuria.[31] Wedemeyer had already, between November 7 and November 13, landed several Nationalist armies at Qinghuangdao, whence they had thrust into Manchuria and attacked the Communist-led forces. One of Marshall's assignments was to complete the movement of Nationalist troops into Manchuria even if the Communists made concessions in the peace talks. By May 1946, the Americans had ferried six Nationalist armies into that region.

Chiang persisted in his Manchurian campaign under the guise of restoring its Chinese sovereignty. Although the Cessation of Hostilities Order of January 10 did not "prejudice military movement of forces of the National Army into or within Manchuria which are for the purpose of restoring Chinese sovereignty,"[32] as Marshall had to admit, "there was no indication, or implication, in the meetings of the Committee of Three that Manchuria was not included within the scope of the Cessation of Hostilities Order."[33] He and Zhou Enlai, Communist Party representative on the Committee of Three, time and again proposed that the Cessation of Hostilities Order was applicable to Manchuria and that truce teams should be sent there. But Chiang rejected these proposals. According to Marshall,

One reason for his refusal to approve such action lay in his desire to avoid recognition of the Communist Party forces in Manchuria. Also it appeared to me that his commanders in that region desired to avoid any interference by Executive Headquarters teams directed toward halting the sporadic fighting then in progress.[34]

Indeed, his commanders in Manchuria referred to the Communist-led forces as "bandits" and sought expressly to destroy them. Chiang's insistence on excluding Manchuria from the cease-fire order proved that his chief aim in these provinces was not to restore Chinese sovereignty but to eliminate the Communist-led forces. In mid-April the Soviet authorities announced that their forces occupying Manchuria in the war with Japan would complete their withdrawal by April 30. With neither Japanese nor Soviet troops any longer occupying Manchuria, the issue of Chinese sovereignty was no longer in question. Nevertheless, immediately after this announcement the Kuomintang forces intensified their assaults on all important Communist-held strongpoints.

Marshall, the mediator, knew of these assaults. He therefore proposed a series of programs which would, allegedly, avert war. But ironically he continued to allow transport of Kuomintang armies and supplies into Manchuria. He also, during a month's stay in the United States in mid-March, arranged an enormous loan for the Kuomintang government. On Marshall's return to China, Zhou Enlai told him that there was a growing awareness that "the American government is carrying on a double policy toward China." The continued movement of Kuomintang troops and the granting of a loan, Zhou had warned in an earlier conversation with Marshall, would only encourage the Kuomintang to wage war.[35]

Under this encouragement, the Nationalists staged an offensive aimed at the capture of Changchun, a large city in the heart of Manchuria. On May 23, the Nationalist forces, after the Communists had withdrawn, entered that city; on June 6, Chiang issued a cease-fire order for Manchuria, with a stipulated limit of only fifteen days. At the same time, Chiang put forth a set of exceedingly harsh terms to the Communists as a condition for the cease-fire's prolongation. He demanded that the Communists evacuate vast liberated areas and major railway lines, not only in Manchuria but also in north China. He did not expect the Communists to accept these terms but instead planned to use their refusal as a pretext for spreading the war to the whole of central and north China. Although the cease-fire had been extended to June 30, four days before that day, on June 26, Chiang unleashed his forces in a siege against the liberated area near Hankou. It was the starting point of a full-fledged counterrevolutionary war, a civil war unprecedented in Chinese history in scope or intensity.

The capture of Changchun, in fact, marked the beginning of the end of Chiang's power in Manchuria. The incursion had placed the Nationalists in a dangerous military position, with overextended lines and an increasing dispersion of troops. The Communist-led forces, on the other hand, grew larger and more concentrated in the hinterland. The annihilation two years later of the Nationalist forces in Manchuria heralded the collapse of the Kuomintang regime in north China, a collapse that then spread to the whole country.

But in 1946, the Nationalists took the capture of Changchun as a sign that, with their American-equipped divisions, the defeat of the Communists would be easy. One Kuomintang general even boasted that Chiang's armies could crush the Communists in three months. Decisive in encouraging the arrogance of Chiang and his generals was the fact that they enjoyed America's unquestioning support.

In the months when the war spread south of the Great Wall, more than a hundred thousand American troops, mostly marines, guarded, on Chiang's behalf, China's major ports. The U.S. Army had not only furnished the Chinese navy with vessels, but had also sent two fleets to China, one stationed at Qinghuangdao and the other at Qingdao. Moreover, the Sino-American Cooperative Organization, set up by the U.S. Navy and Chiang's secret police in 1942, expanded their repressive activities, to the outrage of thousands of Chinese revolutionaries and liberals. That Americans participated in that repression also did America's reputation little good either. By mid-1946, the American government had established both army and naval advisory groups in China, assisting Chiang in military training and the planning of operations. From the end of the war with Japan to October 1946, the value of lend-lease aid to the Nationalists amounted to more than $800 million, of which more than $600 million was for ammunition. A special surplus property agreement of August 30, 1946, transferred an additional $855 million worth of American equipment to the Nationalists. On the eve of the eruption of the all-out civil war, the U.S. Congress initiated more measures in support of the Nationalist military power.

Marshall acknowledged that American military aid to Chiang caused difficulty and embarrassment to his efforts at mediation. He also admitted it encouraged the Nationalists "to push forward with a campaign of determination against the Communists."[36] But embarrassment could not shake America's will to suppress the Communists and to increase its influence in China. John Lucas, head of the U.S. Army Advisory Group, assured Washington that if it gave him the authority and wherewithal, he and his group could build a first-rate army and defeat the Communists. His counterpart in the Naval Advisory Group exhibited the same confidence that American technology and know-how could determine the outcome of an Asian civil war.[37] But the outcome proved contrary to their expectations.

Still, American aid was not without some rewards. As early as October 1945, a report of the Joint Chiefs of Staff had recommended that, in return for the military assistance rendered, Chiang should grant America special economic concessions and should put the Chinese economy under overall American guidance. The State Department's John Carter Vincent, who opposed this proposal, could not but point out that, by its statement of concessions desired, the United States seemed to be moving toward a relationship in which China would become a semicolonial protectorate with its army under American direction.[38] The State Department shelved, momentarily, the report of the Chiefs of Staff, but the demands contained in it were finally realized and expanded in the Treaty of Friendship, Commerce, and Navigation, which the United States and China signed at Nanjing on November 4, 1946.[39] The treaty, together with other agreements signed in this period, stipulated that American nationals had the right to reside, travel, and carry on commercial and manufacturing enterprises throughout China. Americans could also acquire and hold lands and property for these purposes, and no prohibitions or restrictions of any kind should be imposed on the importation, sale, distribution, or use of American goods, or on the exportation of any articles destined for the United States. The treaty gave American vessels the liberty to enter all ports, places, and waters, to navigate China's territorial seas and air spaces, and to erect naval bases in China's ports. Although all these rights were supposed to be reciprocal, this was a mutuality between a poor and weak dependency and a rich and powerful overlord.

Chiang was not unwilling to sell out his country, if it gave him the power to crush the Communists. John Leighton Stuart, U.S. ambassador to China since July 1946, reported to the State Department that Chiang

has recognized with cold realism the inherent weakness of his country both human and material and has disciplined himself to paying the price for American monetary aid in having it accompanied by a large measure of American control.[40]

America's dream of a hegemony in China had come true—but too late. The United States' treaties with Chiang not only exposed that mix of fear of Communism and desire for the profits of trade that underlay American imperialism, but they also revealed Chiang's treasonous proclivities, proclivities that incurred the wrath of the people. They called the Treaty of Commerce "the new Twenty-One Demands" and made November 4 a day of national humiliation. An anti-American movement, evoked by the rape of a University of Beijing student by two American soldiers, broke out a month after the conclusion of the treaty. "American forces out of China!" the masses shouted.

On the military front, the Communist-led army, whose strategy was to annihilate the enemy's effective strength rather than seize or hold territory, defeated in battle more than 710,000 enemy troops. After eight months of fighting, they had smashed the Kuomintang offensive.

America's ambivalent strategy of combining peaceful mediation with military aid to Chiang failed. Chiang's offensive, encouraged by American aid, had ended in defeat. General Marshall, whose mediation had become a farce once Chiang had launched the nationwide civil war in the summer of 1946, returned to Washington in January of 1947. But American aid to Chiang did not end. On the contrary, the deteriortion of Chiang's situation made the Americans even more anxious to save him. They had to safeguard their dominant position in China. Acting Secretary of State Dean Acheson had telegraphed Marshall in November 1946:

From our point of view there is no power vacuum in the Far East. It seems to have been filled by Russia and ourselves. Therefore, the principal problem is adjustment of our relations there with the Russians without prejudice to our legitimate interests. It has been our hope . . . that a peaceful settlement of China's internal problems would be conducive to such an adjustment. . . . Furthermore, although we welcome the cooperation and assistance of third powers in seeking a solution, we do not intend to relinquish our leadership.[41]

Acheson had confessed that the United States and the Soviet Union filled the power vacuum in the Far East. By 1947 the hope of absorbing the Chinese Communists into the Kuomintang regime had evaporated. But the United States still refused to relinquish its "leadership"; there seemed no way to extricate itself from the "vacuum" it had largely filled. Chiang Kai-shek also knew that the United States, deeply fearful of Communism and fully aware of China's strategic position, could not abandon him.

On the eve of his departure from China, Marshall saw that, in the Kuomintang-controlled areas, a vicious inflation had combined with the low salaries of public officials to cause a widespread corruption damaging to the reputation of the government. Marshall, considering economic collapse within a few months a definite possibility, concluded that Chiang could not defeat the Communists. He even added that the United States was not going to be dragged through the mud by the Kuomintang reactionaries.[42] Nevertheless, after returning to Washington and becoming secretary of state, he still continued to provide military materiel to the Kuomintang government. He likewise had to help drag the United States through the mud of Chinese reaction. True, Marshall was dissatisfied with Chiang, but that was because he perceived that Chiang was incompetent in curbing the Communists. He complained to Gu Weijun (Wellington Koo), Chinese ambassador in Washington, that Chiang had assured him in 1946 that by July of that year Jiangsu Province would be clear of Communists, but even toward February 1947 the work had not yet been done.[43]

The principal question to be resolved was not whether to aid the corrupt Kuomintang regime, but how to make that aid effective.[44] As the first step to solve this problem, Marshall, in July 1947, dispatched Wedemeyer to China to survey the situation. After a month-long tour, Wedemeyer reported that because the situation had grown worse since Marshall's departure, the United States should not only furnish Chiang with large-scale economic and military aid but also provide closer supervision. The role of American military advisors should be enlarged; they should carry out reconnaissance and directly oversee training and supply. He also recommended that the United States should seek to establish a United Nations trusteeship over Manchuria, turn it into a buffer zone, and thus release the Nationalist troops to fight the Communists elsewhere.[45]

Marshall found the proposed trusteeship unfeasible. The problem of direct American military involvement had already arisen in late 1945. Now, two years later, such action was even less possible. The civil war was already a war in which Chiang provided manpower and the United States supplied money and arms. Authorized U.S. aid from V-J Day to early 1948, exclusive of surplus property sales, totaled $1,432 million. The Chinese people had long resented collusions between reactionary rulers and foreign imperialists. Ambassador Stuart admitted that "anti-American feeling was deepening, due chiefly to the belief that we were delaying the Communist Party's overthrow of a rotten government."[46] Marshall felt sure that any direct American involvement would further touch off strong Chinese sensibilities regarding infringement of China's sovereignty. He was also of the opinion that, if the United States assumed a direct responsibility for the conduct of civil war in China, it would have to commit sizable forces and resources over an indefinite period and thus would face grave consequences by making China into an arena of international conflict.[47]

There was thus no effective means of supporting the Kuomintang except by increasing economic and military aid. Meanwhile, since the spring of 1947, Chiang had made desperate pleas for a $1 billion loan and more military supplies, pledging in return to make effective use of these aids. In February 1948 the State Department sent Congress a proposal for a one-year appropriation of $570 million for assistance to Chiang, and on April 3, $463 million was authorized in a China Aid Act. At that time, the Americans still expected that, although the Nationalists could not wholly overcome the Communists, they might hold out for a certain length of time.

But the rapidity of the Chinese Revolution overtook Chiang and his American ally. Chiang, after his major offensive on the liberated areas had been defeated, turned instead to the strategy of "attacking key sectors"—that is, northern Shaanxi in the northwest and Shandong in the east. But the Communist-led army and people in these sectors hurled the Nationalists back. Then, in the summer of 1947, the Communist-led People's Liberation Army took the offensive, carrying the war into the Kuomintang areas. One year later, starting on September 12, 1948, they fought three decisive campaigns in Manchuria, the Beijing-Tianjin area, and northern Anhui and northern Jiangsu. Within only four months and nineteen days they annihilated

1.54 million enemy troops, the crack forces on which the Kuomintang had relied for ruling the country.

As the People's Liberation Army approached the gate of the Kuomintang capital, Nanjing, Chiang appealed to the United States for
rescue, using his ambassador, his foreign minister, a personal letter
to Truman, and finally his wife. He sent Madame Chiang to Washington to take charge of the matter, for, it was said, "he believed a
woman could do more than a man." [48] He urged the American government to increase the supply of military materiel, to issue a statement of support, to dispatch a high-ranking military officer to direct
the war, and to allow American officers to take command of the
Kuomintang armed forces in the field. The American government
responded to these requests with firm rejection and to Madame
Chiang's visit coolly. The rapidly deteriorating situation was much
more disappointing to the Americans than could possibly have been
contemplated; the government, especially General Marshall, felt that
not even American military aid could salvage the Nationalist cause.

But this was not the only reason for rejection of Chiang's proposal.
The Americans also intended to resort to peace talks again. As Ambassador Stuart, who as late as October 1948 still pleaded for an
American takeover of Nationalist military planning, emphasized to a
Kuomintang high official, "The all but universal desire of the people
was for peace." [49] But the renewal of peace talks now required a
precondition. Chiang, by plunging the country into civil war, had
lost so much popular sympathy that he had to retire to the backstage:
already in January 1948, Marshall had asked Zhang Junmai (Carson
Chang), chief of a small Chinese political party, what alternative there
was to Chiang's regime. [50] On December 13, Stuart told Chiang's
trusted follower Zhang Qun, as reported in a telegram, that

it was certainly [the] impression of most of [the] Americans that I
had talked to that [the] great mass of Chinese people felt that [the]
Generalissimo, as principal obstacle to termination of [the] hostilities, should step down from his position of authority; that what
[the] people of China thought and wanted was [the] dominant factor
in our policy formulation. [51]

America's refusal of Chiang's request for rescue added a tremendous
weight to the pressure exerted on Chiang by Stuart. At the same
time, Li Zongren, Chiang's vice-president and head of the Guangxi
clique within the Kuomintang, incited his followers to appeal for

peace so that he, Li, could supersede Chiang. Encouraged by Stuart's attitude, the clique became more and more vociferous in pressing Chiang to give way to Li.

On January 1, 1949, Chiang issued a New Year's statement suing for peace. The Communist Party responded to the appeal by advancing eight conditions, including punishment of a list of war criminals—with Chiang as the number one criminal—reorganization of all reactionary troops, and abrogation of treasonable treaties. On January 21, Chiang retired (not resigned), and Li entered the stage as acting president. Li continued to push for peace so as to win a breathing spell in which he could rally his forces and prevent the Liberation Army from advancing into the areas south of the Changjiang River. Stuart placed great hopes on Li. He regarded Li as the man

who can be counted on to make every effort to develop that part of China under his control into [a] constructive positive force in [the] Far East. He wants to maintain China's friendly cooperative policy with the West. We believe his present intentions are to resist unreasonable Communist demand in Peiping, hold out for reasonable settlement and if necessary resume armed resistance eventually. His usefulness to [the] cause of world peace as [an] effective instrument for containment of communism in [the] Far East should not be underestimated.[52]

However, Li, the new instrument, was no more effective than Chiang, the old one. Li never realized his intentions. When he sent a delegation to Beijing for negotiations with the Communist Party, the latter insisted that the Liberation Army must cross the Changjiang River and reorganize all reactionary troops. Li, seeing his hopes shattered, refused to approve the terms which his delegation had accepted.

On April 21, 1949, the Liberation Army crossed Changjiang River. Two days later, they freed Nanjing, an event which proclaimed the downfall of the Kuomintang regime. Then, like a whirlwind that sweeps away the autumn leaves, they pursued the reactionary armed forces and, within one year, liberated the entire country except for Taiwan Province. On October 1, 1949, Mao Zedong declared the establishment of the People's Republic of China. The Kuomintang's dual tactics of war and peace, tactics largely supported by the United States, proved to be bankrupt.

A hundred years after the conclusion of the Treaty of Wangxia, the United States had become the dominant power in Asia. It was, with its atomic bombs and limitless resources, a power with no parallel in history or rival in the world. This awesome strength, which had come quickly and almost unwittingly, engendered in its leadership an illusion of omnipotence and a tendency to forget that, after a hundred years of struggle, the Chinese people had also matured and that they were competent to overthrow feudal and imperialist rule in China. In the past the United States, in league with other major powers, had helped repress the Taiping insurrection, the Boxer movement, and the revolution of 1911. Why should it not, now that its power was unrivaled, help repress the Chinese Communists, who were a part, the American ruling circles mistakenly thought, of a worldwide conspiracy? They did not know, or want to know, of the strength, maturity, tenacity, and popularity of the Chinese Communists, that they were completely independent of the Soviet Union. They therefore aided Chiang, whose weaknesses they also overlooked. Their failures of understanding, their obsessive anti-Communism, and their feeling of superior dominance in Asia led them to cling to anachronistic views. And the continuance of these profoundly mistaken views of the Chinese Communists entailed a great injury to the relations between the United States and China, an injury that lasted more than two decades.

9

On June 30, 1949, three months before the establishment of the People's Republic of China, Chairman Mao Zedong announced his policy of "leaning to one side." China, he asserted, will ally itself "with the Soviet Union, with the People's Democracies and with the proletariat and the broad masses of the people in all other countries, and form an international united front." [1] It was a policy derived from the conclusion Dr. Sun Yat-sen had drawn from his forty years' experience conducting China's revolution. The Chinese people, he had said, should not look for help from the imperialist countries but should instead "unite with those nations of the world which treat us as equals." "Leaning to one side" meant that the New China belonged to the anti-imperialist front, from which front alone genuine help could be expected.

The policy did not, however, indicate that the New China would refuse to establish diplomatic relations with the capitalist countries. On the contrary, on April 30, 1949, Chairman Mao declared that the People's Government was willing to establish diplomatic relations with all foreign countries on the basis of equality, mutual benefit, and a mutual respect for territorial integrity and sovereignty. Recognition, Mao added, also depended on severance of relations with the remnant Kuomintang forces. [2] These requests were only natural, especially in dealing with the United States, a nation which had long helped the Kuomintang oppose the Chinese Communist Party. The People's Government time and again expressed its willingness, as part of its foreign policy, to establish diplomatic relations with all nations. In fact, according to Leighton Stuart's report of May 13, 1949, Huang Hua, the chief of the People's Government's Office of Alien Affairs in Nanjing, had told Stuart that China was interested in the United States' recognizing the New China on terms of equality and mutual benefit. In reply Stuart said that "such terms together with accepted international practice with respect to treaties would be [the] only proper basis."[3] China, in short, must first accept the "treaties."

Stuart's reply was ominous. It foreboded little good, for it suggested that the United States would not agree to China's demand for a relationship of equality and respect. When the Kuomintang government fled its capital, Ambassador Stuart decided to remain in Nanjing, a decision approved by the State Department. He hoped thereby to promote America's interests in the newly liberated areas, as well as to evaluate the attitude of the new government toward the United States and to exert some influence on the new regime. Stuart, having lived in China for fifty years, had witnessed how the imperialist powers, by undermining the Revolutions of 1911 and 1926–1927, had kept intact those privileges which the unequal treaties guaranteed. Perhaps he still imagined that his efforts might bring about some modification of the new government's anti-imperialist position.

According to Stuart's report, in early June, 1949, his secretary had asked Huang Hua if it would be possible for Stuart to travel to Beijing and visit Yanjing University, of which he had once been president. On June 28, Huang replied that Mao Zedong and Zhou Enlai would welcome such a visit. Stuart considered that this trip would give him a chance to talk with Mao and Zhou, to influence their policies, and to strengthen the "more liberal anti-Soviet element in [the] CCP."[4] But later Secretary of State Dean Acheson informed Stuart that he and President Truman, fearing unfavorable publicity, objected to the proposed trip. On August 2, Stuart left Nanjing for the United States. On January 14, 1950, the American government ordered all its official personnel to leave China. During their stay in China, neither Stuart nor any of the United States' diplomatic personnel treated the People's Government as the de facto authority, in spite of the fact that they had some contact with its officials.

Stuart's behavior revealed two conflicting aspects of the American government's policy toward the New China: it both refused to recognize the People's Government and yet wished to influence its policies. The United States still harbored vain hopes of converting the People's Government into a regime open, as previous Chinese governments had been, to imperialistic interests. In the spring of 1949, Dean Acheson said that the United States could not foretell its future course toward China "until some of the dust and smoke of the disaster clears away."[5] Acheson adopted a wait-and-see attitude, not with a view to reaching in due course an accommodation with the new China, but because he was stalling for time, time he thought he could work with along two lines: first, to separate the People's Republic of China from the Soviet Union, and second, to exact concessions using recognition as a lever.

The United States and its governing classes did not understand that the triumph of the Chinese Revolution in 1949 was the victory of a hundred-year-long struggle against feudal regimes and foreign imperialism. It was not, as many Americans believed, part of a Moscow-directed plan of "Communist world conquest." Some American high officials who had personal experience in China knew that the Chinese Communists' organization, leadership, and morale were far superior to those of the Kuomintang and, most important of all, that they enjoyed far wider and deeper popular support. Even those who were staunchly behind Chiang did not deny the crusading zeal of the Communist supporters. General Wedemeyer, a devoted friend of the Kuomintang cause, recognized the self-developed strength of the Communists. General Marshall, too, held that, although the United States strongly believed that the Soviet Union had surreptitiously aided Chinese Communist advances in Manchuria, three years of careful surveillance had yielded no concrete evidence of such aid.[6] Nevertheless, most American politicians still depicted the Chinese People's Government as a puppet of an international conspiracy centered in Moscow. In the China White Paper of 1949, Dean Acheson asserted that China's Communist leaders were subservient to the Soviet Union. In this case, he said, "the foreign domination has been masked behind the façade of a vast crusading movement which apparently has seemed to many Chinese to be wholly indigenous and national."[7] Acheson's statement was flawed by a fatal inconsistency: how could a foreign-dominated puppet, with a mere handful of men, erect a façade involving a vast, indigenous, and nationalist crusading movement of millions? Blinded by the errors of this appraisal, or perhaps merely using this appraisal as a pretext, Acheson refused to accord China its deserved equality. Before the United States would condescend to grant it recognition, China would have to abandon its anti-imperialist position, accept the treaties signed by the Kuomintang government, and agree to terms most advantageous for the United States.

Because Dean Acheson also knew that the Chinese Revolution had an indigenous nature, he hoped that he could detach the People's Republic of China from the Soviet Union. In late September of 1949, the Kuomintang delegation to the United Nations called upon its assembly to condemn the Soviets for aiding the Chinese Communists and to insist that no member state accord diplomatic relations with China's new government. But the United States had this resolution referred to the Assembly's interim committee, where no action was taken, and instead introduced a vague proposal that merely reiterated the traditional principles of upholding China's independence and of refraining from establishing any sphere of influence within Chinese territory. The proposal did not mention the question of recognition. The United States put forth this substitute resolution not because it disapproved of the Kuomintang action, but because it wanted to drive a wedge between Moscow and Beijing. Though the American delegate to the United Nations, Philip Jessup, did not, in supporting this resolution, attack the Chinese Communists, he nevertheless did assert that the Soviet Union had set up special regimes in Manchuria and Mongolia and that it sought to dominate North China.

On January 5, 1950, President Truman released to the press a statement on Taiwan. After reaffirming the Allies' commitment, as stated in the Cairo and Potsdam declarations, to return Taiwan to China after agreeing to China's exercise of authority over the island, he also professed that "the United States Government will not pursue a course which will lead to involvement in the civil conflicts in China."[8] He thus recognized that the legal status of Taiwan had already been settled, that Taiwan belonged to China, and that the conflict between the Chinese People's Government and the Kuomintang remnants entrenched in Taiwan was a civil war, in which the United States would not interfere.

In a speech on January 12, Secretary Acheson went even further. The strategic line, he announced, that the United States was prepared to defend against Communism in the western Pacific, ran from the Aleutian Islands through Japan, down to the Ryukyus, and on to the Philippine Islands.[9] He pointedly excluded Taiwan and Korea from within this perimeter. One of Acheson's aims in making this definition was to sow dissension between Beijing and Moscow. In the same speech, he charged that the Soviet Union was "detaching the northern provinces of China from China." He also asserted that

we must not seize the unenviable position which the Russians have carved out for themselves. We must not undertake to deflect from the Russians to ourselves the righteous anger, and the wrath, and the hatred of the Chinese people which must develop.[10]

Acheson thus hoped to deflect China's resentment against foreign intervention away from the United States and toward the Soviet Union.

But in fact, it was actually Acheson and some of his colleagues who sought to detach territory from China. As early as January 1949, the State Department had agreed on the desirability of keeping Taiwan out of the hands of the People's Liberation Army. The only question that remained was how to achieve this goal without either angering the Chinese Communists and thus driving them closer to the Soviets or intervening so blatantly that it would offend the international community. They therefore, in 1949 and after, devised various schemes for a separate Taiwan: one would foster an independence movement in the island, and another would place the island under a United Nations trusteeship, thus replacing Chiang Kai-shek with some new tools. These schemes, together with the speech of January 12, were calculated both to "carefully conceal our wish to separate the island from mainland control"[11] and to divert the Chinese people's wrath toward Soviet expansion. As we shall see, after the outbreak of the Korean War, when the United States no longer needed to conceal its wishes and avoid blatant intervention, it did not hesitate to interpose its Seventh Fleet in the Taiwan Straits.

The China bloc in Congress demanded greater support for the Kuomintang and denounced all moves toward recognition of the People's Republic. Acheson not only encouraged "the democratic People's Republic of China" to reassert itself[12] but also strove to win the New China over to the imperialist side. If there was any divergence between the China bloc and Acheson, it was in tactics, not principle. Mao Zedong realized that the two factions were only arguing in their own camp "as to which kind of counter-revolutionary tactics is the more clever."[13] Senator Joseph McCarthy, in February of 1950, charged that the many Communists who had infiltrated the State Department were part of an international conspiracy, which had delivered China, on a silver platter, to Communist rule. This assertion was preposterous but not accidental: it was a manifestation of that rage which the American rulers, because of their embarrassment and shame, felt even more intensely when the Chinese people, who they believed could never liberate themselves from imperialism, did just that. President Truman and Secretary Acheson, of course, denounced McCarthy's accusation; but they also shared, though less extremely, the same deep-seated and frustrated animosity toward China's Revolution and the same fear and hatred of Communism. In October 1949, Acheson told the Senate Foreign Relations Committee that "the fundamental starting point in our relations with China" was the fact that the new Chinese government was "really a tool of Russian imperialism in Asia."[14]

Even if there had been no Korean War, the United States would have been slow to recognize the People's Republic of China, and would only have done so when China proved more accommodating to American interests. The People's Republic would not have accepted U.S. recognition unless China were treated as an equal. Mao had resolutely answered: "We Chinese have backbone." [15]

After the outbreak of the Korean War on June 25, 1950, the United States ceased all attempts to persuade the People's Republic of China to abandon the anti-imperialist front. Instead, it intensified its aggression against China, and did so long before the Chinese People's Volunteers had entered the Korean War.

On June 27, President Truman ordered the U.S. Seventh Fleet to prevent the Chinese people from liberating their own territory, Taiwan, on the grounds that the "occupation" of the island by "Communist forces" would threaten American forces in the Pacific area. [16] Premier and Foreign Minister Zhou Enlai immediately declared that Truman's action constituted armed aggression against the territory of China and a gross violation of the United Nations charter. [17]

Taiwan is Chinese; it is Chinese legally, historically, and ethnically. Since ancient times it has been a part of China: more than a thousand years ago China established government offices in Taiwan and Penghu and administered both places. After the Sino-Japanese War of 1894 the government of the Qing Dynasty, by signing the Treaty of Shimonoseki, ceded Taiwan and Penghu to Japan. With the outbreak of China's War of Resistance against Japan in 1937, in accordance with international law, the treaties between China and Japan became null and void. The United States, Great Britain, and the other Allies also pledged that, upon Japan's defeat, Taiwan and Penghu would be returned to China. In 1945, after Japan fell, the Chinese government recovered Taiwan and Penghu and reasserted sovereignty over both. The legal status of Taiwan, as one of the provinces of China, was thus restored. Truman, in his statement of January 5, 1950, recognized all these facts. The Chinese people had overthrown the reactionary rule of the Kuomintang and had established the People's Republic of China, a republic whose sovereignty extended to Taiwan; the Chinese people's liberation of Taiwan, like their liberation of other provinces of China, belonged to their internal affairs. Truman's statement of January 5 not only recognized this struggle as a "civil conflict," but also solemnly declared that the United States would not intervene in it.

After only six months, however, Truman, on June 27, as an explanation for why he was interposing the Seventh Fleet in the Taiwan Straits, abandoned all the points on Taiwan that he had enunciated on January 5. Perhaps feeling that the interference in the Taiwan issue was too flagrant an aggression to be justified, Truman did not scruple to reopen the question of Taiwan's legal status and to claim that the determination of the future status of Taiwan "must await the restoration of security in the Pacific, a peace settlement with Japan, or consideration by the United Nations." [18] Later, John Foster Dulles confessed to the Kuomintang ambassador to Washington that if the United States had already regarded Taiwan as purely Chinese territory, "[she] would lose her grounds for dispatching the Seventh Fleet to protect Taiwan." [19] The status of Taiwan as an integral part of Chinese Territory had long been settled. To hold the legal status of Taiwan as uncertain only proved the falsehood of Truman's statement of January 5.

Following the Seventh Fleet's move into the Taiwan Straits, contingents of the U.S. Air Force arrived in Taiwan. The United States thus placed Taiwan under its military control. In late July, MacArthur paid a visit to Chiang Kai-shek in Taiwan. In their statements at the conclusion of their talks, MacArthur stressed the importance of "defending" Taiwan, while Chiang declared that "the foundation for Sino-American military cooperation has been laid." [20] On August 25, MacArthur again emphasized the importance of Taiwan by calling it "an unsinkable aircraft carrier and submarine tender" in American strategy. Two days later, U.S. aircraft in Korea began their raids on Manchuria, damaging Chinese property and killing Chinese people. The American government also resumed the shipment of military supplies to Chiang. All these activities demonstrated to the Chinese people that the United States was turning Taiwan into an American stronghold, one that could threaten the Chinese mainland. The Kuomintang remnants on the island became the agent of the United States and a rival "government" to the People's Government in Beijing.

In July and September 1950, India twice proposed that the People's Republic of China be seated in the United Nations. The Soviet Union submitted resolutions that not only would have seated the People's Republic but also would have expelled the Nationalists. In order to preserve the Nationalist remnants on Taiwan as the "government" of all China, the United States actively opposed both proposals. The Generaly Assembly, manipulated by the United States, rejected both resolutions. China was one of the original members of the United

Nations and a permanent member of the Security Council. Because the People's Republic of China, established after the victory of the Chinese people's Revolution, was the continuation of preliberation China, it was unequivocally entitled to China's legitimate seat in the United Nations. But the United States insisted on depriving the People's Republic of its undeniable right to participate in the United Nations. Soon afterward, American forces in Korea crossed the thirty-eighth and pressed toward China's frontier.

These aggressive actions alerted the Chinese people to the fact that the newly established People's Republic was in danger. In the first year of the republic's existence, the Chinese people were resolved on the reconstruction of their country. Long years of imperialist and reactionary Kuomintang rule had left China's economy in a chaotic state. The basic task facing the government and the people was to consolidate the new state power and revive the national economy. For the fulfillment of this task, the Party convoked a plenary session of the Central Committee in June of 1950, to which Chairman Mao presented a written report entitled "Fight for a Fundamental Turn for the Better in the Nation's Financial and Economic Situation."[21] Indeed, the Chinese government and people were determined to accomplish this central task and not to fight in Korea. In the report Mao set partial demobilization of the People's Liberation Army as a key measure to allow manpower and resources to be shifted from the military to the domestic economy. Mao, in a speech at the session, also stressed that "we must not hit out in all directions. It is undesirable to hit out in all directions and cause nationwide tension."[22] His speech indicated that the New China would concentrate on economic reconstruction; but it needed a peaceful environment to achieve its aims, and the United States, by occupying Taiwan and invading the Democratic People's Republic of Korea, threatened China with war. How to tackle the problem? The Chinese people needed peace but they had also resolutely refused to beg the imperialists for it. The People's Government decided that it would both strive, through diplomacy, to avert a military clash and, at the same time, prepare for any contingency.

On August 20, Premier Zhou Enlai cabled the United Nations, pointing out that Korea was China's neighbor and the Chinese people could not but be concerned about the solution of the Korean question. He demanded that the question must be settled peacefully and that China's representation must be invited for discussion of the situation. To this appeal the United States responded merely with a threat. On

September 1, President Truman suggested that if China was "misled" into fighting the United States, the fighting in Korea would become a general war.[23] General Nie Rongzhen, acting chief of staff of the People's Liberation Army, told the Indian ambassador, K. M. Panikkar, that the Chinese did not intend to sit back with folded hands and allow the Americans to march up to their border.[24] But the Americans insisted on doing just that. On September 27, President Truman authorized General MacArthur to carry the war into North Korea. Three days later, Premier Zhou declared:

It is obvious that the Chinese people, after liberating the whole territory of their own country, want to rehabilitate and develop their industrial and agricultural production and their cultural and educational work in a peaceful environment, free from threats. But if the American aggressors take this as a sign of the weakness of the Chinese people, they will have committed the same fatal blunder as the Kuomintang reactionaries. . . . The Chinese people absolutely will not tolerate foreign aggression, nor will they supinely tolerate seeing their neighbors being savagely invaded by imperialists.[25]

On October 1, the South Korean forces crossed the thirty-eighth parallel. The next day Zhou Enlai summoned Panikkar to a midnight interview at his official residence. Zhou stated that no country's need for peace was greater than that of China, but there were occasions when peace could be defended only by determination to resist aggression. If the Americans crossed the thirty-eighth parallel, they would encounter Chinese resistance.[26]

The American government and military ignored these warnings. On October 7–8, U.S. troops crossed the parallel in force, and advanced rapidly toward the Sino-Korean border. It was only at this moment that Mao Zedong, chairman of the Chinese People's Revolutionary Military Commission, ordered the Chinese People's Volunteers to march speedily to Korea to safeguard the interests of the people of Korea, China, and all the other countries in the East. On October 19, the Chinese People's Volunteers entered Korea.

Just as Premier Zhou anticipated, the American government had underestimated the likelihood of China's joining the resistance to American invasion. It had also underestimated China's resolve and military strength. Secretary Acheson, speaking on September 10, had said that it would be "sheer madnesss" for the Chinese to intervene in Korea.[27] General MacArthur, too, had constantly played down the possibility of China's entering the war: even if the Chinese should intervene, he haughtily declared, the danger was minimal.[28] As late as October 11, when Truman and MacArthur met on Wake Island, the general assured the President that there was no danger of China's intervention.[29] This attitude once again reflected that arrogance and contempt which had long defined imperialist treatment of the semi-colonial China. During the Chinese civil war, from 1946 to 1949, the United States had supplied both the money and the guns with which Chiang Kai-shek's forces had slaughtered the Chinese people. Now, in the Korean War, the Americans employed their money and guns directly against the Chinese. They assumed that the Chinese people could never withstand the fierce fire of a superior nation. Few Americans really thought that the Chinese people, after their liberation, had created a miracle, not only material and military, but also in terms of a morale and patriotism not known for centuries.

The Americans reaped the fruit of their miscalculation. On November 24, MacArthur launched a general offensive aimed at completing the conquest of the Democratic People's Republic of Korea. Two days later, the Chinese People's Volunteers responded with a crushing counterattack. Carrying only light arms, they sent the American forces reeling back in a defeat that fell just short of being a complete and irremediable rout. From October 26, 1950, to June 1951, the People's Volunteers, by conducting five successive large-scale campaigns, drove the Americans back from the Yalu River all the way to the south of the thirty-eighth parallel, where they tied the Americans down.

These setbacks gave the United States an even more traumatic shock than had the overthrow in 1949 of Chiang Kai-shek. Unable to overcome the Chinese on the battlefield, the American government resorted to other drastic measures. It froze China's financial assets in America, established a complete embargo on all trade, forbade U.S. ships to call at Chinese ports, and refused Americans visas for any travel to China. It even resorted to intimidation and slander. Truman clamored that the United States would be prepared to employ "every weapon that we have"—an intimation that included, of course, the atomic bomb.[30] In January 1951 the U.S. Congress passed resolutions that called for the United Nations to declare the People's Republic of China an aggressor. This the U.N. Assembly dutifully did on February 1.

The Assembly's resolution was a slander against China. As Premier Zhou Enlai pointed out, it was "an utter perversion of truth and confound[ed] black and white."[31] China had acted in self-defense.

The Chinese People's Volunteers had not moved into Korea until all diplomatic means had been exhausted, and well after the United States forces had crossed the thirty-eighth parallel and driven right up to the Chinese border. And had not Truman stipulated, when he approved the invasion of North Korea, that no non-Koreans would approach the Manchurian border? But the U.S. forces did just that, and did so despite Truman's pledge. American communiques had boasted that they were racing "unopposed toward the Manchurian border."[32]

Success engenders greater ambition. If this advance were really to be "unopposed," where would the American challenges on China's very border have led? General MacArthur in fact had demanded to carry the war into China and even to support a Nationalist invasion against the mainland. True, President Truman, by recalling General MacArthur, decided to fight a limited war, but he might not have done so had the Chinese People's Volunteers not repelled the Americans at the Chinese border. China forced a limited war on the United States and revealed the limits of American strength.

The same American government that had intervened in Korea and marched to the Chinese frontier had also intervened in Taiwan both to deny China its lawful province and to protect the Kuomintang reactionaries whom the Chinese people had repudiated. It is thus not surprising that when Wu Xiuquan, of the People's Republic, came to the United Nations to participate in the debate on Taiwan, he denounced the American armed invasion of Taiwan and proposed that the Security Council immediately apply sanctions against the United States government for its armed aggression upon the territory of China, Taiwan, and for its intervention in Korea. The United Nations rejected the Chinese accusation that the United States had acted aggressively.

Thereafter, the American government encroached still further on Taiwan, and in a way that seemed to create a chain of islands that would encircle the Chinese mainland. In February 1951, the Truman administration signed a mutual defense assistance agreement with Chiang Kai-shek. In March, it sent a military assistance advisory group to Taibei and resumed direct military aid, sending as the first allocation $300 million. It continued to recognize the Kuomintang remnants in Taiwan as the "government of China" and was more stubbornly resolved in its effort to deny any recognition at all to the People's Republic of China. In May 1951, Assistant Secretary of State Dean Rusk called the People's Government "a colonial Russian government." Though Rusk gave no evidence for this erroneous charge, he added that it did justify nonrecognition.[33] In the United Nations, the United States adopted a special technique to block the People's Republic's recovery of its seat. In each of the ten years after 1951, when a resolution was introduced to expel the Nationalists and seat the People's Republic, the American delegate simply proposed that consideration of the issue be postponed until the following year, and the Assembly, under American influence, accepted this moratorium.

In September 1951, the United States drew up a peace treaty between the wartime Allies and Japan, one that excluded China. The United States also pressured the Japanese government to announce that it hoped to establish normal relations with the Kuomintang remnants and that it had no intention of concluding any treaty with the People's Republic. The Chinese people had been the first to oppose Japanese aggression in the 1930s. The Chinese had made enormous sacrifices in the worldwide war against Fascism. But now the American imperialists deprived them of even the right to attend a peace settlement. The treaty deliberately failed to say anything about the restoration of Taiwan to China, other than a short note that "Japan renounces all rights, title and claim to Formosa and the Pescadores."[34] In drawing up this cryptic provision, Washington hoped to deny the fact that Taiwan had already been returned to China at the end of World War II. Washington wished, by providing a legal basis for its claim that the status of Taiwan was still uncertain, to leave open the various ways that it could perpetuate its control over the island. Concurrently with concluding the peace treaty, the United States signed a mutual security treaty that gave it the right to dispose of its land, air, and sea forces in and about Japan, a plan whose spearhead appeared directed at China. The United States also, on China's southwestern border, extended aid to the French in their colonial war against the Indo-Chinese liberation movement. By the end of 1952, the United States was paying somewhere between one-third and one-half the total cost of that war.

The United States had by 1952 established an aggressive policy toward China. It was a comprehensive policy, involving military encirclement, political isolation, and economic blockade.

By June of 1951 the Korean War had reached a stalemate. The United States could not break the deadlock unless it risked an unlimited war—by invasion of the Chinese mainland—or an atrocity—the atomic bomb. In the meantime the Korean War had become very unpopular in the United States; Americans desperately wanted an end to it. On July 27, the Eisenhower administration was thus obliged to sign an armistice with the Koreans and Chinese. The courageous anti-imperialist spirit of the Chinese people, as expressed in the Korean War, had won out, but at the cost of further embittering the American imperialists.

The Eisenhower administration, moreover, only escalated those hostile attitudes adopted in the Truman years. Eisenhower's first act toward China after his inauguration in January of 1953 was to instruct the Seventh Fleet that, while earlier orders were still in force, it would "no longer be employed to shield Communist China." [35] When Truman, in 1950, had ordered the Seventh Fleet to prevent any attack on Taiwan, he had also instructed that Kuomintang military operations against the mainland be prevented. Eisenhower tore off the mask of Truman's disarming pretenses: an unleashed Chiang could now return to the mainland. Furthermore, the Eisenhower administration, besides helping Chiang prepare for an invasion, also ordered the American forces on Taiwan to support Chiang's harassment of and spying on the mainland.

Since late 1953, the United States and the Chiang regime had been engaged in negotiations that would convert their military collusion into a formal treaty. On December 2, 1954, they signed the so-called "Mutual Defense Treaty," providing for the "defense" of Taiwan, Penghu, and "such other territories as may be determined by mutual agreement." It also gave the United States the right to dispose of its land, air, and sea forces in and about the Taiwan area. [36] An exchange of notes accompanying the treaty stipulated that, for the Chiang regime, the term "territory" included "all territory now and hereafter under its control." [37] On January 29, 1955, the U.S. Congress passed a resolution that granted the President the unprecedented authority to employ armed forces to "protect" Taiwan and Penghu. [38] Premier Zhou Enlai promptly and vigorously protested such a warlike provocation. He denounced the treaty as a treaty of aggression and reaffirmed the Chinese people's determination to liberate Taiwan. [39]

The treaty contained two aspects. First, by treating the Chiang regime as the "government" of all China and by making a military alliance with it, the United States could reactivate, on the pretext of "resisting armed attack," the civil war in China and help Chiang stage a comeback. Second, the United States, by making the Chiang regime a "sovereign state" that existed side by side with the People's Republic, could transform that civil war into an international conflict. Such a transformation would legalize both U.S. intervention in China's internal affairs and its armed occupation of Taiwan, and would thus hinder the Chinese people from liberating that province. It would also open up "other territories" of China to further aggression. These two aspects showed that the American government appeared in many different ways to be threatening China with war. After the conclusion of the treaty, American military assistance to Chiang increased on a scale greater than was needed solely for the defense of Taiwan.

In May 1954, the people in north Vietnam defeated the French colonialists and compelled them to withdraw from Indochina. The major powers concerned met at Geneva where they pledged to respect the independence of Cambodia, Laos, and Vietnam, to accept a temporary demarcation line dividing Vietnam along the seventeenth parallel, to hold elections in 1956 for Vietnam's unification, and to prohibit the introduction of foreign troops into Vietnam. The American delegate, although he had refused to join in the accord, did, however, state that his government would refrain from any threat or use of force to disturb the agreements.[40] Yet only a few months later, the American government extended military assistance to the Ngo Dinh Diem regime in South Vietnam. The United States had decided to establish a stronghold in South Vietnam against both the Democratic Republic of Vietnam and China. In September 1954, the United States brought eight nations to Manila to sign the Southeast Asia Collective Defense Treaty. Its principal target was, of course, China.

The United States had thus forged an arc of military might that encircled the People's Republic of China. Assistant Secretary of State Walter Robertson admitted at a congressional hearing in January 1954 that the heart of America's China policy was "to keep alive a constant threat of military action vis-à-vis Red China in the hope that at some point there will be an internal breakdown."[41] Besides this military threat, the American government also insisted both on the maintenance of the trade embargo and on its unrelenting campaign to block the recovery of the People's Republic's seat in the United Nations. Opposition to the seating of the People's Republic in the United Nations became one of the chief means employed to isolate New China and thus to hasten its breakdown.

No country having the slightest sense of self-esteem can tolerate such aggression and insulting actions. Nevertheless, the Chinese government still pursued a peaceful policy toward the United States, which it conducted with a maximum of restraint. This policy was based upon the principle of peaceful coexistence among nations. Premier Zhou Enlai, in a later conversation with the American journalist Edgar Snow about the United States' many acts of aggression, asked the question "Would we use force to settle disputes with the United States?" and answered resoundingly, "No!"[42] China opposed the U.S. policy of aggression, but it still desired to settle disputes between the two countries through peaceful negotiations.

Attending an Afri-Asian conference at Bandung, Indonesia, Zhou Enlai announced on April 3, 1955:

The Chinese people are friendly to the American people. The Chinese people do not want to have a war with the United States of America. The Chinese government is willing to sit down and enter into negotiations with the United States government to discuss the question of relaxing tension in the Far East and especially the question of relaxing tension in the Taiwan area.[43]

The initial U.S. response was negative. Subsequently, through the efforts of Great Britain and India, the United States and China agreed to hold ambassadorial talks in Geneva on August 1, 1955. On July 26, Secretary of State Dulles said that he hoped to find out whether China accepted "the concept of a cease-fire in accordance with the United Nations principle of avoiding any use or threat of force which would disturb the peace of nations."[44] Since there was no firing at all between China and the United States in the Taiwan area, talk of a cease-fire seemed irrelevant. As for the military action between the People's Government of China and the Chiang regime in Taiwan, this was only the continuation of a thirty-year-old struggle between the Chinese people under the leadership of the Chinese Communist Party and the Kuomintang reactionaries. It was definitely an internal matter, one for the Chinese themselves. The United Nations principle that force should never be used in international affairs had never been relevant for internal conflicts. Basically, then, Dulles was asking China to accept the American scheme of internationalizing the Taiwan issue.

On July 30, Zhou Enlai told the National People's Congress that the tension in the Taiwan area, caused by the U.S. occupation of China's territory of Taiwan and its interference with the liberation of China's territory, was an international issue between China and the United States. The liberation of Taiwan, however, was a Chinese internal affair. These two questions could therefore not be mixed up; only the first question could be subject to Sino-American negotiation.[45]

When the ambassadorial talks started, China proposed that disputes between China and the United States, including that in the Taiwan region, should be settled through peaceful negotiations and without the use or threat of force.[46] But the United States insisted not only that the renunciation of force should be applied to the relations between the central government of China and the Chiang regime in Taiwan, but also that such a renunciation should not prejudice America's "right of individual and collective self-defense" in the Taiwan area.[47] Taiwan, however, was not a separate nation. The Chinese people, to be sure, wished to liberate that province, by peaceful means if possible, but it was the business of the Chinese people alone as to how and with what means the Chinese government was to deal with the Chiang clique and liberate Taiwan. The United States, after all, had already used force against the Chinese territory, a force in no way justified by any right of self-defense. Its treaty with Chiang's faction was illegal and invalid. All of the United States' assertions and schemes at the ambassadorial talks sought to create "two Chinas" and so to deny the right of the Chinese people to liberate Taiwan. The Chinese people, however, firmly opposed any schemes or claims involving two Chinas. All Chinese, including the Kuomintang remnants, recognized Taiwan as a part of China and not a state outside of China. America's insistence on two Chinas brought the Geneva talks to a deadlock.

In the hope of making some progress, the Chinese suggested that the ambassadorial talks be replaced by direct negotiations on the foreign-ministerial level. The United States rejected this suggestion. On August 6, 1956, in reply to their requests, Premier Zhou offered to grant visas to fifteen accredited representatives of the American news media for a month's visit to China. The American government, however, disapproved of such a visit and refused to issue passports. Finally, under persistent pressure from the journalists, the government agreed to send them to China but only on the condition that the United States need not accord reciprocal visas to Chinese journalists who might wish to visit the United States. In the face of this insufferable arrogance, Premier Zhou let it be known in September 1957 that the actions of the American government had put an end to the matter.

The United States' rigid position arose from an irrational fear of any move that might build up the prestige of the People's Republic.

This fear pervaded the outlook of John Foster Dulles and led to illusory hopes. In a speech of June 28, 1957, Dulles thus declared:

We can confidently assume that international communism's rule of strict conformity is, in China as elsewhere, a passing and not a perpetual phase. We owe it to ourselves, our allies and the Chinese people to do all that we can to contribute to that passing.[48]

Even the "two Chinas" policy was thus but a temporary tactic in a far larger policy toward China. By its treaty with Chiang, the United States had established an informal protectorate over Taiwan. This protectorate was also part of Dulles's plan to further the downfall of the People's Republic. The purpose of the two Chinas scheme was thus to occupy by force a province of China, to support the counterrevolutionary faction in gaining control of it, to sever it from China, and to make it a base for toppling the People's Republic. America appeared to be dedicated to preserving its hegemony in the Far East. As Assistant Secretary Robertson admitted, "The United States is undertaking to maintain for an indefinite period of years American dominance in the Far East."[49]

By August 1958, the United States had moved one hundred thousand of Chiang's troops, more than one-fourth of his forces, onto the offshore islands of Jinmen (Quemoy) and Mazu (Matsu). Chiang had long used these islands as a base for commando raids on the mainland and frequent bombardments on coastal villages and towns. In the summer of 1958, the Chiang faction announced an imminent invasion of the mainland. On August 11, the U.S. State Department reiterated that the United States held the view that "communism's rule in China is not permanent and that it one day will pass. By withholding diplomatic recognition from Peiping it seeks to hasten that passing."[50]

The People's Republic immediately denounced the American policy of seeking "to hasten that passing" as "an idiot's daydream." It stated, defiantly, that the Chinese people "have always held U.S. imperialism in contempt and have never cared a jot about Washington's 'recognition.' " It added that the aggressive policy of the United States could not halt the Chinese people in their advance to national unification.[51] On August 23, 1958, in order to punish the Chiang regime for its U.S.-supported military activities against the mainland and coastal areas, artillery units of the People's Liberation Army in

Fujian Province began an intensive bombardment of Chiang's troops on Jinmen Island.

President Eisenhower ordered the Seventh Fleet mobilized in the Taiwan Straits. The American press reported that the U.S. government had issued atomic missiles to its air forces based on Taiwan and that the American military intended to use nuclear weapons. The Chinese government and people were not intimidated; their batteries continued to shell Jinmen. On September 4, China declared a twelve-mile coastal zone to be national waters. On the same day, Secretary Dulles called on China to negotiate, but he simultaneously threatened that the United States would not hesitate to employ armed force to "protect" Jinmen and Mazu.[52] Two days later, Premier Zhou Enlai responded in kind, announcing that "no amount of U.S. war provocation [could] cow the Chinese people"; he further reaffirmed the sovereign rights of the Chinese people to liberate their own territory, repeated his demand for the United States to withdraw from the Taiwan area, and at the same time agreed to reopen the suspended ambassadorial talks to settle the Sino-American dispute over Taiwan.[53]

In the end, American provocations frightened only its own people and its allies in the West. In America, columnists condemned the American action in the Taiwan Straits as a risky adventure in "the worst place, for the worst cause, with the worst ally."[54] Many leaders of both the Democratic and Republican parties criticized Dulles's policy. Disconcerted and isolated, Dulles backed away from his previous unquestioning support of Chiang. On September 30, Dulles said at a press conference, that it had been "rather foolish" for the Chiang faction to insist on maintaining so great a part of their military forces on the offshore islands. He added that "if there were a cease-fire it would be our judgment, military judgment even, that it would not be wise or prudent to keep [those forces] there."[55] He fell back to the cease-fire scheme as a means of maintaining the "two Chinas": in exchange for a cease-fire, the offshore islands would be abandoned. It was a crafty scheme, intended to separate the question of offshore islands from that of Taiwan, and thus carve Taiwan out of China's sovereign territory. Dulles brought the scheme to Taiwan. In a joint communique concerning his talks with Chiang, he had Taiwan accept the so-called "renunciation" of force, in return for which he granted Chiang's regime the exclusive right to represent "free China."[56]

The Chinese government, of course, rejected the scheme, pointing out that since there was no war between China and the United States, there could be no question of a "cease-fire." The United States had no right to butt in on either the Jinmen-Mazu or the Taiwan-Penghu question. The only thing the Americans could do—and must do—was pull their armed forces out from the Taiwan area, lock, stock, and barrel.[57] To counter Dulles's plot to separate Taiwan from the offshore islands, the Chinese vice-premier, Chen Yi, stated that Taiwan and the islands must be liberated as a whole. China would never allow Jinmen to be handed over in exchange for placing Taiwan under trusteeship.[58] Premier Zhou Enlai was confident that the day would come when the United States would have to withdraw its troops from the Taiwan Straits.[59]

Zhou's prediction was based on an irresistible historical trend. He told Edgar Snow in 1960, "We do not believe that the people of the United States will allow their government indefinitely to pursue such a policy. There is no conflict of basic interests between the people of China and the United States, and friendship will eventually prevail."[60] Outwardly, the impasses appeared insurmountable. The American ambassador, at the talks which resumed on September 15, 1958, in Warsaw, did no more than repeat demands for what would amount to Beijing's de jure recognition of the legality of the American armed protectorate in Taiwan. But in reality the demand for a change in the U.S. policy gained ground. The 1958 crisis, in which the United States extended its aggression to the offshore islands, had revealed the imperialist strain in America's foreign policy, thus arousing a greater revulsion toward the Dulles line. An increasing number of the American press corps began to criticize Dulles's policy. Many Americans in their letters to the press, to Congress, and to the State Department denounced these recent Asian adventures.

Other aspects of America's China policy furthered discontent as well. The European allies in particular were anxious to relax the restrictions on the shipment of strategic goods by narrowing the definition of what might be considered "materials of war." In May 1957, the allies compelled the United States substantially to modify its original restrictions. The United States now stood alone in continuing the embargo on trade with China, while China kept expanding its trade with other nations. In the United Nations, the votes cast against excluding the People's Republic rose in the period between 1954 and 1960 from some 18 percent of the total to nearly 35 percent. The People's Republic had not collapsed as Dulles had hoped. On the contrary, it had grown and progressed at an unprecedented rate. Its international status and prestige grew daily. More and more countries established diplomatic relations with the People's Republic, and more and more people demanded that that republic be recognized as the true, sovereign China. The American policy of isolating China had succeeded only in isolating the United States itself in world public opinion. Calls for a review and revision of the China policy were heard both inside and outside Congress. In the presidential campaign of 1960, even John Kennedy, the Democratic candidate, called for reassessment of a stand that had "failed dismally in its principal objective of weakening Communist rule on the mainland."[61]

After the establishment in 1949 of the People's Republic of China, both the Truman and Eisenhower administrations remained blind to the fact that the Chinese people, comprising one-quarter of all humanity, had stood up in support of the People's Republic. Rather, they attempted in every possible way to precipitate the new China's breakdown. But, ultimately, echoing Chiang's battle against the Communist Party in the 1946–1949 civil war, the many U.S. schemes and actions against the People's Republic proved a failure.

10

Though President John Kennedy and his successor, Lyndon Johnson, acknowledged the failure of their China policy, they made no reassessment and no change. Nor did they cease to oppose the restitution of China's legitimate rights to membership in the United Nations. Since 1951 the United States had cajoled and pressured a majority of the General Assembly to postpone any discussion of that issue. But as more and more nations came to favor restoring China's rightful seat, that majority slowly disappeared. Because of this shift, the Kennedy administration in 1961 designed a new scheme whereby the issue of Chinese representation became an "important question," one that required a two-thirds instead of a simple majority. For ten years this trick continued to deprive China of its seat in the United Nations.

The American ruling group also diminished in no way its obstruction to China's reunification with the province of Taiwan, an obstruction that was harder to justify since the American leaders themselves no longer believed the People's Republic of China was a mere passing phase. Indeed, it was because of this disbelief in the evanescence of the New China that they continued to create various schemes for "two Chinas" or for "one China, one Taiwan."

Such obstinacy in the face of reality won less and less support from the American people and from U.S. allies. The American China policy increasingly became an object of derision in the world. Thus the United States, compelled to change its posture and its tactics, announced that its principal objective regarding the People's Republic was not to produce its downfall or to subject it to long-term isolation but to make it impossible for Beijing to "subvert or commit aggression against its free-world neighbors." China would have to make "very fundamental and very far-reaching" changes before the United States could consider "the possibility of a break" in their relations. "We are determined to keep the door open to the possibility of change." [1] For the United States to have moved from burying its head in the sand to a position of keeping "the door open to the possibility of change" seemed a step forward. But, as the *People's Daily* in Beijing commented, the United States' aggressive posture toward China was essentially unchanged. The "open door" was only to allow China to change its basic policies on two important counts: first, to accept a "two China" policy that would allow the United States permanently to occupy, through a puppet regime, Taiwan; and second, to drop its support for the national liberation movements in other parts of Asia. [2]

To these unjust demands, of course, China would never capitulate. Instead it would make the New China even more stable, influential, and determined, a solid reality quite frightful to President Kennedy. At a press conference in August 1963, Kennedy declared: "We find a great, powerful force in China, organized and directed by a government along Stalinist lines, surrounded by weaker countries. . . . This we regard as a menacing situation." [3] Later, Secretary of State Dean Rusk said that American interests would be gravely jeopardized should China succeed in establishing control over Southeast Asia. Since America is "both a Pacific and an Atlantic power," Rusk added, it has "a tremendous stake in the ability of the free nations of Asia to live in peace." [4] Kennedy's "menacing situation" and Rusk's "tremendous stake" reflect less a desire to undermine a resurgent China than a fear of losing American hegemony in East Asia.

The American rulers were in fact increasingly frightened by the upsurge of the national liberation movement in South Vietnam. They felt that they must hold the line in that area, since they considered it a vital strategic point whose loss would lead to the collapse of their front in the whole region. Thus the "deepening shadow" of an "ambitious China" over Vietnam was used to justify American intervention. From 1964 on, the United States vastly increased its military assistance to the reactionary and corrupt regime in South Vietnam and participated more directly in the fight against the national liberation forces. In 1965, it began bombing supply routes and bases in the Democratic Republic of Vietnam. President Johnson stated in April 1965: "The rulers in Hanoi are urged by Peking. . . . The contest in Vietnam is part of a wider pattern of aggressive purpose." [5] Even more pronounced were the views of Richard Nixon. He declared in March 1965 that the Vietnam War was not a war between the North and the South, or between the United States and North Vietnam, but a war between the United States and "Communist China."[6]

But as a matter of fact, no such war existed. Moreover, the Chinese leaders had persistently stated that they wanted no war with the United States. At the Sino-American ambassadorial talks in Warsaw in September 1958, China had repeatedly put forward two principal points: first, that the two countries should agree on peaceful coexistence, and second, that the United States must withdraw all its armed forces from Taiwan and the Taiwan Straits. Since the establishment of the People's Republic, China had never encroached upon neighboring nations. As Premier Zhou Enlai told Edgar Snow in 1960, China "has not a single soldier abroad, and the treaties it has concluded with Asian countries are all treaties of peace and friendship."[7] China supported revolutionary movements, but not by invading countries. Even after the Americans had fanned the flames of war in Vietnam, the Chinese leaders continued to assert that China's armies would not cross its borders to fight. Only if the United States attacked China would China fight. Secretary Rusk admitted that China "acted with caution when they foresaw a collision with the United States."[8] As for military aid to the Vietnamese people, it was not China but the United States which was arming the Vietnamese liberation forces. Just as the Chinese People's Liberation Army relied mainly on American weapons seized from Chiang's troops in the 1946–1949 civil war, so the Vietnamese liberation forces not only seized American weapons but also recruited defeated South Vietnamese troops and officers trained by the Americans.

Talk of war with China by the American right wing and references to the "Chinese menace" by the American government and press to justify the slaughter in Vietnam could not but rouse the Chinese people's indignation. Foreign Minister Chen Yi, at a press conference on September 29, 1965, stated:

We are fully prepared against U.S. aggression. If the U.S. imperialists are determined to launch a war of aggression against us, they are welcome to come sooner, to come as early as tomorrow. . . .

For sixteen years we have been waiting for the U.S. imperialists to come in and attack us. My hair has turned grey in waiting. Perhaps I will not have the luck to see the U.S. imperialist invasion of China, but my children may see it, and they will resolutely carry on the fight. Let no correspondent think that I am bellicose. It is the U.S. imperialists who are brutal and vicious and who bully others too much.[9]

America's bullying actions in Asia exacerbated the resentment of a large part of the American people as well. A "Chinese menace" that was not a reality could scarcely justify the American adventure in Vietnam. Instead, the Vietnamese war only revealed more clearly than ever that America's China policy was unjustifiable. Some years earlier American leaders had called the Chinese People's Government "a colonial Russian government," "a handmaiden of an alien imperialism," and a government which carried the "flag of Communist conspiracy,"[10] charges that reflected that violent hostility which distorted the United States' policy toward China. But China's persistence in following an independent course in foreign affairs, together with its defiant resistance to Soviet efforts at hegemony in Asia, proved to the world that Beijing was no satellite of Moscow. Yet still the American government invoked the specter of China as the embodiment of "Communist expansion."

The world, however, saw clearly that, whereas by 1968 the United States had 540,000 troops in Vietnam, China not only had no troops there, but it had none outside its own frontiers. The premises underlying the American policy lay shattered on the ground. Furthermore, even America's gargantuan force in Vietnam could not sustain U.S. hopes for dominance in East Asia. Since 1945, a major reason for America's reluctance to intervene in China directly was its fear of becoming engulfed in the boundless ocean of the Chinese people's resistance. In regard to tiny South Vietnam, it thought, the case would be different. But alas, Vietnam too proved to be a trap, as the American invaders found themselves mired ever more deeply in the Vietnamese morass. Both the reasons for, and the results of, that intervention in Vietnam were indefensible.

A steadily increasing segment of the American public attacked the government's Vietnam policy and urged a more conciliatory stand toward China. After 1964, some Democratic senators had called for a new approach to Sino-American relations. In a series of public hearings held in March 1966 by the Senate Foreign Relations Committee, a majority of the scholars testifying advocated development of closer relations with China. Professor Doak Barnett, though still favoring "continued pledges to defend areas on China's periphery, including Taiwan," pointed out that the U.S. attempt to isolate China had been "unwise and, in a fundamental sense, unsuccessful." Barnett thus agreed that the United States should encourage informal contacts, restrict trade only to a few strategic items, acknowledge the People's Government as the de facto government of mainland China, and state America's desire to extend de jure recognition. [11]

In response to this new mood, Secretary of State Rusk made a statement on March 16, 1966, that indicated a desire for better relations, on condition that China "abandon the aggressive use of force." Rusk stated further: "We look forward hopefully—and confidently—to a time in the future when the government of mainland China will permit the restoration of the historic ties of friendship between the people of mainland China and ourselves." But except for expressing a hope for enlarging "the possibilities for unofficial contacts" between the two countries, Rusk maintained intact all the aggressive elements of America's policy toward China. [12]

China had no policies of aggression to abandon. Nor could fine words bring about friendship while America was escalating its war efforts on China's periphery. On April 10, 1966, Premier Zhou Enlai declared China's policy toward the United States in four points: first, though China would do nothing to provoke a war with the United States, it would continue to demand that the United States withdraw all its armed forces from Taiwan and from the Taiwan Straits; second, if any country in Asia, or elsewhere, became the victim of an aggressive American-supported imperialism, the Chinese government and people would give it support; third, should the United States impose a war on China, once there, it would find itself unable to withdraw its forces; and finally, once the war broke out, that war would know no bounds. [13] Zhou's statement revealed that Beijing was greatly skeptical of the American government's sincerity in talking of better relations.

The American government in the 1960s differed from its predecessors of the 1950s only in employing the dual tactics of armed force and peaceful talk, tactics adopted because of the pressure of public opinion. On the one hand, it tightened its military encirclement of China, continued to dispatch aircraft and warships into China's airspace and waters, and pushed its war of aggression against Vietnam to an ever graver state; on the other hand, one American official after another indicated a wish for "reconciliation," "building a bridge," and entering into "peaceful cooperation" with China. [14] But dual tactics achieved little, for they rested so much on mere words. Only deeds could display a sincerity that would effectively ease Sino-American relations.

Nevertheless, the change in tactics after more than ten years of hostility did reflect the awkward fact that America's China policy had entered a blind alley. As Premier Zhou had predicted, the American people would not allow the endless and costly pursuit of such a fruitless policy. Because both the threat of force against China and actual force in Vietnam had ended in failure, it was now time for the American government to consider some real modifications.

The American government, though it had poured 540,000 troops and its most sophisticated arms into South Vietnam, could not subdue this tiny country. Week by week in 1968 and 1969, the American people increased the pressure on their government to end the war. Protests and demonstrations throughout the country, especially on the part of young people, reflected the rapidly spreading belief that America's continued involvement in Vietnam was a colossal error. The American people intensified their demands for a thorough reappraisal of America's Far East policy, including its China policy. The American leaders could not turn a deaf ear to the powerful voice of the masses.

As the United States sank deeper into the mire of Vietnam, the other superpower, the Soviet Union, exploited the occasion by expanding its armament, intensifying its efforts at hegemony in the third world, and putting the United States on the defensive. In order to regain the initiative, the American leaders found it necessary to so improve Sino-American relations that China could serve as a counterweight against the Soviets. President Nixon's assistant for national security affairs, Henry Kissinger, realized that in the subtle triangle of Washington, Beijing, and Moscow, it would benefit Washington greatly to "improve the possibilities of accommodation with each as we increase our options toward both." [15] Kissinger had set his sights on a sustained global equilibrium, which, if once achieved, would increase America's options but which he knew would be unrealizable if the United States remained hostile to China.

The cost and futility of America's involvement in Vietnam had vividly demonstrated the limits of U.S. power. The United States was forced to consider reducing its overextended fronts and concentrating on the more vital points. In order to both pare down its "commitments" in East Asia and still keep a favorable balance of power in the region, it had to reach a rapprochement with China. Withdrawal from an aggressive military policy along China's periphery would also make possible a better U.S.-Chinese relationship.

For these reasons, Richard Nixon promised in his presidential election campaign to pull America's military forces out of Vietnam. Immediately after his nomination, Nixon stated: "We must not forget China. We must always seek opportunities to talk with her, as with the USSR. . . . We must not only watch for changes. We must seek to make changes." [16]

China's own policies formed no obstacle to a better relationship. China had consistently held that the Sino-American dispute could be solved by peaceful means. At the same time, it advocated that the peoples of the world should unite against the hegemonism of the superpowers. In the early 1960s, the leaders of the Soviet Union began a polemical attack on China. Arguments once enjoined over matters of principle became intense conflicts in which the Soviets brought enormous political, economic, and military pressure to bear against China. In 1968 and 1969, while America gave signs that it would soon withdraw from China's neighbor to the south, the Soviet hegemonists deployed massive forces along the Sino-Soviet and Sino-Mongolian borders. In March of 1969, the crisis resulted in a series of armed clashes on both the Manchurian and the Xinjiang frontiers. Soviet hegemonism became the most dangerous threat to China's security and to world peace. To resist this hostile expansionism, it was necessary to enlist all available forces, including the United States.

Since Richard Nixon indicated that he would withdraw from Vietnam and was willing to talk with China, China had no reason not to encourage his efforts. On November 25, 1968, the Chinese charge d'affaires in Warsaw suggested to the American ambassador to Poland that the two sides revive their talks on February 20, 1969. The next day a Chinese foreign ministry statement explained that February 20 had been proposed for the sessions because "by that time, the new U.S. president will have been in office for a month, and the U.S. side will probably be able to make up its mind." [17] The statement also solemnly declared that the Chinese government would never barter away the principles it had adhered to over the past thirteen years—that is, that the United States must withdraw its armed forces from the Taiwan area. The United States would also have to sign a Sino-American agreement for peaceful coexistence. Nixon welcomed the proposal for resumption of the Warsaw talks. In February 1969, however, because the United States provided political "asylum" to a defecting Chinese diplomat, the Chinese government canceled the proposed Warsaw meetings.

During 1969, the newly installed Nixon administration continued its attempts to open communication with Beijing, winning thereby the applause of the American people, many of whom urged, to promote establishment of a more normal relationship with China, the adoption of such specific measures, as the lifting of the embargo on trade, the cessation of opposition to People's Republic representation in the United Nations, the withdrawal of American military presence from Taiwan, and diplomatic recognition of the People's Republic. At the same time, the U.S. government noted that since March of 1969 the Soviet encroachment upon China had culminated in a series of armed clashes. The American leaders, thinking they could exploit the Sino-Soviet rift, thus stepped up their approaches to China. As Henry Kissinger put it, they would now move "without further hesitation toward a momentous change in global diplomacy."[18]

In April 1969, Secretary of State William Rogers declared in a policy statement that he would take the initiative for such approaches without demanding any quid pro quo in return and that he looked forward to a long future in the easing of Sino-American tensions.[19] On July 25, 1969, at a press conference held in Guam, President Nixon, in outlining his general view on Far Eastern policy, announced that the United States would reduce its military role and increase economic aid in Asia. Later, in elaborating on these remarks, remarks which became known as the "Nixon Doctrine," he said that he would expect "the nation directly threatened to assume the primary responsibility of providing the manpower for its defense."[20] On August 8, 1969, Secretary Rogers stated that the United States had taken measures "to help remind people on mainland China of our historic friendship for them."[21] In these months, President Nixon also asked the leaders of Pakistan and Romania to convey to the Chinese his desires for good relations. Thus, by public declaration and through intermediaries, the U.S. government communicated to China that it was moving toward a more relaxed and realistic foreign policy in East Asia.

The Americans supported their words with actions in their efforts to remove irritants in Sino-American relations. It began to withdraw its military forces from Vietnam, and by May 1971 had almost halved the number of American troops in that area. It also decided to substantially modify the trade embargo and to stop the U.S. Seventh Fleet's periodic patrol of the the Taiwan Straits.

Confronted by these developments, China realized that American imperialism was on the decline. In the past twenty years, the United States had failed in both its policy of hostility toward China and its dual tactics. Its military adventure in Vietnam, too, had suffered defeat. This situation produced the Nixon Doctrine. It was not, however, an entirely new invention: in the 1940s the Truman administration had supplied arms and aid, and Chiang Kai-shek manpower, in a vain attempt to suppress the Chinese revolution. Nixon's policy of arms and aid but not manpower thus was a revival of Truman's policy; it was also an admission that the United States' global "commitment" to use its armed forces to fight Communism everywhere had so severely strained its resources and morale that it had to retreat to a policy of employing Asians to fight Asians. Only by such tactics could the United States maintain its interests in Asia without heavy and unacceptable casualties to American soldiers. The Vietnam debacle revealed that the United States could not achieve that position of dominance which its illusion of omnipotence after World War II had led it to assert. Crisis at home and losses in Vietnam had diminished its power abroad. But finally the United States had begun to accommodate itself to the reality that its strength was unequal to its ambition. The action taken by the American government to relax tension was also conducive to a better Sino-American relationship. Therefore, when in December of 1969 the American ambassador to Poland, on instructions from his government, proposed the resumption of the Warsaw meetings, the Chinese agreed.

The meeting took place on January 20, 1970. At the meeting, the American ambassador stated that the United States was willing either to send an emissary to Beijing for direct discussion or to receive in Washington, for the same purpose, a representative from China. The Chinese chargé d'affaires also suggested that the talks might be conducted at a higher level. Formerly the Chinese government had made repeated proposals to this effect because, in its opinion, in direct negotiations it would be easier to solve problems. Now the Americans, on their own initiative, did likewise. According to Henry Kissinger, at this time the American government wanted to make a fresh start toward a fundamental change in Sino-American relations.

In October, in granting an interview to *Time* magazine, President Nixon said, "If there is anything I want to do before I die, it is to go to China. If I don't, I want my children to." Later that month, he successively asked the presidents of Pakistan and Romania to tell the Chinese leaders that the United States regarded a Sino-American rapprochement as essential, that it would never join a condominium against China, and that it was willing to send a high-level secret emissary to Beijing.[22] In December, Chairman Mao Zedong told Edgar Snow that the Chinese Foreign Ministry was studying the matter of allowing Americans of all political persuasions to visit China. Even rightists like Nixon, who represented the monopoly capitalists, would be welcomed, because, as Mao explained, the present problems between China and the United States had to be solved and because Nixon was that country's leader. Mao would be happy to talk with him, whether as a tourist or as President.[23]

Mao's utterances were in conformity with China's consistent policy toward the United States of solving problems through negotiations and, if possible, by high-level talks. Since President Nixon had indicated that he was interested in going to China, the Chinese leaders would of course welcome a direct discussion with him. In April 1971, in response to an American message, Premier Zhou Enlai reiterated the idea that a solution to the crucial question of Taiwan could be found only through direct discussions between high-level responsible persons of the two countries. Therefore, the Chinese government was willing to receive publicly in Beijing a special envoy of the President of the United States or even the President himself.[24] In a formal communication, then, President Nixon received an invitation. On May 10, he accepted that invitation.

For the Chinese the subject of the proposed meeting was Taiwan, since the relations between the two countries could not be restored unless the United States withdrew its armed forces from that area. On the other hand, the United States stressed that each side was free to raise any issue that concerned it. Premier Zhou, in response, repeated that the paramount question was the withdrawal of U.S. forces from the Taiwan area, a question of principle, one which could never be compromised. But at the same time Zhou, in agreeing to discuss other issues, showed China's flexibility, since in earlier ambassadorial talks China had claimed that there could be no progress on subsidiary issues until the Taiwan issue was settled. In fact, in April China had already invited the American table-tennis team, along with others that had been competing in a world tournament in Japan, to play in China. Premier Zhou personally received the American players and told them that their visit to China had opened the door to friendly contacts between the people of the two countries. The invitation and visit of the American team opened the way to a friendly atmosphere for the coming of the official American delegation. In certain circumstances, flexibility is necessary for the realization of more fundamental principles.

President Nixon was satisfied with the formal terms of the proposed visit. On June 2, on hearing about Premier Zhou's reply and the steps for arrangement of the talks, he was so exalted that he proposed a toast: "Let us drink to generations to come who may have a better chance to live in peace because of what we have done." Henry Kissinger intepreted this remark as a reflection of "the emotion and the rekindled hope that out of the bitterness and division of a frustrating war we could emerge with a new national confidence in our country's future." [25]

In preparation for his visit, President Nixon sent Kissinger on a secret trip to Beijing to meet with high-ranking Chinese officials. As a result of this meeting, China and the United States, on July 15, 1971, issued a joint announcement:

Knowing of President Nixon's expressed desire to visit the People's Republic of China, Premier Zhou Enlai, on behalf of the Government of the People's Republic of China, has extended an invitation to President Nixon to visit China at an appropriate date before May 1972. President Nixon has accepted the invitation with pleasure.

The meeting between the leaders of China and the United States is to seek the normalization of relations between the two countries and also to exchange views on questions of concern to the two sides. [26]

This was an announcement which shook and excited the world. In the United States, congratulations poured in from all over the globe. The news media were nearly unanimous in their praise. The Chinese people expressed the same positive feelings, feelings which along those in the United States showed that the action taken by the leaders of the two countries, conformed to both the trend of the times and the desire of the people. For the American governing elite it was also a policy furthering their own interests since it confronted, they thought, the Soviets with a possible Sino-American cooperation, one that would give the United States a stronger bargaining position. Moreover, a better relationship with China would facilitate the U.S. retreat from Indo-China. And better relations between China and the United States, the curbing of Moscow's ambition, and the reduction of American armed intervention in Asia were all compatible with popular aspirations.

One of the first consequences of the above announcement was a dramatic change in the United Nations concerning China's representation. Since 1960 the votes for restoring China's seat had continued to increase, with the majority voting in favor of Beijing in 1970. The United States was thus engaged in a doomed rearguard action, one that led the American government in 1971 to change its policy from opposition to the People's Republic being admitted into the United Nations to endorsement of dual representation between Beijing and Taiwan. On August 17, 1971, the American representative to the United Nations declared that the People's Republic of China should be represented, but at the same time maintained that the Kuomintang remnants should not be expelled. On August 20, the Chinese Foreign Ministry announced that this formula would create "two Chinas" in the United Nations, and it added that "should a situation of 'two Chinas,' 'one China, one Taiwan' or 'the status of Taiwan remaining to be determined' . . . occur in the United Nations, the Government of the People's Republic of China will absolutely have nothing to do with the United Nations."[27] The ministry made it clear that China would never take its seat under the dual-representation formula. It was a question of principle, of justice, and so the Chinese government would remain unshakable. For the United States, the tactic of the "two Chinas" was inconsistent with its desire to improve relations with China by resolving the Taiwan issue. For those in the United Nations who supported the American position, Nixon's dispatch of a representative to Beijing made continued exclusion of Beijing absurd. They had long favored the admission of China to the United Nations, but had followed the United States merely because they feared causing offense. That fear now evaporated. On July 15, Albania, Algeria, and sixteen other countries had demanded the recognition of the representatives of the People's Republic of China as the only lawful representatives of China to the United Nations and the immediate expulsion of the Kuomintang representatives. On October 25, when this draft resolution was put to the vote, the General Assembly passed it by a decisive vote of 76 to 35, with 17 abstentions.

A great issue whose solution the United States had blocked for twenty-two years, thus resulted finally in victory for China. Actually, it was also beneficial to Nixon's forthcoming visit, because it removed a major obstacle to Sino-American reconciliation.

From February 21 to February 28, 1972, President Nixon carried out his visit to China, a visit that marked the official beginning of the Sino-American reconciliation. In his welcoming toast at the first state banquet, Premier Zhou Enlai proclaimed that, despite ideological differences, the United States and China could establish normal relations on the basis of peaceful coexistence. He hoped that "through frank exchange of views between our two sides to gain a clearer notion of differences and make efforts to find common ground, a new start can be made in the relations between our two countries." [28] President Nixon, in replying to this toast, said that "if we can find common ground to work together, the chance for world peace is immeasurably increased. . . . What brings us together is that we have common interests which transcend those differences." [29] This spirit—to seek common ground while reserving differences—dominated the subsequent negotiations.

In the joint communiqué issued in Shanghai at the termination of the visit on February 27, 1972, the two sides enumerated their conflicting viewpoints over Taiwan and other issues. However, they did agree that

countries, regardless of their social systems, should conduct their relations on the principles of respect for the sovereignty and territorial integrity of all states, nonaggression against other states, noninterference in the internal affairs of other states, equality and mutual benefit, and peaceful coexistence. International disputes should be settled on this basis, without resorting to the use or threat of force. The United States and the People's Republic of China are prepared to apply these principles to their mutual relations. [30]

The United States, at long last, had accepted sound principles on China and had thus ended a twenty-two-year-old estrangement between the two countries.

Previously the United States had alleged that the status of Taiwan remained to be determined. Now it declared:

The United States acknowledges that all Chinese on either side of the Taiwan Strait maintain there is but one China and that Taiwan is a part of China. The United States Government does not challenge that position. [31]

This declaration committed the United States to devise no scheme of "two Chinas" or "one China, one Taiwan." The United States also promised progressively to reduce its forces on Taiwan as the tension in the area diminished, although it regarded their total withdrawal merely as an "ultimate objective" and linked it to a peaceful solution of the Taiwan question. These acknowledgments and pledges were advantageous to China's hope of returning Taiwan to the embrace of the motherland.

With the principles of normal state-to-state relations established, the United States and China agreed to promote trade between the two countries, and to facilitate contacts and exchanges in such fields as science, technology, culture, sports, and journalism.

Besides bilateral relations, the leaders of the two countries also paid great attention to international order. Both sides agreed that

neither should seek hegemony in the Asia-Pacific region and each is opposed to efforts by any other country or group of countries to establish such hegemony. [32]

Opposition to hegemonism was China's cardinal foreign policy. In the 1970s, in particular, China was anxious that in fending off the threat of American hegemony the Asian countries did not fall prey to a Soviet one. In agreeing to these principles that would govern the future international order in East Asia, the United States went on record as joining China in opposing the hegemonic threats of other powers.

Premier Zhou in his welcoming toast referred to his statement of 1955 in which he had said that "the Chinese people do not want to have a war with the United States and the Chinese Government is willing to sit down and enter into negotiations with the United States Government." Zhou then added, "This is a policy which we have pursued consistently." [33] The agreements reached during President Nixon's visit were the logical and successful result of this policy. Indeed, the gains achieved during this visit would open up new prospects for relations between the two countries.

Yet the gains, though in striking contrast to the more than twenty years' suspension of contacts between the two peoples, were only a fresh start, not a consummation of the process of normalization. Before and after his visit to China, President Nixon specifically affirmed that America's "friendship, diplomatic ties and defense commitment" to Taiwan would remain unaffected. [34] As long as the United States maintained this position, complete diplomatic relations with the People's Republic were impossible. The Chinese government insisted that the achievement of complete diplomatic rela-

tions entailed three conditions: that the United States sever its diplomatic ties with the Chiang regime, that it abrogate its "mutual
defense treaty" with Chiang, and that it withdraw all its forces from
Taiwan. Nevertheless, the tide of history was irresistible. Just as
Premier Zhou said, "At the present time it has become a strong desire
of the Chinese and American peoples to promote the normalization of
relations between the two countries and work for the relaxation of
tension. The people, and the people alone, are the motive force in the
making of world history. We are confident that the day will surely
come when this common desire of our two peoples will be realized." [35]

In 1973, China and America set up liaison offices in each other's
capitals. But these de facto embassies only demonstrated that diplomatic ties still remained unconventional, and unconventional relations cannot last long. There was also, given the reduction of American military involvement in East Asia, no reason for the United States
to keep an alliance with the Kuomintang that was detrimental to the
friendship of a billion Chinese people. Both China and America felt
they needed the other's friendship in order to prevent East Asia from
falling under the influence of the Soviet Union. Furthermore, the
expanding economic and cultural exchanges that followed normalization also required a better-defined and more formal diplomatic relation. Full normalization was merely a matter of time.

In late 1978, the People's Republic of China and the United States
agreed to recognize each other and to establish, as of January 1979,
full diplomatic relations. In the joint communiqué of December 15,
1978, the United States agreed to recognize the government of the
People's Republic of China as the sole legal government of China. The
United States would maintain only cultural, commercial, and other
unofficial relations with Taiwan. The joint communiqué also reaffirmed the principles agreed on in the Shanghai Communiqué, principles that included acknowledgment of Taiwan as a part of China
and a common opposition to hegemonism. [36] An abnormal relationship of nearly thirty years thus came to an end. It was a historic event
in Sino-American relations.

The American government also told the Kuomintang that it would
terminate both its diplomatic relations with Taiwan and the "mutual
defense treaty" and that it would withdraw its remaining military
personnel within four months. [37] The solution of the Taiwan question,

once an obstacle to normalization, now created the conditions for China's national reunification.

Unhappily, the U.S. government also stated that it "continues to have an interest in the peaceful resolution of the Taiwan issue and expects that the Taiwan issue will be settled peacefully by the Chinese themselves." In short, it was still unwilling to abandon totally its interference in China's internal affairs. The Chinese government thus countered that, "as for the way of bringing Taiwan back to the embrace of the motherland and reunifying the country, it is entirely China's internal affair." [38] There were also differing views on commercial relations between the United States and Taiwan. During the negotiations for normalization, the Americans mentioned that after normalization they would continue to sell limited amounts of arms to Taiwan for defensive purposes. China replied that it absolutely disagreed with this policy, saying that sales of arms to Taiwan not only violated the principles of normalization, but would be detrimental to the peaceful liberation of Taiwan and would exercise an unfavorable influence on the peace of East Asia. The two sides still differed on this question.

The American government continued to sell arms to Taiwan in contradiction to its agreed upon principles of normalization because of the power of the American right. These ultraconservatives, who wished to retain their imperialist interests in Taiwan, felt uneasy over normalization. In March of 1979, a little over two months after normalization, the conservatives in Congress adopted the "Taiwan Relations Act." [39] With a brazen disregard for reality they played the old tune of "two Chinas" by stipulating in the act that the policy of the United States was "to maintain the capacity of the United States to resist any resort to force or other forms of coercion that would jeopardize the security, or the social or economic systems, of the people of Taiwan." The act also stated that the President and Congress would determine, solely on their judgment of Taiwan's needs, the nature and quantity of the defense aid sent to that island. The President and Congress would also determine what action the United States would take in response to any threat to the people on Taiwan and to the interests of the United States in that area. The United States still placed under its protection not only Taiwan's security but also its social and economic systems. Though the United States, in the Shanghai Communiqué, had declared that it did not challenge the Chinese position that Taiwan is a part of China, these stipulations gave the opposite impression, namely that "Taiwan is a part of the United States." The Shanghai Communiqué stated that the United States would maintain no more than unofficial relations with Taiwan. But by this act the United States actually maintained a military alliance with it. The act both betrayed the principles upon which normalization was based and impaired the sovereignty of China. It could only obstruct the smooth development of the newly established relations between the two countries.

After over twenty years of confrontation, China and the United States did achieve a reconciliation. The normalization not only greatly reduced past antagonism but also, for the first time since 1844, planted the Sino-American relationship on an equal footing. The conservative forces in America, to be sure, were still up to mischief, but, just as they could not arrest the tendency toward accommodation, they were not able to block forever the progress of good relations.

Conclusion

From the 1840s to the 1970s, U.S. ambitions, aggressions, and fears, along with Chinese resistance, defined the Sino-American relationship. But in most cases, the tactics used by the United States differed from those of other imperialist powers. As early as in the 1860s, when China's semicolonial status was established, American diplomats emphasized the necessity of preventing one foreign power from holding a preponderant position in China, a policy that hoped to insure that each of the powers could exert an equal influence and enjoy equal opportunities of penetration. Only through such a policy, they thought, could the contingency that America be left behind or elbowed out of imperialist gains in China be guarded against. In the late 1890s, when the United States attained preeminence in world industrial production, the American insistence on a balance of power among the foreign states in China evolved into the "open door" policy. U.S. policy ceased to be passive; rather, it was designed both to enhance American economic dominance and to take the lead in Asian politics. After World War I, in the Washington Conference of 1921–1922, the United States even succeeded in converting the open door and equal opportunity doctrine into a convenant that all foreign powers would observe.

The open door policy presupposed that the foreign powers in China should cooperate among themselves so as to exert a joint control over China. But jealous and aggressive powers in China fell far short of a concerted control. Moreover, cooperation proposed by America was not an aim in itself; it was merely a leverage for competition. Tsarist Russia, for example, and then, Japan, sought the conquest of parts of China in order to exclude the interests of other powers. They allowed neither cooperation nor free competition. Eventually they preferred to resort to war rather than cooperate.

The open door policy required a common agent in China both to safeguard and extend the special privilege of the imperialist powers and to repress the resistance of the Chinese people. The United States laid stress on propping up a "stabilizing" force in China, successively supporting the Qing Dynasty, Yuan Shikai, the Beiyang warlords, and Chiang Kai-shek's Kuomintang. Moreover, the American ruling class was always hostile to China's revolutionary movements; it thus helped the Qings to strangle the Taiping insurrection, dispatched expeditionary troops to quell the Boxers, undermined the revolution led by Dr. Sun Yat-sen, and supplied Chiang with billions of dollars in an attempt to suppress the revolution led by the Chinese Communist Party. But the more aid the United States gave to the Chinese reactionary rulers, the more corrupt did those rulers become; and as their servility grew, the more they were discredited. One by one, the imperialist-supported lackeys were overthrown by the Chinese people.

At the end of World War II, the American governing circles believed that all former rivals had left the stage and that the whole of China was open to their dominance. They overlooked the fact that the Chinese people had grown mature and strong and were capable not only of toppling the Chiang faction but also of driving out those imperialist forces that had humiliated them for over a century. Not until after its twenty years of efforts to undermine the People's Republic of China had failed did the United States accept this reality. Yet even at this moment it still retains some vestige of a policy of interference in China's internal affairs. If there is any lesson to draw from the history of Sino-American relations, it is that policies and actions based on anachronistic assumptions are of no avail. Only respect for China's sovereignty and territorial integrity can contribute to the mutual benefits of the two peoples and to the peace of the world.

Appendix

Names and Places In Pinyin (Used in Text) and Wade-Giles

Personal Names

PINYIN	WADE GILES
Cao Kun	Ts'ao K'un
Chen Yi	Ch'en Yi
Cheng Yucai	Ch'eng Yu-ts'ai
Conglun	Ts'ung-lun
Duan Qirui	Tuan Ch'i-jui
Emperor Xianfeng	Emperor Hsiang-feng
Emperor Xuantong	Emperor Hsüan-t'ung
Empress Dowager Cixi	Empress Dowager Tz'u-hsi
Gu Weijun	V.K. Wellington Koo
Guiliang	Kuei-liang
Hengfu	Heng-fu
Huashana	Hua-sha-na
Jierhanga	Chi-erh-hang-a
Li Hongzhang	Li Hung-chang
Li Yuanghong	Li Yüan-hung
Li Zongren	Li Tsung-jen
Liang Shiyi	Liang Shih-yi
Liu Kunyi	Liu K'un-yi
Mao Zedong	Mao Tse-tung
Nie Rongzhen	Nieh Jung-chen
Peng Xuepei	P'eng Hsüeh-p'ei
Prince Gong	Prince Kung
Prince Qing	Prince Ch'ing
Qi Gong	Ch'i Kung
Qing Dynasty	Ch'ing Dynasty
Qiying (Tsiyeng)	Ch'i Ying
Sheng Xuanhuai	Sheng Hsuan-huai

Shi Shaoji	Shih Shao-chi
Song Ziwen	T.V. Soong
Tan Tiangxiang	T'an T'ing-hsiang
Tang Shaoyi	T'ang Shao-i
Wang Chonghui	Wang Ch'ung-hui
Wang Jingwei	Wang Ching-wei
Wang Zhenting	Wang Chen-t'ing
Wang Zhichuan	Wang Chih-ch'uan
Wenxiang	Wen-hsiang
Wu Chaoshu	C.C. Wu
Wu Peifu	Wu P'ei-fu
Wu Tingfang	Wu T'ing-fang
Wu Xiuquan	Wu Hsiu-ch'uan
Xiliang	Hsi-liang
Xu Shichang	Hsu Shih-ch'ang
Yang Hucheng	Yang Hu-ch'eng
Yiliang	Yi-liang
Yilibu	Ilipu
Yu Qiaqing	Yu Ch'ia-ch'ing
Yuan Shikai	Yuan Shih-k'ai
Zaifeng	Tsai-feng
Zeng Guofan	Tseng Kuo-fan
Zhang Junmai	Carson Chang
Zhang Qun	Chang Ch'un
Zhang Xueliang	Chang Hsüeh-liang
Zhang Zhidong	Chang Chih-tung
Zhang Zuolin	Chang Tso-lin
Zhangxun	Chang Hsun
Zhou Enlai	Chou En-lai
Zhu De	Chu Teh
Zongli Yamen	Board of Foreign Affairs

Places

PINYIN	WADE GILES
Aihui	Aigun
Anhui	Anhwei
Baietan	Pai-wo-t'an
Baoding	Paoting
Beihe River	Hai River
Beijing, Beiping	Peking, Peiping
Chahar	Chahar
Changchun	Ch'ang-ch'un

Chengdu	Chengtu
Chiangjiang	Yangtze
Chongqing	Chungking
Dagu	Taku
Dalian	Dairen
Fengtian	Fengtien
Fujian	Fukien
Fushun	Fushun
Gansu	Kansu
Guangdong	Kwangtung
Guangxi	Kwangsi
Guangzhou	Canton
Guizhou	Kweichow
Hainan	Hainan
Hangzhou	Hangchow
Hankou	Hankow
Hebei	Hopei
Heilongjiang	Heilungkiang
Henan	Honan
Huanghe River	Yellow River
Hubei	Hupei
Huguang	Hukuang
Hunan	Hunan
Jehol	Jehol
Jiangsu	Kiangsu
Jiangxi	Kiangsi
Jiaozhou	Kiao-chou
Jilin	Kirin
Jinan	Tsinan
Jinmen	Quemoy
Jinzhou	Chinchou
Jiujiang	Chiuchiang
Lanzhou	Lanchcow
Longkou	Lung-k'uo
Luoyang	Lo-yang
Lüshun	Port Arthur
Mazu	Matsu
Nanchang	Nan-Ch'ang
Nanjing	Nanking
Ningxia	Ningsia
Penghu	P'eng-hu (Pescadores)
Qingdao	Tsingtao
Qinghuangdao	Tsinghaungtao

Shaanxi	Shensi
Shandong	Shantung
Shanhaiguan	Shanhaikuan
Shenyang	Mukden
Sichuan	Szechuan
Taibei	Taipei
Taonan	Taonan
Tianjin	Tientsin
Wangxia	Wanghia
Weihaiwei	Weihaiwei
Wuhan	Wuhan
Wuhu	Wuhu
Xi'an	Sian
Xinjiang	Sinkiang
Xinmintun	Hsin-min-t'un
Yan'an	Yen-an
Yanjing	Yenching
Yunnan	Yunnan
Zhili	Chihli

Notes

1 From "Peace and Amity" to "Cooperation"

1. The Qing government placed foreign trade under its control. Foreign merchants had to observe official regulations as to the duration of their stay, the choice of their living quarters, and the scope of their activities in Guangzhou. They could trade and do business only with authorized Chinese merchants and were not allowed to deal directly with Chinese government organs.

2. John Foster, *American Diplomacy in the Orient* (Boston and New York, 1903), pp. 6–7.

3. Besides Guangzhou, the Treaty of Nanjing opened Xiamen, Fuzhou, Ningbo, and Shanghai to foreign trade.

4. Earl Swisher, *China's Management of the American Barbarians* (New Haven, 1953), p. 107.

5. Kenneth Latourette, "The History of Early Relations Between the United States and China 1784–1844," *Transactions of the Connecticut Academy of Arts and Sciences,* vol. 22 (1917–18), p. 126.

6. Jules Davids, ed., *American Diplomatic and Public Papers: The United States and China,* series 1 (Wilmington, Del., 1973), vol. 1, p. 64. (Series 2 of this work appeared in 1979 and series 3 in 1981.)

7. Swisher, *China's Management,* p. 107.

8. Ibid., p. 111.

9. Davids, *American Diplomatic and Public Papers,* series 1, vol. 1, pp. 151–152.

10. Swisher, *China's Management,* p. 134.

11. *American Diplomatic and Public Papers: The United States and China,* series 1, vol. 1, pp. 151–152.

12. Ibid., pp. 204–205.

13. Ibid., p. 232.

14. Ibid., vol. 2, p. 37.

15. Ibid., p. xx.

16. Tyler Dennett, *Americans in Eastern Asia* (New York, 1922), p. 160.

17. Davids, *American Diplomatic and Public Papers,* series 1, vol. 2, p. 228.

18. Teng Yuan Chung, "American China Trade, American-Chinese Relations and the Taiping Rebellion, 1853–1858," *Journal of Asian History* 3, no. 2 (1969): 94.

19. Davids, *American Diplomatic and Public Papers,* series 1, vol. 2, p. 128.

20. Swisher, *China's Management,* p. 217.

21. Tong Te-kong, *United States Diplomacy in China, 1844–60* (Seattle, 1964), p. 216.

22. S. T. Tong, *The Taiping Rebellion and the Western Powers* (n.p., n.d.), pp. 222–223.

23. Davids, *American Diplomatic and Public Papers,* series 1, vol. 10, p. 59.

24. The Taipings, imbued with the integrity of the revolutionary people, were not prepared to barter away their country's rights. They required foreigners to be subject to Chinese jurisdiction. They welcomed international trade, provided opium was not imported and a reasonable customs duty paid.

25. Teng, "American China Trade," p. 252.

26. Swisher, *China's Management,* p. 226.

27. Ibid., p. 231.

28. Davids, *American Diplomatic and Public Papers,* series 1., vol. 6, pp. 26–27.

29. Ibid., vol. 14, p. 131.

30. Ibid., p. 180.

31. Ibid., p. 385.

32. Ibid., p. 386.

33. Swisher, *China's Management,* p. 431.

34. Ibid., p. 455.

35. Ibid., p. 463.

36. Ibid., p. 479.

37. Ibid., pp. 481–482.

38. Ibid., p. 505.

39. Davids, *American Diplomatic and Public Papers,* series 1, vol. 14, p. 181.

40. Ibid., series 2, vol. 1, p. 29.

41. Frederick Williams, *Anson Burlingame and the First Mission to Foreign Powers* (New York, 1912), p. 22.

42. Sheng Hu, *Imperialism and Chinese Politics* (Peking, 1955), p. 51.

43. Davids, *American Diplomatic and Public Papers,* series 2, vol. 1, p. 29.

44. Harley MacNair, ed., *Modern Chinese History Selected Readings* (Shanghai, 1927), p. 357.

45. Davids, *American Diplomatic and Public Papers,* series 2, vol. 1, pp. 27–30.

46. *Chouban Yiwu Shimo* (The Beginning and End of the Management of Barbarian Affairs: The Xianfeng Period), vol. 71 (Taipei, 1970), p. 18.

47. Swisher, *China's Management*, p. 691.

48. *Chouban Yiwu Shimo,* The Tongzhi Period, vol. 5, p. 55.

49. Davids, *American Diplomatic and Public Papers,* series 2, vol. 1, p. 43.

50. Ibid., p. 31.

51. *Chouban Yiwu Shimo*: The Tongzhi Period, vol. 55, p. 9.

2 From Rivalry to "Open Door"

1. Thomas McCormick, *China Market: America's Quest for Informal Empire, 1893–1901* (Chicago, 1967), p. 131.

2. Ibid., p. 130.

3. Davids, *American Diplomatic and Public Papers,* series 3, vol. 8, pp. 36–37.

4. McCormick, *China Market,* p. 60.

5. Davids, *American Diplomatic and Public Papers,* series 3, vol. 8, pp. 28–30.

6. McCormick, *China Market,* p. 95.

7. Harvey Pressman, "Hay, Rockhill, and China's Integrity: A Reappraisal," *Papers on China* 13 (1960): 68.

8. Davids, *American Diplomatic and Public Papers,* series 3, vol. 8, p. 45.

9. McCormick, *China Market,* p. 122.

10. Pressman, "Hay, Rockhill, and China's Integrity," p. 71.

11. Swisher, *China's Management,* pp. 406, 413.

12. *Yihetuan Dang'an Shiliao* (Archival Historical Materials on the Boxer Movement), vol. 1 (Beijing, 1959), p. 140.

13. Ibid., p. 187.

14. Ibid., p. 203.

15. Davids, *American Diplomatic and Public Papers,* series 3, vol. 8, p. 100.

16. Ibid., 8: 100.

17. Pressman, "Hay, Rockhill, and China's Integrity," pp. 72–73.

18. Davids, *American Diplomatic and Public Papers,* series 3, vol. 8, p. 100.

19. McCormick, *China Market,* p. 164.

20. Sheng Hu, *Cong Yapian Zhangzheng Dao Wusi Yundong* (From the Opium War to the May Fourth Movement) (Beijing, 1959), p. 619.

21. Davids, *American Diplomatic and Public Papers,* series 3, vol. 8, p. 100.

22. Marilyn Young, *The Rhetoric of Empire: American China Policy 1895–1901* (Cambridge, Mass., 1968), p. 211.

23. Davids, *American Diplomatic and Public Papers,* series 3, vol. 5, pp. 273–274.

24. Ibid., 5: 311–322.

25. Young, *American China Policy*, p. 163.

26. Davids, *American Diplomatic and Public Papers*, series 3, vol. 5, p. 176.

27. *Zhongguo Jindai Shi Ziliao Congkan: Yi He Tuan* (Collections of Materials of Modern Chinese History: Yi He Tuan), vol. 4, p. 249.

28. Davids, *American Diplomatic and Public Papers*, series 3, vol. 5, p. 306.

29. Ibid., 5: 274.

30. Alfred Count von Waldersee, *Denkwürdigkeiten* (Stuttgart and Berlin, 1923), vol. 3, p. 92.

31. *The Parliamentary Debates*, 4th Series, vol. 87 (London, 1900), p. 486.

32. *Yihetuan Dang'an Shiliao*, vol. 2, p. 945.

3   "Open Door" Put to the Test

1. Paul Varg, *The Making of a Myth: The United States and China, 1897–1912* (East Lansing, Mich., 1968), p. 74.

2. Davids, *American Diplomatic and Public Papers*, series 3, vol. 9, pp. 27–28.

3. Liang Wang, comp., *Xi Xun Dashiji* (A Chronicle of the Westward Inspection Tour) (Beiping, 1933), vol. 5, p. 36.

4. Ibid., vol. 6, p. 8.

5. Ibid., p. 5.

6. Ibid., p. 18.

7. Zhang Zhidong, *Zhang Wenxianggong Chuanji* (Collected Works of Zhang Zhidong) (Beiping, 1937), vol. 55, pp. 2–3.

8. Varg, *The Making of a Myth*, p. 76.

9. Davids, *American Diplomatic and Public Papers*, series 3, vol. 9, p. 51.

10. Thomas Etzold, ed., *Aspects of Sino-American Relations Since 1784* (New York, 1978), p. 51.

11. Michael Hunt, *Frontier Defense and the Open Door: Manchuria and Chinese-American Relations, 1895–1911* (New Haven, 1973), p. 78.

12. Raymond Esthus, "The Changing Concept of the Open Door, 1899–1910," *Mississippi Valley Historical Review*, vol. 46 (1959–60), p. 445.

13. Hunt, *Frontier and the Open Door*, p. 72.

14. Wang Yunsheng, ed., *Liushi Nian Lai Zhongguo Yu Riben* (China and Japan in the Last Sixty Years) (Tianjin, 1934), vol. 4, p. 205.

15. Hunt, *Frontier and the Open Door*, p. 89.

16. Paul Varg, *Open Door Diplomat: The Life of W. W. Rockhill* (Urbana, 1952), p. 86.

17. Lee En-han, *China's Quest for Railway Autonomy 1904–1911: A Study of the Chinese Railway Rights Recovery Movement* (Singapore, 1977), p. 56.

18. Etzold, *Aspects of Sino-American Relations*, p. 41.

19. Arthur Smith, *China and America Today: A Study of Conditions and Relations* (New York and Chicago, 1907), pp. 165–166.

20. Ts'ai Shih-Sham, "Reaction to Exclusion: The Boycott of 1905 and Chinese National Awakening," *The Historian* 39, no. 1 (1976): 109.

21. Ibid., p. 95.

22. Xu Shichang, *Tuigeng Tang Zhengshu* (Public Papers of Xu Shichang) (Taipei, 1968), p. 368.

23. Hunt, *Frontier and the Open Door,* p. 152.

24. Etzold, *Aspects of Sino-American Relations,* p. 56.

25. Ibid., p. 56.

26. U.S. Department of State, *Papers Relating to Foreign Relations of the United States, 1910* (Washington, 1915), p. 234.

27. Wang, *Liushi Nian Lai Zhongguo Yu Riben,* vol. 5, p. 348.

28. Etzold, *Aspects of Sino-American Relations,* p. 59.

29. Wang, *Liushi Nian Lai Zhongguo Yu Riben,* vol. 5, p. 293.

30. Hunt, *Frontier and the Open Door,* p. 227.

31. Sheng Xuanhuai, *Yuzai Cungao* (Collected Papers), vol. 30 (Taipei, 1974), p. 23.

4 "Special Interests" Recognized

1. Roy Curry, *Woodrow Wilson and Far Eastern Policy, 1913–1921* (New York, 1957), p. 29.

2. Ibid., p. 30.

3. Sheng Hu, *Imperialism and Chinese Politics,* p. 212.

4. Ibid., p. 217–18.

5. Curry, *Woodrow Wilson,* p. 31.

6. Sheng Hu, *Imperialism and Chinese Politics,* p. 220.

7. Russell Fifield, *Woodrow Wilson and the Far East* (New York, 1952), p. 58.

8. Department of State, *Foreign Relations: 1914,* supplement p. 162.

9. Wang, *Liushi Nian Lai Zhongguo Yu Riben,* vol. 6, p. 42.

10. Department of State, *Foreign Relations: 1914,* supplement p. 172.

11. Ibid., pp. 189–190.

12. Paul Clyde, *United States Policy Toward China: Diplomatic and Public Documents, 1839–1939* (Durham, 1940), p. 259.

13. Fifield, *Wilson and the Far East,* pp. 39–40.

14. Department of State, *Foreign Relations: The Lansing Papers, 1914–1920,* vol. 2, p. 408.

15. *Zhongguo Jindai Shi* (Modern History of China) (Beijing, 1979), p. 489.

16. Paul Reinsch, *An American Diplomat in China* (Taipei, 1967), p. 303.

17. Department of State, *The Lansing Papers,* vol. 2, p. 434.

18. Clyde, *United States Policy,* p. 266; Wang, *Liushi Nian Lai Zhongguo Yu Riben,* vol. 7, p. 104.

19. Reinsch, *American Diplomat,* pp. 307–308.

20. Curry, *Woodrow Wilson*, pp. 182–183.

21. Department of State, *The Lansing Papers*, vol. 2, p. 434.

22. Curry, *Woodrow Wilson*, p. 134.

23. Department of State, *The Lansing Papers*, vol. 2, p. 437.

24. Ibid., p. 435.

25. Curry, *Woodrow Wilson*, p. 185.

26. Clyde, *United States Policy*, p. 268.

27. Wang, *Liushi Nian Lai Zhongguo Yu Riben*, vol. 7, p. 167.

28. Curry, *Woodrow Wilson*, p. 262.

29. Fifield, *Wilson and the Far East*, p. 125.

30. Ibid.

31. Ibid., p. 130.

32. Curry, *Woodrow Wilson*, p. 264.

33. Thomas Barnes and Gerald Feldman, eds., *Breakdown and Rebirth: 1914 to the Present* (Boston, 1972), p. 40.

34. Fifield, *Wilson and the Far East*, p. 253.

35. Barnes and Feldman, *Breakdown and Rebirth*, p. 40.

36. Fifield, *Wilson and the Far East*, p. 273.

37. Ibid., p. 279.

38. Ibid., pp. 286–287.

39. Paul Reinsch, *American Diplomat*, p. 372.

40. Ibid., p. 368.

41. Wei Hongyuan, *Zhongquo Xiandai Shi Gao* (A Draft History of Contemporary China (Harbin, 1980), p. 37.

42. Hua Gang, *Wusi yundong* (The May Fourth Movement) (Shanghai, 1954), p. 94.

43. Thomas Bailey, *A Diplomatic Hisotory of the American People* (New Yor, 1940), p. 611.

44. Fifield, *Wilson and the Far East*, pp. 339–340.

5 "Open Door" Reasserted

1. Westel Willoughby, *China at the Conference* (Baltimore, 1922), p. 292.

2. Reinsch, *American Diplomat*, pp. 334–337.

3. Fifield, *Wilson and the Far East*, p. 351.

4. Ibid., p. 346.

5. Ibid., p. 357.

6. Willoughby, *China at the Conference*, p. 9.

7. Russell Fifield, "Secretary Hughes and the Shantung Question," *Pacific Historical Review* 23 (August, 1954): 375.

8. Sheng Yunlong, *Personal Chronological History of Mr. Huang Yingbai* (Taibei, 1976), p. 121.

9. *China Review* 2 (1873): 74.

10. Merlo Pusey, *Charles Evans Hughes* (New York, 1951), p. 506.

11. Russell Fifield, "Secretary Hughes and the Shantung Question," *Pacific Historical Review* 23 (August, 1954): 374.

12. *Weekly Review of the Far East* 18, no. 1 (1921): 3.
13. *China Review* 1 (1873): 171.
14. Willoughby, *China at the Conference,* p. 371.
15. Robert Pollard, *China's Foreign Relations 1917–1931* (New York, 1933), p. 246.
16. *Weekly Review of the Far East* 18, no. 1 (1921): 4.
17. Willoughby, *China at the Conference,* p. 41.
18. Ibid., p. 251.
19. Ibid., p. 101.
20. Ibid., p. 259.
21. Pollard, *China's Foreign Relations,* p. 223.
22. *Weekly Review of the Far East* 18, no. 1 (1921): 4.
23. Willoughby, *China at the Conference,* p. 365.
24. Ibid., p. 373.
25. Pusey, *Charles Evans Hughes,* p. 517.
26. Chen Duxiu, "The Pacific Conference and the Weaker Peoples in the Pacific Area," *Xin Qingnian* (New Youth) 9, no. 5 (1921): 573.
27. *Weekly Review of the Far East* 18, no. 1 (1921): 4.

6 "Open Door" Lost

1. Foster Rhea Dulles, *China and America* (Princeton, 1946), p. 167.
2. Sheng Hu, *Imperialism and Chinese Politics,* p. 304.
3. Department of State, *Foreign Relations: 1923,* vol. 1, p. 517.
4. Ibid., p. 522.
5. Ibid., p. 556.
6. Ibid., p. 566.
7. Ibid., p. 575.
8. Department of State, *Foreign Relations: 1927* vol. 2, pp. 350–353.
9. Yi Xun, *Jiang Dang Zhenxiang* (The True Features of Chiang's Party) (n.p., 1949), p. 25.
10. *Dongfang Zazhi* (The Eastern Miscellany), 24, no. 2 (1926): 167.
11. Harold Isaacs, *The Tragedy of the Chinese Revolution* (London, 1938), p. 150.
12. *China Weekly Review* 40, no. 12 (1927): 317.
13. *China Weekly Review* 39, no. 1 (1926): 3.
14. *China Weekly Review* 43, no. 9 (1928): 222.
15. Pollard, *China's Foreign Relations,* p. 338.
16. Department of State, *Foreign Relations: 1928,* vol. 2, p. 331.
17. Ibid., p. 333.
18. Ibid., p. 332.
19. Pollard, *China's Foreign Relations,* p. 341.
20. Department of State, *Foreign Relations: 1928,* vol. 2, p. 476.
21. Ibid., p. 456.
22. Ibid., p. 195.
23. Ibid., p. 403.

24. Huang Yuanqi, ed., *Zhongkuo Xiandai Shi* (Current History of China) (Zhengzhou, 1982), p. 329.

25. Ibid., p. 330.

26. *China Weekly Review* 58, no. 4 (1931): 132.

27. Department of State, *Foreign Relations: Japan, 1931–1941*, vol. 1, p. 9.

28. U.S. Department of State, *Peace and War*, p. 159.

29. Dulles, *China and America*, p. 192.

30. Sara Smith, *The Manchurian Crisis, 1931–1932* (Westport, Conn., 1970), p. 200.

31. Department of State, *Foreign Relations: Japan, 1931–1932*, vol. 1, p. 76.

32. Department of State, *Foreign Relations: 1932*, vol. 3, p. 8.

33. Russell Buhite, *Nelson T. Johnson and American Policy Toward China, 1925–1941* (East Lansing, Mich., 1968), p. 69.

34. Dorothy Borg, *The United States and the Far Eastern Crisis 1933–1938* (Cambridge, Mass., 1964), p. 32.

35. *China Weekly Review* 62, no. 6 (1932): 240.

36. T. A. Bisson, *American Policy in the Far East 1931–1940* (New York, 1939), p. 30.

37. Department of State, *Foreign Relations: Japan, 1931–1941*, vol. 1, p. 224.

38. Ibid., p. 232.

39. Dulles, *China and America*, p. 209.

40. Department of State, *Foreign Relations: Japan, 1931–1941*, vol. 1, p. 319.

41. Ibid., p. 321.

42. Dulles, *China and America*, p. 210.

43. Department of State, *Foreign Relations: 1937*, vol. 4, p. 198.

44. Bisson, *American Policy*, p. 105.

45. Cordell Hull, *The Memoirs of Cordell Hull* (New York, 1948), vol. 1, p. 278.

46. Borg, *The Far Eastern Crisis*, p. 295.

47. Joseph Grew, *Ten Years in Japan* (New York, 1944), p. 270.

7   Aid to Chiang Against Japan

1. Dulles, *China and America*, pp. 221–222.

2. Buhite, *Nelson T. Johnson and American Policy*, p. 92.

3. Ibid.

4. *Jiang Zongtong Milu* (Inside Records of President Chiang) (Taipei, 1974), vol. 12, p. 93.

5. Department of State, *Foreign Relations: 1940*, vol. 4, pp. 673–674.

6. Ibid., pp. 473, 476.

7. Department of State, *Foreign Relations: 1939*, vol. 3, p. 308.

8. Ibid., p. 208.

9. Michael Schaller, *The U.S. Crusade in China, 1938–1945* (New York, 1979), p. 43.

10. *Jiang Zongtong Milu,* vol. 12, pp. 115–116.

11. Department of State, *Foreign Relations: 1942, China,* p. 15.

12. Department of State, *Foreign Relations: 1939,* vol. 3, p. 513.

13. Walter LaFeber, "Roosevelt, Churchill, and Indochina: 1942–1945," *American Historical Review* 80 (December 1975): 1280–1281.

14. J. W. Pickersgill and D. W. Forster, *The Mackenzie King Record* (Toronto, 1960), vol. 1, p. 553.

15. David Dilks, ed., *The Diaries of Sir Alexander Cadogan, 1938–1945* (New York, 1972), p. 488.

16. Ibid.

17. Department of State, *Foreign Relations: 1941,* vol. 5, p. 768.

18. Department of State, *Foreign Relations: 1942, China,* p. 111.

19. *Jiang Zongtong Milu,* vol. 13, p. 83.

20. Department of State, *Foreign Relations: 1942, China,* p. 114.

21. Schaller, *U.S. Crusade in China,* p. 113.

22. Department of State, *Foreign Relations: 1942,* vol. 1, p. 713.

23. Charles Romanus and Riley Sunderland, *Stilwell's Mission to China* (Washington, 1953), p. 279.

24. Department of State, *Foreign Relations: 1943, China,* p. 166.

25. David Barrett, *Dixie Mission: The United States Army Observer Group in Yenan, 1944* (Berkeley, 1970), pp. 27–28.

26. Charles Romanus and Riley Sunderland, *Stilwell's Command Problems* (Washington, 1956), p. 383.

27. *Jiang Zongtong Milu,* vol. 13, p. 150.

28. Romanus and Sunderland, *Stilwell's Command Problems,* pp. 445–446.

29. *Jiang Zongtong Milu,* vol. 13, p. 157.

30. Romanus and Sunderland, *Stilwell's Command Problems,* p. 453.

31. Schaller, *U.S. Crusade in China,* pp. 173–174.

32. Elliott Roosevelt, *As He Saw It* (New York, 1946), p. 154.

33. Department of State, *Foreign Relations: 1944,* vol. 6, p. 243.

34. Ibid.

35. Ibid., pp. 745–749.

8   Aid to Chiang Against the Chinese Communist Party

1. *Selected Works of Mao Tse-tung* (New York, 1954), vol. 4, pp. 13–20.

2. Schaller, *U.S. Crusade in China,* p. 209.

3. William Leahy, *I Was There* (New York, 1950), p. 337.

4. Department of State, *Foreign Relations: 1944,* vol. 6, pp. 687–688.

5. John Davies, *Dragon by the Tail* (New York, 1972), p. 372.

6. Russell Buhite, *Patrick J. Hurley and American Foreign Policy* (Ithaca, N.Y., 1973), p. 172.

7. *Selected Works of Mao Tse-tung,* vol. 4, p. 14.

8. *Jiang Zongtong Milu* vol. 14, p. 7.

9. Department of State, *Foreign Relations: 1944,* vol. 6, pp. 706–707.

10. Ibid., p. 573.

11. Ibid., p. 738.

12. Ibid., p. 703.

13. Ibid., p. 747.

14. Schaller, *U.S. Crusade in China,* p. 207.

15. Ibid.

16. *Selected Works of Mao Tse-tung,* vol. 4, p. 21.

17. Department of State, *Foreign Relations: 1945,* vol. 7, pp. 886–887.

18. Ibid., p. 433.

19. *Selected Works of Mao Tse-tung,* vol. 4, p. 20.

20. Department of State, *Foreign Relations: 1945,* vol. 7, p. 319.

21. *Selected Works of Mao Tse-tung,* vol. 3, p. 336.

22. Department of State, *Foreign Relations: 1945,* vol. 2, pp. 527–528.

23. Schaller, *U.S. Crusade in China,* p. 280.

24. *Jiang Zongton Milu,* vol. 14, p. 27.

25. Davies, *Dragon by the Tail,* p. 417; Herbert Feis, *The China Tangle* (Princeton, 1953), p. 402.

26. Paul Varg, *Closing of the Door* (East Lansing, Mich., 1973), p. 242.

27. Ernest May, *The Truman Administration and China, 1945–1949* (Philadelphia, 1975), p. 59.

28. John Morton Blum, ed., *The Price of Vision: The Diary of Henry Wallace 1942–1946* (Boston, 1973), p. 520.

29. May, *Truman and China,* pp. 59–60.

30. *George Marshall, Marshall's Mission to China* (Arlington, 1976), vol. 2, p. 7.

31. May, *Truman and China,* p. 58.

32. *Marshall's Mission to China,* vol. 2, p. 24.

33. Ibid., vol. 1, p. 50.

34. Ibid., p. 51.

35. Department of State, *Foreign Relations: 1946,* vol. 9, p. 952.

36. Ibid., p. 1202.

37. May, *Truman and China,* pp. 14–15.

38. Department of State, *Foreign Relations: 1945,* vol. 7, pp. 614–617.

39. *China Weekly Review,* no. 16 (1946): 319–329.

40. May, *Truman and China,* p. 13.

41. Department of State, *Foreign Relations: 1946,* vol. 10, p. 560.

42. Ibid., pp. 603–604.

43. Wellington Koo, *Memoirs* (Glen Rock, N.J.: NYT Microfilming Corporation of America, 1978), vol. 6, p. D-15.

44. May, *Truman and China,* p. 77.

45. U.S. Department of State, *United States Relations with China, with Special Reference to the Period 1944–1949 (The China White Paper)* (Washington, 1949), pp. 766–774.

46. John Leighton Stuart, *Fifty Years in China* (New York, 1954), p. 188.

47. May, *Truman and China,* p. 82.

48. Koo, *Memoirs,* vol. 6, p. H-106.

49. Kenneth Rea and John Brewer, eds., *The Forgotten Ambassador: The Reports of John Leighton Stuart, 1946–1949* (Boulder, 1981), p. 287.

50. Koo, *Memoirs,* vol. 6, p. F-9.

51. Rea and Brewer, *Forgotten Ambassador,* p. 285.

52. Ibid., pp. 314–315.

9   Aggression Against the People's Republic of China

1. *Selected Works of Mao Tse-tung,* vol. 4, p. 415.

2. Ibid., p. 402.

3. Rea and Brewer, *Forgotten Ambassador,* p. 325.

4. Ibid., p. 333.

5. Dean Acheson, *Present at the Creation: My Years in the State Department* (New York, 1969), p. 306; Foster Rhea Dulles, *American Policy Toward Communist China, 1949–1969* (New York, 1972), p. 34.

6. Dorothy Borg and Waldo Heinrichs, eds., *Uncertain Years: Chinese-American Relations, 1947–1950* (New York, 1980), p. 156.

7. Department of State, *United States Relations with China,* p. xvi.

8. Roderick MacFarquhar, ed., *Sino-American Relations, 1949–1971* (New York, 1972), p. 70.

9. Ibid., p. 75.

10. Ibid., p. 74.

11. Borg and Heinrichs, *Uncertain Years,* p. 79.

12. Department of State, *United States Relations with China,* p. xvi.

13. *Selected Works of Mao Tse-tung,* vol. 4, p. 442.

14. Borg and Heinrichs, *Uncertain Years,* p. 54.

15. *Selected Works of Mao Tse-tung,* vol. 4, p. 437.

16. MacFarquhar, *Sino-American Relations,* p. 83.

17. Chiu Hungdah, *China and the Question of Taiwan: Documents and Analysis* (New York, 1973), pp. 230–231.

18. MacFarquhar, *Sino-American Relations,* p. 83.

19. Chiu, *The Question of Taiwan,* p. 237.

20. Dulles, *American Policy Toward Communist China,* p. 100.

21. *Selected Works of Mao Tse-tung,* vol. 5, pp. 26–31.

22. Ibid., p. 35.

23. Allen Whiting, *China Crosses the Yalu* (Stanford, 1968), pp. 97–98.

24. K. M. Panikkar, *In Two Chinas* (London, 1955), p. 108.

25. *Weidade Kang Mei Yuan Chao Yundong* (The Great Movement to Resist United States Aggression and Aid Korea) (Beijing, 1954), p. 27.

26. Panikkar, *In Two Chinas,* p. 110.

27. Robert Blum, *The United States and China in World Affairs* (New York, 1966), p. 113.

28. Dulles, *American Policy Toward Communist China*, p. 99.

29. Ibid., p. 100.

30. Ibid., p. 107.

31. *Oppose the New United States Plots to Create "Two Chinas"* (Beijing, 1962), p. 60.

32. Dulles, *American Policy Toward Communist China*, p. 99.

33. Robert Newman, *Recognition of Communist China?* (New York, 1961), p. 10.

34. Chiu, *The Question of Taiwan*, p. 126.

35. MacFarquhar, *Sino-American Relations*, p. 107.

36. Chiu, *The Question of Taiwan*, pp. 250–252.

37. Ibid., p. 253.

38. Ibid., p. 257.

39. Ibid., pp. 253–256.

40. Dulles, *American Policy Toward Communist China*, pp. 145–146.

41. Blum, *The United States and China*, p. 120.

42. Edgar Snow, *The Other Side of the River: Red China Today* (New York, 1971), p. 89.

43. Chiu, *The Question of Taiwan*, p. 147.

44. Ibid., p. 263.

45. Ibid., p. 147.

46. Snow, *Other Side of the River*, p. 91.

47. MacFarquhar, *Sino-American Relations*, pp. 126–127.

48. Ibid., p. 141.

49. Dulles, *American Policy Toward Communist China*, p. 134.

50. MacFarquhar, *Sino-American Relations*, p. 154.

51. *Peking Review* 1, no. 25 (August 19, 1958): 6.

52. MacFarquhar, *Sino-American Relations*, pp. 159–162.

53. Ibid., pp. 162–165.

54. Herbert Aptheker, *The United States and China: Peace or War?* (New York, 1958), p. 3.

55. MacFarquhar, *Sino-American Relations*, pp. 165–166.

56. Chiu, *The Question of Taiwan*, pp. 286–288.

57. *Peking Review* 1, no. 33 (October 14, 1958): 9.

58. Chiu, *The Question of Taiwan*, p. 153.

59. *Peking Review* 1, no. 33 (October 14, 1958): 9.

60. Snow, *Other Side of the River*, p. 92.

61. Dulles, *American Policy Toward Communist China*, p. 190.

10   From Hostility to Reconciliation

1. MacFarquhar, *Sino-American Relations*, pp. 210–205.

2. Ibid., p. 208.

3. Ibid., p. 200.

4. Dulles, *American Policy Toward Communist China*, p. 214.

5. Ibid., p. 213.

6. Ibid.

7. Snow, *Other Side of the River,* p. 89.

8. MacFarquhar, *Sino-American Relations,* p. 224.

9. Ibid., p. 227.

10. Dulles, *American Policy Toward Communist China,* pp. 121, 135.

11. Akira Iriye, ed., *U.S. Policy toward China: Testimony Taken from the Senate Foreign Relations Committee Hearings, 1966* (Boston, 1968), pp. 127–131.

12. MacFarquhar, *Sino-American Relations,* pp. 222–225.

13. Ibid., p. 226.

14. Ibid., p. 231.

15. Henry Kissinger, *White House Years* (Boston, 1979), p. 165.

16. Ibid., p. 164.

17. *Peking Review* 11, no. 29 (November 29, 1968): 31.

18. Kissinger, *White House Years,* p. 171.

19. Dulles, *American Policy Toward Communist China,* p. 241.

20. Ibid., pp. 244–245.

21. Kissinger, *White House Years,* pp. 181–182.

22. Ibid., p. 699.

23. Edgar Snow, *The Long Revolution* (New York, 1972), pp. 171–172.

24. Kissinger, *White House Years,* p. 714.

25. Ibid., p. 727.

26. Ibid., pp. 759–760.

27. *Peking Review* 14, no. 35 (August 27, 1971): 5–6.

28. *Peking Review* 15, nos. 7–8 (February 25, 1972): 8–9.

29. Ibid., p. 9.

30. Richard Stebbins and Elaine Adam, eds., *American Foreign Relations 1972: A Documentary Record* (New York, 1976), p. 309.

31. Ibid., p. 310.

32. Ibid., p. 309.

33. *Peking Review* 15, nos. 7–8 (February 25, 1972): 9.

34. Kissinger, *White House Years,* p. 1053; Stebbins and Adam, *American Foreign Relations 1972,* p. 316.

35. *Peking Review* 15, nos. 7–8 (February 25, 1972): 8.

36. *Peking Review* 21, no. 51 (December 22, 1978): 8.

37. Ibid., p. 12.

38. Ibid., pp. 8–9.

39. *United States Statutes at Large, 96th Congress, 1st Session, 1979,* vol. 93, stats. 14–21.

INDEX

Acheson, Dean: policy toward Far East, 128–29; policy toward PRC, 135, 137–38; perception of Soviet control in China, 136; speech of January 12, 1950, 137; and Korean War, 142

Amau, Eiji, 93

Amau doctrine, 93–94

American China Development Company, 38

American merchants, in China, 1–3, 19

Anglo-Chinese War (1856–60), 10–13; U.S. mediation of, 11–12; settlement reached, 13, 14

Anglo-Japanese Alliance, 1, 53, 67; abrogation of, 76

Anti-American boycotts, in China, 39, 40, 80

Anti-Chinese movement, in U.S., 39–40

Anti-imperialism, in China, 6, 25, 37, 63–64, 82, 83. *See also* Anti-American boycotts; Boxer movement; Rights recovery movement

Arita, Hachiro, 97

Army Observer Group, U.S., 110–11

Baker, John Earl, 77

Baker, Ray Stannard, 63

Balfour, Arthur, 68, 74, 75

Bandung Conference, 148

Barnett, Doak, 157–58

Barrett, David, and U.S. Army Observer Group, 111

Beijing, opening to foreigners, 7, 9, 13, 14

Beijing-Shenyang railway, 41, 42

Belgian syndicate, in China, 38

Bisson, T. A., 96

Bliss, Tasker, 62

Board of Foreign Affairs, 16

Borah, William Edgar, 64

Bowring, John, 9

Boxer indemnity, 30

Boxer movement, 24–25; and Chinese nationalism, 29; implications for U.S. policy, 25–26, 28; and Protocol of 1901, 30; U.S. participation in, 27, 172; U.S. remission of indemnity, 42, 43

British-Chinese Corporation, 42

British East India Company, 1

Broderick, Sir John, 28–30

Brussels Conference (1937), 95–97

Bryan, William Jennings, 53

Buchanan, James, 11